ROSE'S RAMBLIN'S

AN ITALIAN-AMERICAN LOVE STORY 1930-1940

ROSE BO MARENCO

PUBLISHED BY FASTPENCIL, INC.

Published by FastPencil, Inc.
3131 Bascom Ave.
Suite 150
Campbell CA 95008 USA
(408) 540-7571
(408) 540-7572 (Fax)
info@fastpencil.com
http://www.fastpencil.com

The Publisher makes no representations or warranties with respect to the accuracy or completeness of the contents of this book and specifically disclaim any implied warranties of merchantability or fitness for a particular purpose. Neither the publisher nor author shall be liable for any loss of profit or any commercial damages.

First Edition

I dedicate this to the memory of Sue Sarbaugh, the Memoir Writing Class teacher who encouraged me so much to write this book.

❧

ACKNOWLEDGEMENTS

Thanks to my mother and Carlo's mother for sharing so many stories while they were alive as we sat around the kitchen table. Also thanks to my family for putting up with me while I wrote these stories and I appreciate the proofreading my brother, Louis and his wife Betty did for me.

CONTENTS

1

1953

Whenever I think of my birthday coming up in July, I realize that in that same month in 1953 I was so relieved that I had finally reached my 18th birthday. About a year and a half before that I had a dream, or perhaps I should call it a nightmare, that I would die during my 17th year. I kept thinking and worrying that it would come true. Of course during my senior year in high school I had so much going on that I didn't think about it too much and when graduation time came near, my mother announced that she and I would take a trip to Italy so she could see her family again as she hadn't seen them in twenty four years. Well, never having been on a plane, I immediately thought that that was how I was going to die.

Twenty four years before, my father, Stefano Bo, (Steve) had been living in America for 10 years having come to America with his mother and sister to join his father, Luigi Bo, who had been here for 9 or 10 years.

Paternal grandfather Luigi Bo

Baralis & Bo family—Back row, Lena Baralis Memeo, Stefano Bo, Angela Baralis & Mary Baralis —Middle row: Stefano Baralis & Anna Donadei Baralis, Maddalena Baralis Bo & Luigi Bo — Front row: Steve Memeo & Maria Bo around 1920

My father went to Italy just for a visit with two other men and also with the task of buying property for my grandfather because he wanted to go back to Italy to live. At that time the three who were working, my grandfather, my father and my aunt, were combining all their wages so that they could go back to Italy and retire comfortably in the little town of Franchini.

Well, someone played "matchmaker" and introduced my dad to my mom and two months after he arrived in Italy, they were married in the church of San Dalmazio in Quargnento, in the province of Piemonte in northern Italy.

Marina Stanchi & Stefano Bo wedding, Dec. 12, 1929

My mother was a young teen-age bride of seventeen when my father married her and two months later they sailed to America leaving behind her family of father, mother, two brothers and a young sister.

Newlyweds Stefano & Marina Bo & Stanchi Family, Jan. 1930—Mother & father Rosa & Domenico Stanchi, brothers Evasio and Giuseppe Stanchi and sister Adriana Stanchi

They arrived in February, 1930 in New York. A cousin living in New York met them at the dock and later my mom remembered going shopping with her to buy a hat. A few days later they boarded a train to come across the United States to California. Now, 24 years after their marriage, my mom and I were going back for a visit so that she could see her family again. My parents couldn't go together because they owned a supermarket and they both couldn't leave at the same time. My father had gone back alone in 1951 so now he and my brother Louis stayed home to mind the business.

We left on the 4th of July from the old Mills Field in South San Francisco. The gates were covered breezeways with barriers that were waist high. You had to walk out to the airplanes and up the stairs. We flew to New York by way of Chicago. Then we stopped in Gander, Newfoundland, Shannon, Ireland and finally landed in Milano (Malpensa). At that time the customs area seemed like a chicken shack. There were windows along the sides that were painted white and one was broken. As our bags were being checked out, my uncle found his way to the broken window pane and of course peeking through he could see where we were. He yelled my mom's name "Marina" and she immediately left me there at the counter and ran to him to have her head pulled through the broken pane and kissed by all the relatives waiting for us. The customs agent finally came over and stopped all the hugging and herded us on our way out the exit.

Outside there was the taxi driver who went to school with my mother, my mother's two brothers, their two young daughters and my father's sister. So we were six adults and two children riding in the taxi along with our luggage. What a load!

The weather was hot and very humid and it seemed as if it was going to rain any moment. We stopped to get a soda at an outdoor café and the taxi driver was very nervous because he wanted to get on his way. I didn't understand why he was so nervous. When we continued on I could see what looked like brick smokestacks sending up columns of smoke and was told that people were firing them to break up the thunderclouds so that it wouldn't hail. I still don't understand why they did this. I immediately said to myself— "I want to go home!" It took almost two hours to get to the farm house where we would be staying for the next two months. The weather looked very gloomy and the driver kept speeding up more and more. When we got to the dirt road off the main highway, it started to sprinkle a little and after two miles we got to the farm house. The driver jumped out, quickly unloaded us and the luggage, gave my mom a big hug and dashed off. I couldn't understand why he didn't stay for a coffee which wouldn't have taken so long. I later found out that if he stayed and it rained, it would be three days before he could leave the place as the dirt road would become impassible for the car. The dirt became a very wet, sticky mud that clung to everything that passed on it.

At the farmhouse there was the wife of one of my uncles, my grandparents, my great-grandmother who lived in one side of the farmhouse. In the other side of the farmhouse there was a great-uncle and aunt (my grandfather's brother) and also a laborer and they were all waiting for "the Americans". There was much hugging and kissing and then it started to thunder and lightening and pour rain. It was late afternoon so my aunt made coffee and served a delicious fig tart and then she lit a kerosene lantern on the table which cast dark shadows of us on the walls as we all sat around the table. Of course I had to use the bathroom soon and asked if I could use the facilities. I wanted to go home even more when they told me it was outside and pointed to a brick structure with a beautiful orange trumpet vine growing all over it. Here I was at this farm away from the comforts of the city and my mother didn't warn me about anything. She didn't see the need to tell me that there was no running water, no electricity and we would be stranded for three or four days without transportation because she grew up with all that, and she just thought I would automatically know. Wrong!!

The next day was Monday and I asked my uncle when the mailman would arrive as I was already anticipating a letter from my boyfriend. He laughed and said that there was no mailman and mail had to be picked up in town so I would have to wait until the road dried — three or four days. The only transportation at the farm was a horse drawn two-wheeled buggy and bicycles.

The next morning my young cousins went to help my uncle cut some alfalfa. He was using a big scythe and my cousins were using hand sickles. I figured I was older than my cousins and even though I had never used such a tool I could do it. After only about an hour of cutting I swiped the tool and the point of it went into my leg. Good going clumsy one! It wasn't a bad wound and a band aid took care of it but my uncle didn't want me out there. It was as if he didn't want me getting hurt on his watch.

My aunt told me that there was a "festa" in Quargnento and there was a dance that evening. It was to celebrate the patron saint of the town. Since this was a working farm, work was started early in the morning, then a rather substantial lunch and afterwards everyone rested during the hottest part of the day because you could get heatstroke. Then work started again around 4:00. Work was done in the field until the sun went down. Then a light supper was eaten and we had to get ready to go to the dance. To get ready we had to use candles to get dressed in our rooms. The mode of transportation that evening was our own two feet. We brought our dancing shoes in a bag and put on an old pair of shoes for walking and we cut across pastures and wheat fields. We walked about a mile having cut off about three miles by not going on the muddy road and the main road to town finally arriving around 10:00. In town there was a temporary dance floor put up with a roof and benches on the sides.

In such a small town of about 500 people any stranger is a curiosity especially Americans in 1953. Some of the young men who asked me to dance immediately asked questions about America after asking if I was from South America or North America. I thought it was odd that they would ask if I was from South America. Later I learned that many Italians migrated to South

America as well as North America. Some of the young men who knew my relatives felt free to say "You Americans came over and bombed Italy during the war," as if I had something to do with it. Being my age, between six and eleven during World War II, I was not interested in what was going on then and my parents never really talked about the war. At the time we were living in Northern California in the small mill town of McCloud and we were sort of secluded from everything - no radio and not much activity as in the larger cities.

At the dance my uncle was so happy to re-introduce my mother to many of the people she had known before she left for America. It seemed as if every third person was a relative. In the neighboring town of Fubine it was even worse because my great-grandmother was one of 10 children and of course they all had children so I couldn't keep up with first cousins, second cousins, third cousins, etc, etc. After having a good time and enjoying the music and dancing we walked home and got back at 2:30 in the morning.

The next day the road was passable and my grandfather took my mother and me to see my paternal grandparents with the horse and buggy. I wasn't feeling well but I had to go to meet them. The sun was very hot and there was no "top" on the buggy. The law in Italy did not allow three adults in these buggies and on the way home my grandfather realized that the police had just pulled onto the road behind us. My mother got down and walked as I wasn't well and she pretended that she didn't know us and had nothing to do with us. She was just a stranger walking on the road and we happened to be riding by. Technically the police couldn't do anything but I felt bad that she was walking and I'm sure the police just shook their heads and said, "There's the Americans."

My paternal grandparents whom we had just visited were the ones who had been in America. My grandfather was Luigi Bo, born in 1876 in the little town of Franchini. In 1900 he married Maddalena Baralis who was born in the town of Acceglio near the French

border. My father Stefano Bo was born in 1905 and my aunt Maria
Bo was born in 1910. My grandfather decided to come to America
in 1911 when he was called for by his brother-in-law Stefano Baralis and sailed from La Havre, France aboard the ship "La Pro-
vence." He arrived in New York on June 24, 1911. He joined his
brother-in-law in working in the copper mines of Copperopolis,
California and then in the lumber mill in Weed, California. My
grandfather kept working and saving money and finally his brother-
in-law said "Isn't it about time you sent for your family?" So on
January 31, 1920 my grandmother, my father who was 14 at the
time and my aunt who was 9 finally arrived in New York aboard the
ship "America". The Bo family lived in Weed for two years and
then moved to McCloud, CA which was also a lumber town.
McCloud was a company town owned by the McCloud River Railroad Company.

During the visit with my grandparents my grandfather talked
about the little towns around Copperopolis which he remembered
such as San Andreas, Murphys, and he also remembered some
American words.

A year after my parents arrived in McCloud from Italy, my
brother Louis was born in February, 1931. Everyone lived together
in the house in Tucci Camp and the three who worked for the
company put all their money together. Near the end of 1931 my
grandparents decided to go back to Italy along with my aunt. I
really don't think my aunt wanted to go back, but in those days you
didn't go against your parents. They went back to Italy taking all
the savings and leaving the furniture and whatever was in the house
to my parents so basically my parents started all over again. My
grandfather had the house in Italy which my father had arranged to
be built and put his money in the bank or post office savings. Then
later the lire devalued and all my grandfather had left was the house
and land.

The house in Franchini was not a farm house as the one we were staying in but it was similar to a villa with some land around it for a small vineyard, some fruit trees, again no running water but they had electricity.

The farm house in Quargnento was about two to three times larger than the one in Franchini because there was more than one family and there was a hay loft on one side of the structure. There were also animals on both ends. They didn't send the cows to pasture. My uncle brought the feed in to the animals. There was a system for water for the animals. There were about 8 head of cattle which were fattened up to sell or for milk. They also raised chickens and rabbits. If you slept upstairs in the bedroom above the stable you could hear the animals moving their chains or making noises. The land was used for wheat, corn, alfalfa and hay. At that time my uncle didn't have a tractor and did everything with oxen which pulled the plows and rakes. When it was time to thresh the wheat a cooperative threshing machine with a crew came and worked for a day or two on the property. Then my aunt and grandmother would really cook up a storm because there were so many extra people to feed. We were there one time when the threshing machine came. Even my young cousins, ages 7 and 11 had the job of cutting the lengths of wire to go around the bales of straw. It was almost "party time."

It was almost a celebration when someone would come to visit. First there weren't any noises other than the birds and animals at the farm so if the noise of an automobile could be heard, the person who heard it would immediately yell, "Someone's coming." Everyone would go and stand outside awaiting the company. Sometimes the car was still a mile away and it would sound like a bee buzzing its way up the road.

One of these time, the taxi driver (Pino) came to tell my mom that he was going to the town of Franchini and if she wanted to go there for a few days to visit with my other grandparents. Usually if we wanted to go somewhere my uncle would bicycle into town to make an appointment with Pino to pick us up on a certain day at a certain time. Since he stopped by on the spur of the moment we just threw some clothes and shoes in a small box. He said he would pick us up for a return trip in a couple of days which was fine with us. It rained while we were in Franchini and when Pino came to pick us up again we asked if the road was passable and he assured us that it didn't rain too hard at the farm and he thought everything would be fine. It was about 10:00 p.m. and when we turned off the main road onto the dirt road Pino went about 1/2 mile before he started to slip and slide. He went a bit further so he could turn around almost getting stuck in the process and said we would have to turn back or get out. My mom said we would be fine and would walk the rest of the way. We took off our shoes, carried our box and began on our way walking up to our ankles in the mud. Pino had to try several times to get the car out of the mud and finally was able to get on his way. There was a full moon and we set off. The mud was hard to walk in and slippery. We decided to walk in the fields of wheat which had been cut so we were walking in the stubble which was poking our feet. I was worried about animals or "bogey men" and my mom started to laugh. Then I had to also laugh at this funny situation. I thought—if only my friends back home could see me now! They all thought I was going to have such a glamourous vacation.

Our talking awoke the dog and he started barking and soon my Zio (uncle) Evasio came downstairs with a lantern to see what was happening. My grandfather was so happy to see me laughing and without the frown on my face which I had worn for the last few weeks.

2

LA CASCINA (THE FARMHOUSE)

From now on I will refer to the farmhouse as the *cascina*, my grandparents as *nonno* and *nonna*, or the plural as *nonni*, my uncle and aunt as *zio* or *zia* or *zii* for plural.

The cascina as I said was a large structure as it had two families living in it. It was built in the 1850's by my nonno's father, Giuseppe Stanchi who came from Valenza, Italy.

Maternal great-grandfather Giuseppe Stanchi

Valenza is not too far from Quargnento and is known for its gold and artisans of gold jewelry. My great grandfather met Maria Mairo of Fubine and married her and they constructed the cascina with other family members. The cascina has walls that are at least 18 inches thick and stays cool in summer.

My nonno who was born at this cascina in 1876 was Domenico Stanchi

Maternal grandfather Domenico Stanchi

and he married Rosa Zeppa who was born in 1888 in Fubine.

Grandparents Rosa Zeppa & Domenico Stanchi circa 1907

They had four children, Giuseppe, Maria or Marina (my mother), Evasio, and Adriana.

Across the cement walkway in front of the cascina there was a well which was about 30 to 40 feet deep and had good cool water. My nonno loved his wine a bit cooler than room temperature so he would pull up a bucket of water about an hour before a meal and put a bottle of wine in this bucket to cool it off. Then when he was ready to eat he would pull up another bucket of fresh cool water and put the bottle in it. If he had a refrigerator during the time he was alive I'm sure he would love to use the ice that it made and my nonna would be nagging him because she would say that drinking very cold beverages would tie up your intestines in a knot. My nonno also loved the American black pepper and my mother always made packages to send her family and always put in a large can of black pepper. He claimed that Italian black pepper was not as strong as American pepper. I remember seeing nonno sprinkle pepper on his food and nonna nagging him. He would just shrug his shoulders and keep doing what he was doing. He was a very patient, quiet and calm man and my nonna was a little spitfire.

At the cascina there was also a large outdoor brick oven. It was housed in a structure that was about 10 by 20 feet. They usually lit a fire in the oven once a week and some of the people from neighboring farms would come over when they knew the oven would be in use and ask if they could bake their bread or whatever they could. The fire was started using old grape vines which were then shoved to the side of the oven and cleaned out by a wet mop. The oven could probably handle about 50 loaves of bread though I don't know if these were small individual loaves or what. I was told recently that my nonno would test the temperature of the oven by placing a straw on the bread peel and count to 60 and if the straw turned a dark brown the oven was too hot so he waited a while until it was the right temperature. After the bread was baked the oven temperature was low enough to bake cakes or tarts and also meat casseroles or meats such as roasts or poultry.

I mentioned earlier that the cascina did not have running water, so to wash up we had a basin with a pitcher of well water in our bedrooms. The water was cold in the mornings and it took a bit of getting used to it. To brush my teeth was a bit difficult, also to pour water from the pitcher holding my toothbrush in one hand and pouring water with the other.

The cascina had a name "Casa Pace" which means peaceful house or house of peace as it was about three miles from town and was out in a peaceful area. During World War II it was never bothered by anyone. The cascina also sat on a small knoll and you could look all around it and see the valleys and fields. The photo on the cover is of the cascina.

3

THE FESTA OF FUBINE

The festa of Fubine was similar to the festa of Quargnento but Fubine is a much larger town. The festivities
started on the weekend with a dance on Saturday and
Sunday. Again, this festa was in honor of the patron
saint of Fubine which is San Cristofero. There were two
or three booths with the nougat candy called Torrone
for sale which I found to be delicious but hard on the
teeth. During the weekend everyone had relatives or
friends over for dinner and that is when they cooked perhaps twice the normal amount of food.

First they start off with antipasto which is usually sliced meats
such as prosciutto, mortadella, coppa and then some cured olives,
or marinated vegetables. Then comes some form of pasta or rice in
a spaghetti sauce. Then there is chicken and beef or veal and two
or three vegetables. There was also a dish which is typical of the
area which is a mixture of fried items such as small pieces of liver,
small pieces of breaded veal, carrot sticks, breakfast sausage links

and an item which I really love. This item is cooked cream of wheat which also contains grated lemon rind, then it is poured into a dish and left for a few hours to harden. Then this is cut into squares or diamonds, coated with egg and then breadcrumbs and fried. All these ingredients are mixed onto a dish and is always included for festivals. Then there are two or three varieties of cheese and dessert is usually fruit and cookies. Of course there is always an abundance of wine and at the end there is espresso coffee.

On Wednesday during this festa there was always "The Picnic." Everyone of the town and outlying farms went to a meadow which was about a half mile from town with a little hill next to the meadow. Since it was close everyone walked to this meadow and if people had cars they just drove right on the grass and parked. Blankets or tablecloths were spread and baskets of food were laid out. It was a chance for everyone to visit and eat and forget about work or worries for the day. It was a very relaxing and enjoyable day.

During this time I met some cousins who were visiting from New York. Ada Peri was the daughter of a brother of my great grandmother. Ada had a daughter a little older than myself and another daughter younger. I enjoyed their company. Another relative of one of my great grandmother's brothers happened to be Luigi Longo of Rome. Ada made us all laugh when she said that she was going to Rome with her two daughters to see this cousin and then to see the Pope. The reason we laughed was that Luigi at that time was the Deputy Secretary of the Communist Party in Italy so she would visit her cousin first and then go to see the Pope to be absolved of her "sins"? Luigi later became the Secretary General of the Communist Party from 1964 to 1972 and I have read that he was a very nice man.

New York had a very large contingent of people from Fubine and there was a club called "La Fubinese." I don't know how many members belonged to the club but I think it was in the hundreds. It is still going strong today and there is a yearly dinner dance and I recently heard from a friend in New York that he attended the last gathering. This friend is in his nineties and still going strong.

The cousins from New York had traveled to Rome and Venice and other cities and my mother could see that I was a bit bored just visiting relatives in the small towns so we decided to go to Venice. We took the train from Milano and arrived in Venice around 9:00 in the evening with no reservations. (We were very novice travelers.) My mom wasn't afraid to ask whomever, such as porters as to the availability of rooms. One of the porters knew of a family that rented out rooms so our first night was a room in a house which was very clean and nice but my mother made sure to put a chair under the doorknob. The next day during our walk around the city we found a room at a very nice hotel.

The only other big city we visited was where my mother's older brother, Zio Pino lived and that was Torino. He and his wife Zia Francesca had a latteria. A latteria is a store that sells mostly dairy products but they did sell some soda pop, eggs, candy. Stores in Italy in that time were very specialized and sold only certain items. There were meat markets which sold only veal, pork and poultry. Then there was a salumeria which sold sausages and salamies or meats of that type. There was also the butcher who sold horse meat. A housewife went to at least four food shops every morning to get fresh food to prepare the day's meal. I think many of the housewives just loved visiting with all the shopkeepers whom they knew and catching up on the gossip. This was very true in the little towns. Now there are very large supermarkets which put our Costco to shame.

A few doors down from my zio's store there was a reataurant and some afternoons my zio would send my cousin Rosanna to get some ice cream cones. This was a special treat to me as on the farm there was no refrigeration. I think gelato is the best ice cream in the world and the chocolate and lemon are especially delicious.

Now you can guess how I put on quite a bit of weight while in Italy with my mother.

Another trip my mother and I took besides Venice was to the Italian Riviera and it was only because my mother's first cousin who was married to a doctor was spending the summer there. The doctor who was staying home because of his practice arranged to pick us up to take us to the train station so that we could visit her along with their small daughter. He didn't have time to come all the way to the cascina so it was planned to pick us up on the main road. The two of us along with our luggage could not fit on the buggy so my zio loaded us on the big farm cart which was pulled by two oxen. We stood up in the cart and rumbled along the dirt road. It was an ugly foggy morning and I had my usual frown on my face. The doctor picked us up on the paved road and took us to the train station which we took to the town of Laigueglia and met up with the cousins. We stayed two or three days and then returned back to the cascina. I remember the Mediterranean ocean being so calm and warm, unlike our beach at Santa Cruz. Also the sand was more pebbly instead of sticky sand.

Many of the people who live in the big cities of Italy go to the beaches or mountains for the summer so that they can at least breathe healthier air and relax. The husbands usually stay home and visit the family on the weekends. I enjoyed the few trips away from the cascina because I could enjoy having a nice bath just like home and not having to use the "outhouse."

When I thought of all the hard work and what had to be done at the cascina, it was easy to appreciate how comfortable we had it in America. To cook, a two-burner propane stove was used. I couldn't believe the multi-course dinners served while we were there. I am sure they weren't the normal fare but I know they were celebrating the fact that we were there. The dinners were like an orchestrated play as to what was cooked first and last and kept warm by setting dishes holding food onto pots which were still cooking to keep things warm. Sometimes there were three items stacked up on one burner. Then to wash the dishes, two buckets of water were pulled up from the well, one was warmed on the burner for soapy water and one was used for rinsing and dishes were washed in a very small space almost like a long closet with a sink minus the faucet but with a drain. Water was not wasted. A chair was set up with a dishpan and dishes were placed in this pan to drain.

For washing clothes, a few buckets of water were pulled up from the well and heated and a large tub was set up in a small room next to the stable in the winter or outdoors in the summer and clothes were scrubbed on a washboard, rinsed and hung up to dry. My mother told me about the years before she married in 1929 when the linens had to be washed. They wouldn't do them as we do them every week. They would save up the wash and when spring time arrived they would do all the linens at once, often taking the whole week. They folded the sheets and then pleated them accordian style and stood them up in a large vat similar to a small wooden hot tub. When the tub was full, they would place a white cloth or another sheet over the ones which were standing up. Over this they spread ashes from the fireplace and then poured hot boiling water over all of this. This procedure was repeated until the water from the drain came out clear. The sheets were spread over the grasses or alfalfa to dry as they didn't have enough lines to dry all of them.

The fireplace was used to hang kettles of water from hooks of iron and my grandmother also made polenta in the fireplace by stirring the water and cornmeal in the pot hanging from the hook.

Cakes or tarts were made in the large oven outside when bread was made but I saw my other zia in Franchini make a cake in the fireplace as she didn't have a large oven as on the farm. She made a fire and let it burn down to just some coals and mostly ashes. She placed the cake pan with a lid among the ashes and heaped the

ashes onto the cover. Of course it was with quite a bit of experi-
ence that the cakes came out just right without being burned or not
baked enough.

To iron clothes, my Zia Pina was an expert. She had an old iron
which opened from the top. Hot coals were placed into the iron
which had holes just above the sole plate and all around the base.
Her ironing board was the table with a blanket spread onto it and a
clean white cloth over the blanket. Sometimes I would see her
swing the iron to "fan" the coals to keep them hot. My Zio Evasio's
white dress shirts looked like a work of art—so white and without a
single wrinkle. Very rarely a spark would fall out of the iron and
burn a hole in whatever zia was ironing. My Zio Evasio always
changed from his work clothes to go to town and Zia Pina always
made sure his clothes were hanging and ready for him to change
into. In later years (1990's) their daughter Rosita was working in
Milano and would take the train home on weekends and Zio
Evasio would go to pick her up at the train station in Alessandria.
He would change from work clothes to his Sunday suit to go there
but of course he would do some errands in that city so he didn't
want to look like a peasant even if it was only the grocery store.

During our time in Italy we celebrated my saint day which was
August 30. Italians at that time celebrated the saint day more than
birthdays. The saint for which I was named, besides being my
grandmother's name is Saint Rose of Lima. Besides myself and my
grandmother, my cousins were also named Rosanna and Rosita so
there were four of us and of course a big dinner was prepared.
Rosita was the daughter of Zio Evasio and Zia Pina and Rosanna
was at the cascina during the summer so her parents, Zio Pino and
Zia Francesca came from Torino. Raviolis were made for this special occasion and gifts were also given to the honorees. My grandmother gave me a beautiful 18 karat gold ring with two small rubies
which I still wear quite often. I picked it out and I still remember

the price. It was $17.00 and I'm sure the price would have been many times more if it was here in America at that time.

When we returned home in September another "Rose" was born in October. My mother's sister, Adriana who came to America in 1950, gave birth to a girl named Rosemary. You could say our family had a bouquet of roses because of my grandmother.

4

MC CLOUD

I was the first born Rose to be named after my grand-mother. Four and a half years after my brother Louis was born, I was born on July 17, 1935 in McCloud, California on what my mother said was the hottest day of the summer. The doctor visited my mother the day before I was born and suggested that since she was about ten days overdue she should take a dose of castor oil to hasten my arrival as he was going on vacation in a few days. My mother hesitated taking the castor oil so I decided it was time to come out the next day with the help of two midwives, Nanda Isoardi and Caterina Marchetti. My father had shaved my brother's head bald in order to stay cool during the summer heat and my brother was so happy to have a baby sister that he went all around the neighborhood telling everyone that "mia mamma ha comprato una sorrellina." My mother bought a baby sister. Our neighbor, a jovial Tuscan lady saw him getting sunburned on his bald head so she brought him home telling my mother to keep him in but he was just too happy and wanted to tell the world.

We were living in New Mill Camp of McCloud at the time and you could say that McCloud was segregated where there were three separate neighborhoods which were away from the center of town and were inhabitated by Italians. There was Tucci Camp, where my brother was born, Old Mill Camp and New Mill Camp where I was born.

Bo family, Marina & Steve Bo, Maria Bo - Grandparents Luigi & Maddalena Bo with baby Louis 1931

New Mill Camp was 1 1/2 miles from town.

Steve (Stefano) Bo, Marina Bo, Rose and Louis Bo, 1937

There were about 40 homes on two streets, North Street and Firenze Street, which is the Italian word for Florence. Since almost everyone in the neighborhood spoke Italian, my mother learned English along with my brother when he went to school. My brother and I spoke the dialect Piemontese and our neighbors spoke mostly the true Italian but everyone understood each other.

I don't remember too much of the years before going to school but I do remember my little friend next door. Mirella Bortolin was born when I was 4 years of age and after she began walking she was like my little shadow.

Before I started school there was no Kindergarten class so my first day of school began with the first grade. The day before the first day, my mother suffered a miscarriage. My father had to take my mother to the hospital, then take me to school and explain to the teacher what had happened. Of course I didn't know what had happened, just that my mother was sick. The teacher paid special attention to me and had me right next to her side while she registered the children in her class. In the first grade our teacher was Mrs. Farnham and what I remember most was that we had to have clean fingernails and a clean handkerchief.

From our neighborhood all the school children walked to school together. Of course the older high school children would walk far ahead of the younger ones but my mother would always tell my brother to keep an eye on me. One of my friends was Franca Peretto who came from Italy the year before and spoke just Piemontese. I was her interpreter at the school. When the war started there were rules to observe in the bathroom such as two squirts of soap and one sheet of paper towel. I couldn't make her understand this and she was always in trouble with the bathroom police and made to stay in at recess. If I was ill and didn't attend school her mother said that she would really have a hard time making her go to school because I wasn't there for her. Unfortunately she was held back a year because of her language skills.

Almost none of the mothers in the neighborhood drove cars so most of us walked to school even through snow, rain, wind, etc. It was a mile and a half but with eight or ten children walking together the time passed quickly. When Mirella started school four years after I started, her mother was younger, more aggressive and I was happy because very often Mirella was running late and her mother would say, "Just a minute as Mirella isn't ready yet and I will drive you to school." Three or four of us soon learned to stop by Mirella's house on our way to school and if we were lucky her mom would drive us.

Walking home from school we passed by the park where there were swings, a very wide slide and monkey bars. We would forget about the time and play on the bars. Arriving home late I would be admonished by my mother. I tried to lie and say that I had to do something for the teacher but one look at my dirty hands would prove that I had been playing at the park. The next time we stayed a bit too long at the park I prepared for my lie by licking my hands and wiping them on my dress.

McCloud was a company town and everyone worked for the company whether it was at the mill, the box factory, the big general store, etc. One could not live in the town and not work for the company. Also when something was purchased at the general store, you could pay for it in cash or just charge it to your account with the purchases being deducted from the pay check at the end of the month. After the age of ten, my brother and I were allowed to go to the general store and buy a nickel ice cream cone if we wished and we would say "charge it." Can you imagine the trouble it was for the clerks to write the date, name of the account, the address and the item — 1 ice cream cone — 5 cents and have us sign it. Then the clerk would give us the duplicate and send the original in a pneumatic tube up to the general office to be added to our account. I don't think we took advantage of the situation but perhaps if we lived closer to the store, who knows?

There were two doctors in town, Dr. Runkel and Dr. Dickenson, and the hospital was situated on a hill. Dr. Runkel's son was on the ship USS Arizona when it was sunk in Pearl Harbor on Dec. 7th, 1941. I remember going with my parents to visit Dr. Dickenson and he reminded me of the doctor in the Norman Rockwell painting sitting at the roll top desk. After any visit with the doctor he would open the middle drawer of his desk and pull out one stick of Black Jack gum and give it to me. That was my reward for being a good girl.

Our camp was right next to the pine forest. To the north was the majestic Mount Shasta which was almost always covered with snow, even during the summer time. I always thought Mount Shasta was where Santa Claus lived, right up on the very top.

It was great fun to play in the woods. Some of the teenagers put up an iron pipe between two trees and did chinups or just played on the bar. There was also a bocce court which the men played on Sunday afternoons. I remember playing hide and seek, kick the can, red, white and blue and any other game we could think of. There were small wooden sheds, perhaps two or three to a block and they contained a fire hose. These were great places in which to hide. We would remove the front door and go inside and hold the door in place. We always found something to do, we were never bored. Mirella and I also made a teeter-totter with a saw horse and an eight-foot ladder. She sat in between the rungs on one end and I sat at the other end. We had great fun. Her grandfather had the saw horse and my father had the ladder and she and I would go down the street carrying the ladder to her grandfather's house. Nowadays I think teeter-totters are not allowed in parks anymore. What a shame.

There was a swimming pool in McCloud but since it was in town, we had our own swimming hole in the woods. There were two railroad tracks which led to the mill and they were only five minutes from our house. There was a stream which came from the mountain and went under the tracks. Some of the boys dammed up the stream in between the tracks so that it made a small pond. This was our swimming hole and we had a great time even if the water felt like 20 degrees.

When I mentioned that McCloud was segregated, we also had a black neighborhood. There were 20 or 30 homes of African-American people living in this neighborhood. I didn't realize it then that we were segregated because I had two of them as friends in my class. Leroy Slocum and Betty Pitts walked home with us from school every day as we came to their camp before we reached New Mill Camp. I didn't realize until years later that they were not allowed at the pool in town and they were limited to a certain section at the theater. I also learned that they had their own swimming hole but instead of one of the streams, their swimming hole was because of a hole in the water pipeline that passed near their neighborhood, they dug a hole in the ground and let the water fill up the hole. Then they would plug the hole in the pipeline. Of course it was standing water and muddy. I felt so bad when I saw this mud hole.

I never felt the racial bias that some Italians felt during the first years of the war but my brother did when he heard a teacher tell some of the young boys who were speaking Italian that they should all go back where they came from. Since there was a majority of Italians living in McCloud she probably felt outnumbered. My father served as a trustee on the school board and many years later told me of the problems with the teacher because of her prejudice with the blacks and the Italians.

McCloud was a small town of 2,300 people. The main industry was the lumber mill where my father worked. He ran the transfer which was a large platform that ran on very wide railroad tracks which were about 25 to 30 feet across. He would transfer rail cars full of cut boards from the dry kilns where the green lumber was placed to dry out. After a certain number of days the kilns would be opened up and the cars of lumber would be pulled out and transferred to the outside. I think the kilns held two or three cars of lumber each in a line. I don't remember how many kilns there were. On Sunday if my father had to work it was always exciting to walk to the mill to see him working. He would allow me or my brother to sit on the covers for the motors as long as we behaved and we enjoyed riding up and down the track. Sundays were not busy so even the bosses didn't mind us being there. Can you imagine what Cal Osha would say now of this situation? The best part of visiting my dad was that there was a Coca Cola machine there and he would allow us to have a nickel to get a soda from the machine. We never had Coke at home so it was a big treat. I also loved to meet my dad when it was quitting time. The men would line up at the time clock which was like a huge regular clock with numbers all around it and holes below each number. There was a large arm on it and the arm was swung around until you came to your employee number and punched it in the hole. My father would pick me up and let me swing the arm around to his number and punch it in the hole. I felt so important.

My parents went through the depression in McCloud but they said they did not suffer. The company was good to them, rent being only $9.00 and later going up to $12.00. Also they had insurance paid for them by the company with dependents costing $1.00 a month. The families were given sacks of flour so that they could make bread and pasta. My mother made some form of pasta everyday and I hated it. We also had chickens for meat and eggs and a huge vegetable garden. I was a poor eater and my mother tried to do everything she could to make me eat. She made pasta with red sauce, meat sauce, butter sauce, cheese sauce but I turned up my nose at all of these. She also gave me a spoonful of Scott's fish emulsion every morning to keep me healthy and help to give me an appetite. Nothing worked until I became a teenager. At school we didn't have a cafeteria so we brought our lunches every day. My mother would usually put in a sandwich, cookies, a banana or apple and a thermos of milk during warm weather or hot chocolate during cold weather. She always included a cloth napkin on which she had embroidered a squirrel or dog or cat.

During the first three years of my schooling my mother was ill quite a bit. In first grade she had a miscarriage, the second year she had an appendectomy and two years after that she had a hysterectomy. During the last two illnesses I stayed with a family, Iole and Giovanni Puccini who lived about five houses down the street and they had a daughter Marisa who was six years older than I. I really felt so lucky to have someone like an older sister and she really treated me as such. Her parents spoiled me rotten during these times. Also Iole made different foods than I was used to such as different fillings for sandwiches and cupcakes with frosting on them and then Giovanni would tease me and play tricks on me so that I would be happy and not think of my mother being sick. When my mother came home from the hospital my father came to take me home and I was terrible by saying, "Oh no, I think I'll stay here." The Puccini family had spoiled me too much.

The weather in McCloud was hot and dry during the summers and the winters usually had a lot of snow. I don't remember the year of 1936 but I was told that it snowed so much that the company made all the men working in the mill go out and shovel the snow off the roofs of the homes. I do remember one year when my brother and I were walking to school while it was snowing and he let the snow pile up on his hat. When we arrived at school there was at least 4 or 5 inches of snow on his head. Being a child I thought it was great when I would wake up and see that it had snowed during the night. As we went out I loved to hear the crunch, crunch of the snow as we walked on the sidewalks.

Speaking of sidewalks, we had wooden sidewalks instead of cement sidewalks. The only cement sidewalks were downtown where the general store, post office, theater and hotel were. In the camps the sidewalks were wooden and we had to be careful so as not to drop money or anything of value because it would fall through the cracks and be lost. If it was near our house, my father had to pull up the boards with a hammer. I remember my friend next door losing a ring at her house and I lost money once or twice. After that my mother always tied whatever money I had in the corner of my handkerchief. I also remember losing rosary beads in the wooden steps of the catholic church and I really cried because I couldn't ask anyone to take up the boards. Years later I visited the church again and was dismayed to see that the wooden steps were replaced with cement steps going into the church. I wonder how many rosary beads or how much money was found under the steps.

Wooden sidewalks were not suited for roller skating so no one had roller skates in our camp except for Freddy. He had a pair of skates and he let my friend Alice Reginato and I borrow them. We didn't know how to skate but we would each put on one skate and try to skate on the street which was also full of pot holes. We soon gave that up.

McCloud was also a fisherman's paradise. My father loved to fish but did not like to eat them. It was always fun to go fishing in the late afternoon. When my dad had the early shift at the mill he would tell mom to have a picnic ready and we would go fishing around four or five in the afternoon. The limit of trout then was 15 and we always caught the limit. Then he would clean them and send me with plates of the fish to our neighbors. My mother did fry some and marinate them and that is the only way my father liked to eat them.

The company had a big Fourth of July picnic every year and they would transport the people who didn't have cars by truckloads out to one of the rivers where there was a huge flat area. Then we would have a huge picnic with the company furnishing some of the food. I don't remember but my mother told me that one year the picnic had to be canceled because it snowed during this holiday.

Another interesting fact about McCloud is that William Randolph Hearst had a home on the McCloud River. The family still has this home and it is like a Bavarian home right next to the river. I have been told that Mr. Hearst would send his chauffer into town and round up children on the street and bring them to his home and treat them to hot dogs and hamburgers. This home is called Wintoon. Mr. Hearst would also have the first editions of the San Francisco Examiner newspaper flown up from San Francisco to the airfield in Dunsmuir, so the people of McCloud were privileged to be among the first to get the news.

The McCloud River goes right through the Hearst property and people have gone down the river in rafts but one cannot get out of the raft onto his property. We know some people whose raft got hung up on a rock and while they were wrestling with the raft, a guard with a shotgun appeared and said "You people are not thinking of stopping on this property are you?" They assured him they were not stopping and quickly disengaged their raft from the rock.

The woods around McCloud are also great for mushroom hunting and my family would often go mushroom hunting. My parents and brother were good at finding mushrooms but I was not. I think I was always worried about getting lost and not finding my way back to the car. When we did come home with mushrooms my parents would clean them and slice them and spread them on screens which were taken down from the windows. They dried in about a day or two depending if the weather was warm. Then they were used in cooking.

With all the fishing, hunting, and mushroom hunting my husband often asks why my family moved from this paradise. During the winter my father was usually sick with pleurisy or bad colds so when he went to San Jose to attend a Sons of Italy Convention in February and there were trees in bloom and flowers blooming, he said "Let's move."

Although we moved to San Jose in 1946 there were many fond memories of McCloud. In fact, many people referred to it as "Mother McCloud." The people were not treated as just another number. I'm sure it was because of the supervisors, bosses, etc. The person who was the liaison between the Americans and Italians was John Peracchino. Many of the Italians did not speak English and when and if they had problems they would go to him and he with his mild manner would usually come up with a solution. John was a single man living with his brother and brother's wife and two children. One of the children died and then his brother died. He kept living with the sister-in-law, Margarita and her son John. If he had not been living with them, they would have had to move because one could not live in a company house and not be working for the company. I will not forget their house because it sat up on the side of a hill. The lawn on the side of the house sloped down toward the road. Whenever we went to visit, John, my brother Louis and I would lay horizontally across the top of the lawn and roll down the hill. It was such fun. We would entertain ourselves with so little.

Near the Christmas holidays the company would invite everyone with children to the theatre and would hand out presents to the children. One year I remember receiving a very thick coloring book and a box of crayons. The book was about two inches thick. It kept me busy for months. Toys were quite scarce in our house and I still remember almost all of them.

During the depression the company also took care of workers by having them work at least one or two days a week at $2.00 a day so that they would at least have some money coming in. We didn't have natural gas for the stoves, they were wood burning stoves. Almost all of the families had a wood shed where they would store wood and also a part that was for storing anything else. The woodshed had an opening at the back alley with a wooden "window." We would call for a load of wood and it would be delivered by the company and dumped by the window. The wood was usually the ends "cut-offs" or scrap lumber of boards or 2 x 4's and the size of the truck was about 3/4 ton. My brother went around when he saw the truck deliver the wood and ask the people if he could throw the wood into the woodshed for 50 cents a load. My brother was an enterprising young man of 12 or 13. He would also go around and see who had a dirty car and offer to wash it for 50 cents. The priest was always willing to get his little coupe washed and then he would tip them money for an ice cream cone. Louis and another young boy would also run the coat or hat check room at the dances. I remember seeing them make double cards with numbers on them. At the dances which were usually organized by the Sons of Italy Lodges everyone went to the dance. There were no baby-sitters in those days, at least my parents didn't use them. They took me to the dances and if I got sleepy I would just fall asleep on the bench. Everyone knew each other and had a great time. During intermission the other kids and I would slide on the dance floor which had been sprinkled with something they called "spangles" in order to make the floor easier for dancing.

We didn't get a telephone in McCloud until around 1942 and then it was a party line. I think there were about six other families on our line. The telephone was a wooden box on the wall which had the mechanism in it. Next to the box was a small platform on which rested the black tall phone with a hook on which to hang the earpiece. There was a small crank on the right side of the box. Our ring was one long and two short. There was one person who loved to listen in on conversations. It was easy to pick up and listen when you recognized the ring of one of the other parties. I remember hearing about this person in later years when her son who was in the service telephoned his girlfriend instead of his mother and when the mother recognized the ring, she picked up the phone to listen. Hearing her son's voice, she cut right in and was so happy to hear his voice. The girlfriend was pretty upset to have the future mother-in-law cutting in.

Before we got the telephone we improvised with our neighbor. Other then walking right next door to talk to them, on winter evenings especially if it was cold, we would shine a flashlight in their kitchen window which faced our kitchen window. When we got their attention they would open the window and we would say whatever we had to say.

A fond memory of our neighbor was that she made bread in a large brick oven in her back yard. She made large loaves of a chewy bread much like the ciabatta bread which can be purchased nowadays. She sold the bread for 25 cents a loaf and they were about 12 inches in diameter and tasted so good. My brother and some of his friends would hang around when she made bread about three times a week and when it came hot out of the oven she would give them pieces of the bread and they would sit on her cellar steps chewing away. This lady was Laurina Barsanti and was the mother of the founders of Race Street Fish and Poultry Company in San Jose. We are still friends today with the family and still recall the good old days of McCloud.

Beginning in 7th or 8th grade Louis was allowed to go to the general store and buy things for my mother and go to the post office. We did not have mail delivery or newspaper delivery. The lady next door to us on the north side also asked my brother to pick up a newspaper for her family. Besides paying my brother for the newspaper she would "tip" my brother with a candy. She would wrap a Luden's cough drop in a bit of wax paper and twist the ends so that it looked like an Italian caramella or hard candy. My brother caught on and didn't care for the cough drop so he would have me deliver the newspaper to her. I would do his work and bring the paper next door and she would always say, "Wait a minute, I'll give you a caramella." Wow, I would think—bring it home and discover it was a Luden's coughdrop. Well, she meant well.

Another good memory of McCloud was that my father made wine. When the season turned to fall, some of the men would go downtown with pickup trucks and get the grapes they ordered so that they could make wine. The grapes came either by train or sometimes came by individual trucks from the Napa Valley. My father didn't have the equipment and neither did most of the other families in our camp. There was usually one family that had the equipment to crush and press and then it was loaned out to all the others. We did have a large tank for fermentation in our wood-shed. The grapes were crushed and put into the large tank. When-ever we walked into the woodshed for the next week, there would be a heavy smell of grapes fermenting. Then when the grapes were ready to be pressed, the juice at the bottom of the tank would be drawn off and then the remaining grapes would be pressed. I would see the wine press being dragged on skids behind the car of the owner of the press. Then the press would be brought to the different houses in our camp. The big screw in the middle of the wine press would have a long handle and 3, 4, or 5 men would push this handle around and make the screw press down on the blocks of wood which were pressing the grapes. I always thought I was helping my father if I pushed him on his backside. I'm sure I was a bit of a bother but he never scolded me or shooed me away. The juice was placed into the barrels in our basement.

In our basement along one side were the barrels of wine and on the opposite side were shelves where my mother placed the fruit she canned. My brother loved to arrange the jars by color. The dark red cherries, the white pears, the yellow peaches and the orange apricots. I don't remember if she canned vegetables, perhaps because I didn't like vegetables. Louis and I both loved cherries and my mother portioned out the same number of cherries to each of us. However, you could say I was a little devil when I would swallow a few pits and then tell my mother she miscounted because I had less pits than he did. So she would give me a few more. He didn't catch on for a while. Then I was worried that a cherry tree would grow in my stomach.

My mother was a good cook making raviolis, gnocchi, pasta but I think I didn't appreciate that fact then as I was so picky. The gnocchi were my brother's favorite dish. I didn't really have a favorite.

Mom was also an excellent seamstress and made all of my clothes. She had a friend who worked in the dry goods department of the general store and she would tell my mom if some nice material came in to make a dress for me. I especially remember a brown velveteen dress with gold buttons she made and then made a short white imitation fur jacket with a hat to go with it. I loved that outfit.

Louis and Rose with outfits sewed by mom

She also made a double breasted suit for my brother and it looked very professional. She made my First Communion dress and veil and the suit was for my brother's Confirmation.

My First Communion dress and veil made by mom, 1942

I always had a new dress for the first day of school, Christmas, and Easter. Those were special days with special outfits to wear. Of course she made other dresses but they were not as fancy as those.

Mom also did fancy embroidery, cutwork and filet. Filet work is like a fisherman's net but much more delicate and then usually has a design worked in it. When she was a teenager in Italy, she made a black dress with beautiful filet work on the skirt. The work was red roses with green leaves. A few years ago when we celebrated her 80th birthday the invitation was a photo of her wearing the dress. She still had the dress and we hung it up on the wall at the party. One of the gentlemen who was older than she by a few years said he remembered when she arrived in McCloud wearing the dress. He thought the dress was beautiful and unforgettable.

5

OUR VACATION IN KLAMATH FALLS

When I was about five years old our family was invited by our cousins to spend two weeks in Klamath Falls. They had a farm so this was completely different from living in a lumber town. My father took my mother, brother and myself to the farm and then he went back to work in McCloud. This was like a fantasy for me. There were pigs, chickens, a horse, cows, etc. In fact I was so unfamiliar with farm life that my cousins have yet to stop teasing me about how I didn't know very much about farm animals.

When we first arrived my cousin Guy took us around for a tour showing us just about everything. He took us near the bull, a big white and black bull behind a double fence and told me not to go too close to it as it was mean. Later on that day I went to see Guy milking the cows and I saw him milking a huge black and white animal. I immediately asked, "Guy are you milking the bull?" He knew I didn't know the difference so he said "Yes, I am." Boy I was scared and ran like lightning to the house and announced, "Guy is milking the bull!" They never let me live that down along with another proclamation that I made. Since we always had very simple breakfasts of coffee and milk and bread or hot chocolate and toast or crackers, the breakfasts at the farm were really a treat and I soon enjoyed all the different things my cousin made. One especially good breakfast was pancakes which I had never tasted. When my mother said she would like to have the recipe for the pancakes I informed her that she couldn't make them because we didn't have cow's milk because our milk came from a bottle left on the porch by the milkman. Up until that time I had never seen cows in McCloud. There were cows but not where I ever saw them.

My cousin Guy also let us ride on the horse behind him. The horse seemed huge to me and was named Dolly. One day the neighbor children came over and we were all playing and then everyone ran next door to play. I was the last one after them and ran out of the gate and didn't want to close the big farm gate because I might not catch up with them. Well, Dolly knew immediately that the gate was open and ran out. It was a good thing she ran after us to the same neighbor's farm and we saw her, plus she was running in the vegetable garden and eating vegetables. I was scolded and told the importance of always closing the farm gate.

One of the chores I liked to do everyday was to go and pick the eggs. We would end up with quite a few buckets of eggs and then we would clean them with sand paper and candle them to see if there were any blood spots in them. I think during the two weeks I only broke one or two eggs but I felt bad about that. We also went with my cousin to slop the hogs which I didn't like because it smelled. They also grew hay and potatoes. One time I was sitting behind a hay stack and my cousin didn't know I was there because I was little. He started to pick up the stack with a pitchfork and the tine went into my leg. Boy, did I holler and he felt bad about that but I lived.

Since there were so many irrigation canals or ditches around Klamath Falls it was a good breeding place for mosquitoes. I was covered with mosquito bites and my mother's remedy for the itch was to apply vinegar on my bites. I went around smelling like a salad.

The Fourth of July parade occurred while we were in Klamath Falls. Number one, I had never seen a parade and number two, I had never seen a live Native American Indian. There were many Native Americans in the parade on horseback in their full headresses and native clothes. I was really impressed.

That summer we were also introduced to ice cream sundaes. We went to town and ordered ice cream sundaes and I was in heaven. It was a small one, one scoop with strawberry syrup and a special shaped spoon. I had never tasted anything so delicious.

Another thing we did was to get together with the four neighbor children and play softball around the farm house. Since they didn't have that many cows, they let them roam around to eat the grass. When we played softball we learned to watch where we put our feet, we didn't want to step into an unexpected gift from the cows.

We did go another time during the summer to our cousins and I will never forget the good times spent there with them. I was always so happy to see them because we didn't have any relatives here, they were all back in Italy. These cousins were related to us in this manner. My grandmother on my father's side had a brother, Stefano Baralis. He had three daughters, Lina, Angela and Maria or Mary. Angela married Tony Galletti and had two children, Eleanor and Gaetano or Guy. Angela's family was the one in Klamath Falls. I actually felt deprived because many of the children talked about their grandparents, aunts and uncles and cousins. I didn't have anyone, just our family, but at least I had a good family and good friends, I was just too young to realize it.

6

THE MOVE

My father had been thinking about moving from McCloud because of the weather and the fact that there wasn't much future for my brother and me other than to work in the mill. He and my mother didn't talk too much about their plans so I didn't know a thing. One day when I was in fourth grade my friend Alice said as we were walking home from school, "Your parents told my parents that you were going to move to Davis." This was the first I heard about it so I denied it and she insisted that my family was going to move because my dad bought a gas station with a little grocery store attached. Then I was worried that they might have moved without me so I ran all the way home to see if they were still there. When I questioned my parents they said they were looking into this but decided not to move to Davis. The following year, however, they did decide to move to

San Jose. They went into a partnership with Franca's parents and the two families bought a corner "mom and pop" grocery store on 17th and Empire in San Jose in a predominantly Italian neighborhood and called it Siskiyou Market after the county we moved from. The grocery store had living quarters attached to it but it was a house with only two bedrooms in it and one bathroom. Our two families comprised of seven people. The other couple took the smaller bedroom. Their daughter, Franca slept in the dining room. My parents and I slept in the larger bedroom. My brother, Louis slept in the detached double garage that also served as the warehouse for the store. The garage was just wood siding with knotholes letting the breezes in. My brother never caught a cold the two years he slept out there. He really loved having his own private bedroom. My father and the other man, Vince got jobs in a lumber factory and a cannery. The two ladies ran the store.

I thought San Jose was great. Coming from a small town of 2,500 to a city with just under 100,000 people I thought I was really something. The city bus line stopped right at our store and we could get on and go downtown which seemed like a big metropolis to me. When we moved to San Jose it was the end of school after my fifth grade. In September I began the sixth grade at Grant Grammar School on 12th and Empire. There were two classes of each grade. After the first two weeks of school, the principal called my mother in and told her that I was finishing my work faster than the other students and then I was bored. Since McCloud was a small town with a small school, the classes had only 20 to 30 students and each child got a lot of attention so I was a bit ahead of the students at Grant. The principal suggested that my mother enroll me in the 7th grade which meant my going into junior high school where students changed classrooms for every period. My mother thought about it but told him that she didn't want me to skip a grade because then I would be at the bottom of the class.

Then the principal suggested that I go into the accelerated 6th grade and also to let me participate in extra curricular activities. I was put on crossing guard duty so I got out ten minutes before everyone else, wore a "patrol" hat and had a hand stop sign to help the students cross 12th street at the crossing. I was also put to work in the cafeteria. Every day, fifteen minutes before lunch, I had to report to the cafeteria with about seven other girls to set up the tables for the students who ate in the cafeteria. We had to set the tables with a napkin, a straw, cartons of milk and utensils. Then we had to monitor the tables and then clean them up. I happened to have two tables of second graders and our neighbor's son was at my table. He was just like me when I was young, very picky and very thin. He didn't want to eat his lunch. When his mother found out that Frankie was at my table, she told me to be sure he ate everything and not to let him out to play until he finished his lunch. I felt so bad when I told him he could not go out to play and he was the very last one in the lunchroom. I knew how he felt. Sometimes I would just relent and say, "All right Frankie, go out and play".

Our pay for working in the cafeteria was our lunch and we got more than they normally gave to the students. I gained 20 pounds in that year. I had never before tasted tamale pie, mashed potatoes with hamburger gravy, Waldorf salad, and I thought everything was so delicious.

Another activity I had was to be a "bank teller". About twice a month on Mondays, about six of us were assigned to sit behind tables and the students would line up in front of us and bring money, $2.00, $5.00 or even $10.00 to deposit to a bank account. It was to teach the students how to save money. We would take the money, write in their little bank books, give them a receipt and we would turn them in, and the money would be deposited in the bank.

During this year in the 6th grade, our teacher, Miss Maxey, chose some of the students to be in the Christmas Pageant. She chose me to be the angel. I had one whole line to say and I think it was "Behold! A child is born and he shall be named Jesus!" We practiced and Miss Maxey couldn't hear me as she stood at the back of the auditorium. At recess, Miss Maxey told me to go and get the speech teacher and tell her that she wanted to see her. She did not tell me why so I went and found the speech teacher and brought her back. I immediately ran off to play. Soon another student came after me and said Miss Maxey seemed angry and wanted me back. When I got back to see her, she said to me, "Rose, you were to stay here with the speech teacher to practice your part as the angel. You don't have any initiative." I didn't even know what the word initiative meant. I just knew I was being reprimanded and I didn't like it. Well, I practiced and practiced but I just couldn't project my voice. Well, the day of the Christmas Pageant was approaching and about a week before that my mother decided to have my hair cut. My hair by now was down to my hips and I wore it in braids. In the winter time my mother would wash my hair and have me sit in front of the open oven so that my hair would dry as it was very thick. In the summer I would sit outside in the sun and at that time we didn't have the handheld hair dryers we have nowadays. My hair after the cut was just below my ears. When I arrived at school Miss Maxey just about had a heart attack. She almost yelled "What happened to your hair? I wanted you to let your braids down and have long hair for the part of the angel." Well, she never told me that. I thought it was my "acting ability" to be the angel. Needless to say, she was very disappointed in this event.

My brother was a junior in high school at San Jose High while I was in 6th grade and he got a job at a coffee shop/truck stop which was open very late at night and was located on North 13th Street near the Bayshore Hiway. He peeled potatoes and washed dishes. He was barely sixteen and would walk home around midnight. He was not afraid to walk home but sometimes dogs would start barking as he passed the houses. The following year at seventeen he got a job at the Mission Theater on First Street as an usher. Soon after he was offered the job of assistant manager. He looked older and he was tall for his age. The manager told him he would have to get a tuxedo or use the tuxedo which the present assistant manager wore as he would no longer need it because he was leaving. The tuxedo needed to be altered as the former assistant manager was a bit stout. Louis said he would take the suit home as his mother could probably alter it herself. Louis said my mom took the entire tuxedo apart and redid it for him. When the manager saw it he said he didn't believe it was the same tux but my brother pointed out the name of the prior owner in it and then he complimented my mother on the beautiful job she did.

When I started the seventh grade at Roosevelt Junior High I got involved in the Drum and Bugle Corps. I began by playing cymbals as I had no musical talent whatsoever and then gradually began playing the snare drums. We marched in parades and I really liked playing them. We would practice early in the mornings on the field before school. When we were in parades, we were one of the largest groups taking up almost a city block. My best friend then also played the drums and we would compete for first chair. The way we did this was to challenge each other during class. The teacher, Mr. Taix would send us into the equipment room so that the other students couldn't see who was playing and we would each play on our drum. Then the students would vote as to who they thought was the better player. That player got to be first chair. We alternated during the year and we couldn't challenge each other more than once a month.

While I was at Roosevelt, I would ride my bicycle to school which was five long blocks and three short blocks away from home. I would ride with my friend, Edna. One day on the way home, she was ahead of me as she had a better bicycle and I had an old clunker and was not as good a rider. As I approached Julian Street and 17th Street at the stop sign, I didn't want to stop completely as it would slow me down more so I slowed down and looked both ways, saw a car in the distance and just started pedaling instead of stopping. Well, I miscalculated and the driver of the car probably panicked and skidded into me after stepping on his brakes. I didn't feel a thing though I did hear the squeal of the tires and my friend screaming my name. I woke up lying in the street with a crowd of people around me. I was embarrassed because my dress was up around my hips. I pulled it down and started to get up and a gentleman said, "Don't move young lady." I told him that I wanted to sit on the curb so he said it was all right. In the meantime my friend, Edna, had pedaled home to tell my mother that I was hit by a car. She lived two doors away from us and her father happened to be home, so he drove my mother to where I was which was three blocks away. The gas station owner on the corner had called the ambulance to come and pick up a body as he had seen the incident and thought I was dead. My mother rode with me in the ambulance and I was taken to San Jose Hospital which was within a mile of the accident. I was so very lucky as I had no broken bones, a cut on my nose, a scrape on my forehead, a huge bruise on my left thigh where the fender of the car connected with my leg and a scrape on my knee where I landed on the street. The doctor sewed up my nose with five stitches and treated my scrapes. My father was notified at work and came to pick me up along with my mother. Later I developed water on the knee and had to have some penicillin shots but I can truly say that I was very lucky to have my guardian angel looking after me. The gentleman who was driving the car came to visit me and to see if I was all right. He was probably hoping my parents wouldn't sue him but he wasn't really at fault. I was the one who was not careful.

Near the end of two years, my parents and the other couple weren't getting along too well, there were always little discussions when the men came home and the ladies would be ready with their little complaints. Well for seven people in one house and two ladies running the store it was no wonder that something had to give. So my father and Vince decided to bid for the business. They started like an auction and when a certain price was said, my father said that Vince could have the business. Then my dad had to look for something.

In the month of May when I was to finish the seventh grade my parents informed me that we would be moving to Sunnyvale. Wow, what a fuss I made. Now I was used to San Jose, the metropolitan city. I did not want to move to the hick town of Sunnyvale. I had never heard of Sunnyvale and I would have to be going to an elementary school which was old and not like junior high school where we changed classes like high school. My mother went to the superintendent of the Sunnyvale School District to see about enrolling me in McKinley Grammar School. She also told him about my not wanting to go to the school. He told her that if there was a reason that was valid for me to stay in San Jose, I could give the address of my best friend there and continue attending Roosevelt Jr. High. Well, I was taking catechism classes to be confirmed that following year as they did this every year in San Jose but in Sunnyvale, at that time, the bishop only came around every two years, so I would have to wait another year. The superintendent said that was a valid reason. So I continued to attend Roosevelt through the eighth grade. My brother would have to go to San Jose to the produce market almost every day, so he drove me to school in the morning. In the afternoon to get home, I would take the city

bus lines from 20th and Santa Clara Streets to Market and Santa
Clara Streets. Then I would take a Greyhound Bus to Sunnyvale
which would drop me off in downtown Sunnyvale, and then I
would walk a mile home. I was thirteen at the time. When my
brother didn't go to the produce market, I would wait for the Greyhound bus on the El Camino Hiway in the dark at 7:00 a.m. and
reverse the procedure. This just proves how spoiled I was and I am
sure I would not let my thirteen-year old daughter do this, especially nowadays. I do have to say that I think I was a bit mature
then. When I rode the bus, sometimes ladies sitting next to me
would strike up a conversation with me and ask if I was going to
San Jose State University. I would then reply that I was in eighth
grade and they were a bit shocked. I thank my parents for giving
me the independence and trust and allowing me to do this and also
to get a driver's license at fourteen just before the law was changed.
They also allowed me to drive to Santa Cruz when I was sixteen
and basically to use the car when I wanted to. I never abused the
privilege.

Regarding the move, my father found a grocery store to buy in
Sunnyvale right across from Bishop Elementary School which was
under construction. Sunnyvale had 9,000 people and our store was
at the north edge of Sunnyvale. Behind our store there were
apricot orchards and not much else until the Bayshore Highway.
We moved in May of 1948 into the living quarters above the store.

I loved the living quarters above the store. The kitchen was
large with a corner bench seat and we could use our round table. It
also had a drop down ironing board which I had never seen. I
almost loved ironing because I could use this board. There were
three bedrooms, a bathroom and a living room with a fake fireplace. There was a laundry room with a door that went out on the
roof above the warehouse of the store. We could hang clothes out
on the clothesline over the roof.

Sunnyvale was growing and homes were soon constructed behind the store and along with them our business was booming. After a year my dad told the landlord that our business was out-growing the building. The landlord had quite a bit of property and offered to build a larger building right next to the present business. At the end of 1950 our new Bo's Market opened with great fanfare. We had a grand opening with a searchlight, contests, a clown for the children and at that time we were the largest super market in Sunnyvale, although in a few months another super market opened in downtown Sunnyvale which was just as large. My father deserved a lot of credit as he had only a third grade education in Italy and came to America not knowing the language at age 14. He went to night school to learn English and in McCloud was on the board of trustees of the elementary school and also sold Farmer's Insurance on the side. Now he was the owner of a large grocery store and did all of his own accounting. I was quite proud of my father. In fact, the owner of Race Street Fish and Poultry Company told me at one time that he looked up to my father as a mentor because he had the guts to move from McCloud to a big city like San Jose and then Sunnyvale and he wasn't afraid to take a chance. When he said this to me I was surprised as I looked up to this friend as a true success story.

My parents worked hard in the store, the butcher shop was leased out and besides my parents and brother we had four full time employees. I was still going to school but I could help after school though they didn't count on me too much as I was always involved in something at school. When we moved to Sunnyvale I was 13 years old and as the business grew my father counted on my brother and me to do errands. I learned to drive at 14 as Sunnyvale was still considered a rural town and if there was a reason or neces-sity for a family one could get a driver's license at 14. Since my mother did not drive my father came to rely on Louis and me more and more. I passed my driver's test two months before the law

changed to 16 years of age for driving. The law was also that I had
to have an adult in the car with me but with Sunnyvale having only
about 9 or 10 policemen on the force we knew almost all of them.
Some came in the store and would always tease me by saying
"Rose, didn't I see you driving in town without an adult in the car?"
Well, I had to go to the bank or some other place for my dad and I
think they just looked the other way. It was thirty-five years before
I ever got a single ticket so I think I did all right.

My driver's license also came in handy when my father had a
heart attack at the age of 45 and was taken to the nearest hospital
which was San Jose Hospital. He was there for eleven days and I
drove my mom there to see him every day. I was 15 at the time.

7

THE STORE

Bo's Market had many good memories. It opened with all the latest equipment in grocery stores and our family was happy to show it off. The purveyors who sold to us were also happy to show it off to other potential buyers and many of them sent huge bouquets of flowers or plants when we had our opening. We lined up the baskets and vases on top of the produce cases and I think there were 35 in all. It looked like a floral shop. One of the public relations people for the Borden Company was around quite a bit with politicians and interesting people. He brought in Richard Nixon, Charles Gubser, Jack Anderson and another time he brought in the world's tallest man. I was in school and missed all the people who were there.

We also had many Navy families living in the newly constructed homes behind the store because of Moffett Field and later

Lockheed. Two of those families who came in our store quite fre-
quently were the James Lovell and Walter Schirra families. The
two men later became astronauts. The Lovell family became good
friends with my brother as they were living only a few houses from
him. They did a lot of their shopping at our store because it was so
close rather than drive to the PX at Moffett.

Other memories though not too nice but some times funny was
the shoplifting that went on at the store. There were five or six
aisles and since you couldn't keep your eyes on all of them sometimes people were tempted to "lift" something. We had a few spots
where we could "hide" and keep an eye on the aisles where people
slipped things inside clothing, etc. One time my father caught a
young mother who was putting things in the storage area of the
baby carriage which was under the baby. Another time my father
caught the wife of a police office who would shoplift when he was
out of town. We didn't call the police on her — he just warned her
that he didn't think her husband would like knowing what she was
doing. That was all she needed to stop her from stealing in our
store. When youngsters were tempted to steal and were caught we
didn't call the police, we would tell them to go home and tell their
parents and have the parents call us back to acknowledge what
their child had done. If we didn't hear within a couple of hours we
would call them. One time a person confessed to me forty years
after the fact that he had shoplifted in our store and he never did it
after that. We were at a party together and he said he had stolen
some candy and was caught. The prospect of having to go home
and tell his parents that he stole and they had to call us back was
worse than anything he could think of. He said he never ever took
anything he wasn't supposed to after that. Another person who
confessed to me was a young man who called me up seven years
after we sold the store. He called and said he took something years
ago and wanted to pay my father back for what he had taken.
When I informed him that my father had died two years prior, he

said he wanted to send me the money. I told him that I didn't want the money but he could make a donation to the Heart Association in memory of my father, he seemed to be so relieved to know that he could somehow pay back for what he had done.

Another young lady confessed to me that she had taken a popsicle once and slipped it in her underpants and the coldness of the popsicle made her very uncomfortable and she was wriggling. Another one foiled in the act. Cigarettes were a popular item to be stolen by teenagers. One rather tall young man stole a carton of cigarettes and when my brother stopped him outside the store he tried to get away. My brother grabbed him by the arms and called me to help. Being that this young teenager was tall and I was short, I grabbed onto the belt of his pants. He stopped because he kept telling me that I was pulling his pants down. I didn't let go and the police were called on this one.

My heart would always feel like it was pounding right through my chest when I saw someone shoplifting. We would have to be sure of what we saw, keep track of them so that they didn't put the item back on a shelf, go up to the checkstand when they checked out and then stop them outside the store because if you stopped them inside they could always say that they forgot or they were going to pay for it before they left.

My father was also so good with customers especially when they were short of money. We did not carry charge accounts but if someone said they were a bit short that week, he would let them sign the back of the cash register receipt and it went into the cash register drawer. After we sold the store, more than one person came up to me to say that they missed our store and how they would never forget my father for letting them sign the tab when they were short of money. I don't recall that we ever lost money on these people.

My mother always said that the store was a good place for our children. My brother married and had three children and I later married and had two.

Elizabeth Rakowski & Louis Bo wedding, August, 1951

They would come to the store and play in the storage area for cardboard boxes or up in the office and look down on the butcher shop or sit in the comic book or Little Golden Books section. A few funny things happened when they were small. When my brother's first born son, Steven, was about three years old, he was going down the aisle and at that time we didn't refrigerate eggs. The cartons of eggs were on the bottom shelf. He was curious and opened a carton and began pulling out the eggs and cracking them on the edge of the shelf, just like mommy did when she made breakfast. He broke three or four before anyone caught him.

My brother's second son, David, was watching the produce clerk putting up the lettuce, carrots, etc. and the clerk sprinkled them with a water hose that was kept under the counter. The clerk went in the back room leaving a shopping cart in the aisle. David saw his opportunity to "wash" the cart, pulled out the hose and started hosing down the cart, shelf, aisle. When the clerk returned, his first reaction was to yell, "No! David, turn that off!" Well, you can imagine, David didn't want to get spanked so he aimed the hose at the clerk. The clerk, cart, floor, shelves were all soaked. David didn't get spanked but he had a good talking to and we had a job of wiping and drying everything and the clerk went home to change clothes.

8

HIGH SCHOOL AND
BUSINESS COLLEGE

My four years of high school were normal and really uneventful though I was involved in quite a few activities. I didn't attend elementary school in Sunnyvale but started Fremont High School after we moved to Sunnyvale. Many of the friends I met had been friends all through the eight grades of McKinley Grammar School which was the only elementary school in the area. Jarvis Bishop Elementary was just being built when we moved in 1948 and then came the middle school right after that. I enjoyed school and my grades were good. In my sophomore year I became class treasurer and I also worked on the sophomore dance with the decorating committee. In the yearly Variety Show I got together with a male friend and did a pantomime of the song "Anything You Can Do, I Can Do Better". The morning of that show, I

was carrying my dress for the number on a hanger and a
gust of wind came along and the dress was blown off the
hanger and into a puddle of water. I called home, my
dear brother came to the school, picked up the dress, my
mother washed, dried and ironed the dress and he delivered it back to me all before the show in the afternoon.
  How is that for being spoiled? My mother always
reminded me with "Remember when I had to wash, dry
and iron that dress for you all in a couple of hours?" Yes,
I always remember and appreciate the facts of everything
they did for me. I also got away with not working too
much at the store because I had things any teenager
loves to do such as hanging out with my friends, being
involved with activities, but I did put in some time
working and I didn't get paid for my work, it was just
expected of me to help the family.

  During the summer I did work more hours in the store and I
would run errands for my parents such as going to the bank, going
to different distributors since I had a driver's license, so I felt that I
did pull my weight, I just regarded it as having fun rather than
working. I also did some of the bookkeeping which I learned in
school. I also took shorthand and typing with the idea of becoming
a secretary. Most of my friends took college prep courses and were
going into nursing or teaching.
  In my junior year I became Student Body Treasurer and that
entailed working one period in the main office, paying bills
incurred by the student body and getting the checks ready for the
principal to sign. I also had to go to the football games and collect
the money paid at the ticket booths and then count the money

which amounted to a great deal. The "constable" or deputy sheriff who was in charge of escorting me to where we counted the money was a very nice man whom we knew from the store. He was Mr. James Goodacre and I told him I didn't think I needed an escort but of course he explained to me it was really his job and it would be a lot safer for me. Since I was always used to carrying money from the bank to the store, etc. I didn't think it was such a big deal. Up until a few years ago when he died he would always mention how he enjoyed the times he protected me while I had all that money.

One of the things I did with my friends in high school was "cruise" the El Camino Real, go to Johnny Mac's Drive In in Mtn. View or Spivey's Drive In on Grant Road and the El Camino. Sometimes the cars would be three or four deep and if the front car wanted to leave, the cars behind would all be asked to pull out so that the front one could leave. Sometimes we would sit there talking and drinking a coke and eating an order of french fries. The length of time would stretch to about an hour or more. The poor owners of the drive ins. Of course we were young and didn't think about that, we were just interested in seeing everyone.

My good friend Marge Silveira had parents who owned a fruit stand on Sunnyvale-Saratoga Road right where Highway 280 now goes under the road. I didn't really get to know her until my sophomore year as she lived in Cupertino and I lived in Sunnyvale. We became the best of friends and one or our favorite things to do was to drive to the San Francisco Airport on Sunday afternoons and watch the planes take off and land and just watch the people going by. It was really interesting.

In our senior year the seniors were given 100 points at the beginning of the year. Points would be taken away for infractions such as smoking, cutting school, too many tardies, not maintaining a C average, etc. If we lost 30 points we could not go on the yearly trip to Yosemite which took place just before graduation. There were 198 seniors and only 85 or 90 students went but not because they lost points, some couldn't afford to pay the cost which was about $70.00 or they just didn't want to go. We had to pay for the food we ate and we had to bring our own tents and sleeping bags but otherwise we were transported there by school buses and were chaperoned by some of the teachers. The trip was for four days three nights. We left on a Friday morning at 4:00 in the morning and returned home Monday afternoon. The night before we left quite a few of us spent the night at Liz Moore's house. I think there was Marilyn Lehmann, Carol Acker, June Braun and Gwen Hoskins. We didn't sleep much as we were talking too much and we were excited. As we got closer to morning my voice started to get hoarse and I figured it was because of talking too much. Liz's father drove us to the City Hall where we were all to meet to catch the school buses at 4:00. By the time we got there my voice was all but gone and the Vice Principal, Miss Coombs immediately asked, "What's wrong with your voice?" I said I probably talked too much. She was worried because in less than a week there was the graduation and I was to deliver the valedictory speech. Well, off to Yosemite. This was the first week of June. We arrived in Yosemite and Miss Coombs took me to the hospital to see what could be done for my voice. I had laryngitis. The doctor told me to gargle with warm salt water (I think he forgot that in the campgrounds, there is no warm or hot water) and he gave me some pills. I was to return the next day at 4:00 for a shot. During the night it rained. The next morning the buses took whoever wanted to go up to Half Dome and Glacier Point. Naturally, I was among those going. To come back, I should have gone back on the bus but we were told that if we wanted to hike down to the valley we could and we were told the different routes to take. Four of us decided to take the shortest one since I had to be back by 4:00. The length of the trail was 4 1/2 miles (I think.) Anyway, I thought that since it was only 10:00 we would be back in plenty of time. After all, 4 1/2 miles should only take us about three hours at most. I was so wrong. The trail was up and down, zig-zagged, around waterfalls, a lot of switchbacks, etc. I think the 4 1/2 miles was as the crow flies. We didn't get back until after 5:00. I think Miss Coombs was a bit angry with me. I did go the next morning with her to the doctor and got a shot. Sunday was a beautiful day and we rented bicycles and rode quite a bit. All the time our muscles were crying but we were having too much fun. At night we saw the fire falls which were burning embers dropped from the top of Glacier Point, a height of 3000 feet. I am sure this "glowing waterfall" was discontinued because of the environmental impact on the valley floor. On Monday morning we packed up our gear and headed back to Sunnyvale. The buses dropped us off in downtown Sunnyvale and since we were sitting for about four hours we were stiff as boards when we got off the bus. My legs never ached so badly as that day. Some of us still had to walk about a mile to get home.

Miss Coombs told me to stay home and not come to graduation practice and rest my voice. Carmendale Fernandes, the Speech/ Drama teacher came to my house to have me practice the speech. On Wednesday my voice seemed better but still hoarse. I was also coughing a bit if I inhaled cold air. Our graduation was held on Wednesday, June 10, 1953 in the evening on the football field of the school. Unbeknownst to me one of my friends, Ona Richardson had learned my speech in case I couldn't finish delivering it. Well, my voice sounded different but I didn't cough once and I made it through. Someone took a photo of me walking back to my seat and I had the biggest smug look of triumph on my face. I made it!

During the summer following graduation was when my mom and I went to Italy.

After my mom and I returned from our trip to Italy in September, I enrolled in Heald Business College to become a secretary. I took shorthand, typing, bookkeeping and learned how to use the dictaphone machine and the various calculators of that time. We didn't have the little hand-held ones everyone uses now. We worked at our own pace and when we passed all the required subjects the college would help us find a job. I think it took me eight or nine months to complete the courses and then I was sent for an interview with the Agricultural Extension Office in San Jose. The office was located in the old Post Office building at First and St. John Streets on the second floor. I got the job and was to start within a week. The office was just two big rooms, one room had ten desks for the bosses or Farm and Home Advisors, the other room had five desks for the secretaries. Three of the farm advisors were my bosses. The Farm Advisors were all graduates of the University of California, Davis, and were paid by the University. The secretaries were paid for by the County of Santa Clara. In the early 50's there were still many orchards of prunes, cherries, apricots, etc. and many farmers raising vegetables, and also cattle ranchers and dairies in the county. The purpose of the farm advisors was to advise these people if they had problems or questions. The 4-H Club was also a part of our office. At that time I think there was a membership of over 1,000 young people and leaders. Two of the advisors were the heads of these clubs.

The first thing I had to do when I started my employment was to organize all the pamphlets or booklets which the University published regarding a range of subjects such as raising any kind of livestock, poultry, growing vegetables, fruits, diseases and pests of all of these subjects, and how to prune and graft trees. All of this information was free for the asking. There were also two home advisors who would answer questions on canning, freezing and many other questions for the homemaker. The booklets were all organized much the same as the library with the Dewey Decimal System. I had to organize them as to subjects and subheadings, place them in cubby holes on the bookshelves and then type up the cards that listed them.

I also took dictation and learned many new words such as; armillaria root rot which is oak root fungus, PDB which is paradichlorobenzene, and parathian which I found out is very poisonous. The farm advisors were very patient with me until I learned these words and many others, but when I encountered these words for the first time, I was really flustered. One of my bosses was away on a sabbatical when I started so when he returned he had all of the letters he wanted to answer in a pile and called me in for dictation. I think it was a session of over an hour. One of the words I learned that day was "rathskeller". He had visited some in England and Germany and was writing to a professor at Davis. This boss was very organized, he would speak very clearly, slowly and when he realized I didn't know a word, without even asking, he would spell the word immediately. This boss was the advisor on entomology and also fruits and nuts. One of the other bosses was the advisor on poultry and vegetables and the third boss was the advisor of fruits and nuts and irrigation practices. These people were not limited to their fields and if someone called in with questions any of them could answer them and many times they would send out the information.

Once one of the advisors was on television to demonstrate how to get rid of gophers in the garden. He borrowed a live gopher from the museum at Alum Rock Park. The program was in San Francisco in the late afternoon and since it was too late to return the gopher he left it in a cage in the office. The cage did not have a top on it so he just put a piece of cardboard on top of it. The next morning, I was the first one to arrive. I went into the room of the advisors to turn the lights on and to take a look at the gopher. Oh, my, the gopher was gone. I quickly left the office, closed the door and waited in the hallway for someone to arrive. When one of the farm advisors arrived I gave him the job of catching "Gus the Gopher" while I waited outside.

The farm advisors sometimes held seminars for the different
fruit and vegetable farmers to advise them of the latest practices on
growing different crops. In order to advise the growers of the
upcoming seminar we had an old addressograph machine which
had the names and addresses of the interested people on the
mailing list. The information was on a small metal card about the
size of a credit card. They were held in trays and when we loaded
the tray in the machine, we would plug the machine in and then
step on a lever which would drop one metal card at a time. We
would hold the envelope or card in place and it would be inked
with the information. It was a bit noisy but it was better than
typing or handwriting all the cards or envelopes. When the 4-H
Club had a county-wide event and letters had to go out to all the
members, the secretary that took care of that had to have help if
there was a deadline. Most of the time she did it all by herself. One
good thing was that we didn't have to carry the mail very far. We
just had to go downstairs to the post office. We also used an old
mimeograph machine to run off letters or make leaflets.

Our office also had a booth at the Santa Clara County Fair
which was a big thing during those years. We would have to man
the booth for the week and give out information and answer questions. It was also fun to see the animals and the 4-H members with
their lambs, steers, goats, rabbits, etc.

The other offices besides our office were the FBI and a couple of
recruiting offices for the Army and the Air Force. My maiden
name was Rose Bo. One day an agent of the FBI came to see what
new booklets we had and when he saw my name on my desk, he
remarked that a few years previous they had a secretary named
Rose Bo. It was a coincidence to have an uncommon name and
work in the same building. It did happen that we knew the family
and they were from Gilroy.

I worked for only 2 1/2 years for the Extension Service before
my parents asked me to quit my job and help my brother in the

store as they wanted to go to Italy for a few months, so I quit in the spring of 1956. Also during the spring I met what would be my future husband so I never went back to this job. How I met my husband was sort of a matchmaking job by a couple of caring ladies. A long time friend of ours named Alice Carnini was working in our store. She kept telling me she had a nice young man she wanted me to meet. Of course I wasn't too keen on meeting someone that appealed to a person 20 years older than I was. I didn't know that she was also telling the young man that she had someone she wanted him to meet. He kept telling her to bring this girl around so he could meet her.

Alice and my parents used to frequent the Sunnyview Family Club in Mtn. View. The Club was an organization of Italian people that had dinners once a month on Sundays and you could have dinner and dance with a live band for a nominal price. I didn't want to go with my parents because I thought there were just older people going to these affairs. People could also play bocce ball, cards or just socialize. Well, one Sunday my mother asked me to drive her to a nursery so she could buy some flowers. I told her I would work in the store for my dad so he could take her. She insisted that I drive her to the nursery. I was more than a bit angry and had an ugly frown on my face when we got to the nursery. When we entered the nursery, my mother introduced me to the owners and then a very handsome young man was also introduced to me as the son of the owners. Oh, wow!! Was he handsome!! Well, we picked out some flowers and a tree rose which didn't fit in our car. The owners said their son Carlo would deliver it. The owners were active in the Sunnyview Club of Mountain View, the husband being the first manager of the club and their son helped them. Carlo didn't ask me for a date but I vowed that when another dinner dance was held at the club I would go with my parents. The next event was the Mothers' Day dinner dance so I went with a girlfriend and my parents. Sure enough, Carlo was there and asked me for a date and said he would get a friend for my friend. Little did I know that Carlo was the young man that Alice had in mind for me to meet. So with my mom and Alice working together they finally got the two of us together and it has lasted more than 51 years.

9

OUR COURTSHIP AND WEDDING

After meeting Carlo, we dated for the next few months, going to movies, going to the Sunnyview Club for dinner and dancing. Carlo knew a lot of people since his father had been the manager for the club a few years before. I knew some of the people as they were friends of my parents. There were young and older people. Some of the young people were from Italy visiting or newly immigrated from Italy. It was an ideal place for the young ones to meet Italian speaking people and to have a good time.

Carlo had graduated from Bellarmine High School in San Jose, then attended Menlo Junior College and then Heald Radio and Television Servicing School in San Francisco. While he was attending Menlo he signed up in the Naval Reserve. After Healds, he got a job with Hi Fi Unlimited installing and repairing sound

systems and worked there for two years. When I met Carlo he was
working for Hi Fi Unlimited in Menlo Park during the week and on
weekends he worked for his father in the nursery as his father had
just opened it the end of 1956. In December of 1956 he asked if I
wanted to accompany him on a job for Hi Fi Unlimited to hook up
a sound system at a huge estate in Woodside where there was a performance being staged for the Christmas holidays and he had to be
there in case anything went wrong with the sound system.. It was a
beautiful estate and I later learned it was the famous Filoli estate.
 The performance was in the ballroom where there was the huge
fireplace that had an opening at least 6 feet high After the performance we had to attend services for a gentleman friend, husband of
our matchmaker friend Alice. Since the schedule was tight, he
decided to bring me to his parents' house for dinner unbeknownst
to them. They were cooking in the "tank house" kitchen on their
property and were embarrassed that Carlo had brought me there
without telling them ahead of time. We didn't have cell phones
then. The tank house is a structure which farms had in those days
to enclose the pump for the well water and the water would be
pumped up into a large tank which was up about 20 feet. Many
people enclosed the bottom of the structure and later Carlo's father
converted the tank part into a bedroom. The bottom enclosure
was a small kitchen which they used without dirtying the main
house.   I was perfectly at home eating in the tank house and the
meal was delicious. I guess by that time they were happy that Carlo
had found an Italian girl so I was OK on their list.

     When Christmas time came I was really expecting an engage-
ment ring and was so disappointed that I didn't get one especially
after he had slipped a cigar band around my finger pretending that
it was a ring. But when New Year's Eve came around he surprised
me with a beautiful engagement ring that fit beautifully. He also
asked if I would wait for him while he fulfilled his two years of

active duty in the Navy. A few days after he requested active duty his draft number came up.

The Navy asked where he preferred to serve his duty and of course he said anywhere in Europe such as Germany or Italy. Well, he was sent to Hawaii in February. He was sent to the island of Oahu in the middle of the island among the pineapple fields. It was a radio and communications station where all the communications from the Pacific went to Washington, D.C. It was a highly classified station with not too many service men on base. He had to service the machines and worked shifts that were not your normal eight hour days. He would work shifts and then be off for 72 hours. Since he had this free time he decided to get a part-time job at a radio station as a night engineer. The radio station was KKHU in Waipahu near Pearl Harbor.

Since the work was classified, he was not allowed to leave the island to come to the mainland so my mother and I decided to visit him in the summer of 1957. We were there for about a week and toured around the island when Carlo was off work. When my mom and I left to return home, Carlo took us to the airport. About an hour after departure we had settled down after eating a meal and I kept seeing an officer going back and forth down the aisle with a flashlight and another time it seemed as if he had a small ladder. I thought it was a bit strange. Soon the pilot announced that we were turning back to Hawaii but he didn't say anything else. Of course my mom pulled out her rosary beads and started praying and saying that we were not going to make it back. That didn't help but I just didn't say anything. When we got back and upon landing I looked out the window and saw a line of fire engines near the runway and when we went down the stairs the pilots, mechanics, etc. were all looking up at an engine with flashlights. I don't remember seeing anything. Meanwhile when Carlo arrived back at the base a buddy asked him which airline his fiance was on. He told him that a Pan Am Airways plane en route to San Francisco had to turn back to Hawaii due to engine trouble. Well, we made it back home after quite a delay but it was a long night.

During the second year of Carlo's being in Hawaii, his mother and I visited him during the summer. While there he announced that with the extra money he was making working at the radio station he had decided to take flying lessons. Well, his mother immediately turned white and expressed her concern. He was taking lessons from an Australian pilot named Eric who really loved flying. His mom and I were there for a week and we had an uneventful trip back home.

During the two years that Carlo was away his parents really worked hard in the nursery as there were many new homes being built between Mtn. View and Palo Alto. Their nursery was on the corner of San Antonio Road and Alma Streets. His mother did not drive and they had only one day off during the week when the nursery was closed. To help them I would get a list of groceries that his mom telephoned to me and I would deliver them on Saturdays. One Monday in September Carlo's mom, Lee, called me to say that his father, Marco, was terribly sick and she was calling an ambulance. He was being taken to Stanford Hospital and the paramedics thought it was bleeding ulcers. I met them at the hospital and the doctor said he would have to do exploratory surgery. It was later discovered that they had gone out to dinner on Saturday evening and Marco had eaten frog legs. He inadvertently swallowed a small bone which was broken and he didn't feel it since he had false teeth. This bone punctured his stomach and two places in the intestine causing peritonitis. He was in the hospital for about a week and then came home but had to take it easy. Lee had a rough time working in the nursery but she did have a couple of men helping.

When Marco went to the doctor for a checkup after a month the doctor said that he had good news and bad news. The good news was that he was coming along very well, but the bad news was that he had to have another operation. When the doctor operated on Marco he discovered an aneurysm of the aorta and it would have to be repaired. Of course, Marco wanted a second opinion and the opinion of the second doctor was, "If you want to live you had better have the operation." There were only two doctors on the West Coast at that time that performed this operation. One was in San Francisco and one was in Los Angeles. When Carlo was informed of the pending operation, he put in for emergency leave due to hardship at home so he returned home in December, 1958.

Marco scheduled the operation for mid December. His real name was Marco Carlo Marenco but he went by Charlie. The doctor who would be doing the operation was Dr. Frank Gerbode of the Stanford Lane Hospital in San Francisco. Dr. Gerbode had performed the first open heart surgery shown on television a couple of years prior. Charlie was in the hospital for about two weeks spending Christmas with us in his hospital room. He returned home very weak and a bit depressed. He was 61 years of age and had never been in a hospital for an illness. In fact when he had the first operation he and Lee didn't have a doctor. They had moved from San Francisco 12 years before and still went to their long-time doctor in San Francisco for routine check ups. When the paramedic asked who their doctor was, they just had to go to emergency and get whomever could take them.

Meanwhile when Carlo returned home from Hawaii we started making plans for our wedding and we set a date for February 8 depending on how his dad was feeling. We proceeded with the plans and everything was coming along fine although his father was still a bit weak.

I was given two wedding showers and received many beautiful gifts. There were 500 guests invited to our wedding. A week before the wedding, on Saturday, I was working at the store and I felt as if I was coming down with the flu. My stomach was upset and I was nauseous. I went home at lunchtime and ate just soup.

Two couples, friends of the family came to visit and bring gifts. One brought an armload of daphne which made the house smell so sweet and perfumy. After they left I just couldn't go back to work. I vomited and felt worse and I thought it was the very strong smell of the flowers which made me sick. My mother being worried because of the impending wedding called our doctor. Of course being a weekend, the doctor was off and out of town. She insisted that the doctor on call come out to the house which he did. When he saw all the gifts stacked in the bedroom he asked about the wedding and came to the conclusion that it was nervous stomach or gastritis. He did not do the routine exam for appendicitis. He prescribed a medicine to settle my stomach. I continued to have dry heaves and I slept fitfully during the night. I awoke the next morning with a low fever and pains in my abdomen. My mother called the doctor again and he said that the pains were from my retching and it would go away.

My father took delivery of a beautiful new Oldsmobile which he ordered especially for the wedding and he brought it home that day. He came in the house asking me to come and see it. I got out of bed all bent over in pain and I didn't care if it was a gold plated car out in front of the house. I went back to bed. That evening my mom again called the doctor who by now was off duty also and another doctor was on call. After explaining everything the other doctor did and said, the new doctor said, "Well, you can try giving her an enema." My mom hung up and was hesitant about what he told her. After consulting with my dad and Carlo who both said, "I wouldn't do that" she called the doctor again and insisted that he had to come out to see me. He said he would after he saw another patient.

The doctor arrived around 10:30 p.m. after seeing a patient whom he had sent to the hospital with a hot appendix. He examined me and said, "I can't believe it. This girl also has a hot appendix. Take her to O'Connor Hospital immediately. My parents and Carlo bundled me up in the car and away we went. I was just so relieved that I was going to be put out of my misery.

I was operated on at 1:00 in the morning. My father and Carlo went home after the operation which turned out to be just in time as my appendix had perforated and I had peritonitis. My mom stayed in my room in a chair at my bedside until someone came back to get her around 12:00 noon. When the surgeon came to see me I asked if I could still get married the following Sunday (silly me). I was on painkillers and drugs and I really felt pretty good. He chuckled and said, "I really don't think so."

My parents and Carlo's parents had to call the invitees to tell them the wedding was postponed. What a job. With such a large number of guests they managed to get to everyone except for one couple. The couple had been on vacation and couldn't be reached. When the lady went to church on the Sunday of the wedding, she shared with a friend that she was going to Rose Bo's wedding. The friend said, "I don't think so—she just came home from the hospital." At least she was told in time. Carlo still says to this day that I had cold feet.

We managed to reschedule everything for four weeks later on the 8th of March. Forget about doing such a thing nowadays. This meant the reception hall (the Sunnyview Family Club), the photographer, the band, the church and the time off for the ushers, bridesmaids, etc. One usher was a pilot for United Airlines and he made the mistake of bidding time off for the 8th of January. Then he found out that it was for the 8th of February and he bid for that day. Then when it was rescheduled he had to bid again for March 8th and the airline really thought something funny was going on.

The wedding came off without a hitch and we had a great time. The reception was at the Club and was served family style. Platters of sliced salami, olives, celery and peppers were on the long tables. Then individual salads, platters of some form of pasta and then platters of roasted chicken and green beans. There were carafes of wine on the tables and then coffee and the wedding cake. The wedding cake was made by Tino Rodriguez of Seijo's Bakery and was a beautiful five-tiered cake. Carlo and I passed out 500 wedding favors of little bells which held three Jordan almonds in netting with a little sprig of fake lily of the valley on top. I recently found the bill for the banquet and it was a mere $5.00 per person.

Carlo & Rose's wedding March 8, 1959

One thing I forgot to mention, my little friend Mirella from McCloud was a bridesmaid in our wedding and her mother was the head cook for the banquet because her family had moved to Sunnyvale a few years prior.

Carlo and I went on a honeymoon of driving to Las Vegas for about a week, then driving up to my hometown of McCloud as he had never been there. When we left McCloud he asked, "Why did your family leave such a paradise?"

10

CARLO'S FAMILY

Now I will tell you a bit about the family I married into. Carlo's father, Charlie was the 10th of 13 children born of Antonio Marenco and Maria Gambetta and he was born on August 23, 1898. He said the siblings were never able to be at the table together at the same time. The oldest sister was 22 when he was born and she went to France to be a maid when he was quite young. Pietro or Pete Marenco who was the fourth born came to America in March of 1907. He was single at the time. After he arrived in America he called for their sister, the second born. She was Maddalena or Manin.

Maria (Manin) Marenco Lepra

Manin came over with Guiseppe Marenco, the 6th born. Manin was married and had a child named Emma born in 1901. Her husband stayed in Italy with Emma and I suspect Manin came to America to see if it was possible to make a living. The two brothers and Manin settled in San Francisco. Charlie's mother took care of Emma while her mother was in America. Charlie was just three years older than Emma and she told me she enjoyed playing with him and the other cousins while she was at the grandmother's house. The house where Charlie grew up was in a level meadow in Pianbotello which today consists of about seven houses or families. It is about two or three miles from Pontinvrea which is a metropolis of 400 compared to Pianbotello. Pontinvrea is about 30 miles north west of Genova. Both Pianbotello and Pontinvrea were owned by a marquis who later lost the property at Monte Carlo while gambling. Charlie's father was a stonemason. He didn't

farm, just raised potatoes and chickens for the family to eat. He
didn't own the house they lived in and the rent was one chicken a
year.

Luigi, Edoardo and Marco (Charlie) Marenco circa 1915

The year after Giuseppe and his sister Manin came to America
Manin's husband and daughter, Carlo and Emma Lepra, arrived in
September of 1913.

Charlie's mother had three other children after Charlie, the last
two dying at the age of 5 and 4 in 1907.

Charlie served in World War I in the Italian Navy on a large,
ocean-going tug which was a rescue vessel for ships in distress.
One time during a big storm everything was wiped out on the deck
and all the communication equipment was gone. A friend of
Charlie's from the same home town was a radio man on another
ship and he reported to Charlie's family that his ship was lost at sea.
They remained "lost" for about a week and finally were able to go

into the port of Odesa in the Black Sea to have their radio repaired
or replaced. He was in the Navy for three years. When he returned
home his brother Pietro called for him to come to America and he
arrived in Boston in October of 1921 aboard the ship Arabic.

The next brother to be called was the third born, Giovanni Marenco who was already 41 years of age, had a wife and four children
in Italy. He arrived in November of 1922. The sad thing about this
brother was that he died at the age of 56 without ever going back to
Italy. Manin also died young at the age of 50 but she had her husband and daughter here.

Marco, Giovanni, Pietro and Giuseppe Marenco here in America circa 1937

Carlo's mother Lee, whose real name was Lucresia which she
disliked, was born in Vandergrift, Pennsylvania on October 27,
1908. She had an older sister Teresa and a younger brother Joe.
Their father worked in the coal mine and their mother ran a
boarding house. There were about 6 men renting rooms in the

house and eating there. Their mother also made the lunches for the men. Lee said the lunch boxes consisted of tin boxes that had three compartments. In the bottom compartment was hot tea or coffee or perhaps soup. The next compartment up was for a sandwich and on top was a piece of cake or fruit. In the evening when the men came home, Lee and her sister Teresa had to wash all the lunch boxes and then all the dinner dishes.

In 1919 Lee, her mother and siblings came to San Francisco by train. Lee attended Daniel Webster School and graduated from the eighth grade.

Stepfather Bert Rosetto, Joseph Gillio, Teresa Gillio, Maria Rosetto and Lucresia (Lee) Gillio

After graduating she got a job in the Gallant Laundry operating the ironer or "mangle" ironing tablecloths and napkins. Her mother was already working there. In those days young people would get together at someone's home and have a party, dancing in the basement. Italians usually had a kitchen on the lower level of

the house so that the "nice" kitchen upstairs was not dirtied. Lee
said she went to a party one night and Charlie was there. He was
dancing on the table and someone suggested to Lee that he was a
nice man. Lee thought this person was crazy to suggest that she go
out with this man who was dancing on the table. Well, a little while
after that they were dating. Charlie also had an Indian motorcycle
which he finally gave up because of Lee.

Charlie loved life in America and was also a hard worker, not
afraid to try anything. When he arrived in America his brothers
were working for vegetable farmers in Colma. He tried it also but
they never saw the sun there. He soon told them that he was going
back to San Francisco where at least he could see the sun sometimes. When he met Lee he was a truck driver. Lee and Charlie
decided to get married when she was 19 and he was 29. They
didn't send out invitations, they went to the homes of the people
they wanted to invite and did it in person and gave the people the
Jordan almonds which are popular with Italians. She said it took
them about a month. They were married on November 12, 1927
in All Hallows Church in the Bayview District of San Francisco.

Marco Marenco & Lucresia Gillio Marenco wedding, November 12, 1927

Soon after their marriage they bought a small neighborhood store. The first day they made $4.00 and Charlie found Lee crying on the steps because it seemed that they had done the wrong thing in buying the store. He reassured her that she could run the store and he would get a better paying job. Lee was taught by her sister, who also had a small store, how to write checks, do the accounting, etc. Her sister, Teresa, was very independent and not afraid to try anything. Teresa and her husband were doing quite well and also had a nice home besides the business. She was only ten months older than Lee but she quit school and got married early. Unfortunately Teresa died at the young age of 24 in 1931 of meningitis. Her husband sold the business and the home and returned to Italy later remarrying and had a daughter.

Lee and Charlie started doing well in the little store, Charlie quit his other job, and they started a ravioli factory in the property behind the store. They called the business Torino Ravioli after the city in Italy. They were married seven years before Carlo was born on October 26, 1934. When Carlo was born they would bring him to the store and put him to sleep in a wooden crate in which cans of olive oil came from Italy. The hum of the ravioli machines would put him to sleep and he would sometimes be covered with a dusting of flour. Charlie sold the raviolis to other markets in the North Beach district of San Francisco. Some of the markets asked Charlie if they could put their labels on his raviolis. He didn't care if his name or the store's name was on the box, as long as he got paid for his merchandise. A funny story was that some of the people who lived near his factory would come in and buy his merchandise during the year but on holidays they would go down to North Beach, then tell him that they hoped he wouldn't be offended if they went down to the other stores for the holidays because their raviolis were just a bit better. He never did tell them they were buying the same raviolis. Another thing they did was to make the raviolis from the fillings the people made. The customers would come in with bowls of filling and Charlie would make the pasta dough and make the raviolis. The tables were long and sometimes there would be a variety of colors when the filling was spread on the dough.

Charlie and Lee worked so hard in the store during the day and then in the factory at night they had a babysitter for Carlo. She was a young girl who spoke the real Italian. Charlie and Lee mostly spoke the Piemontese dialect. To this day Carlo speaks good Italian and I have learned a lot as I spoke only the dialect also when I was young. Carlo spent a lot of time in the store and some of the salesmen who were Italian loved to talk to him in Italian. The owner of the Star Foods Company, Mr. Giurlani would come in and call Carlo, "Carlino" and then he would give him 50 cents and ask him what he was going to do with it. Carlo would always say he was going to put it in the bank, which he did.

In 1936 they sold the store but kept the ravioli factory. In 1938 they bought a new Buick sedan and decided to go to Italy for their first vacation in 11 years.

I forgot to tell a little story that happened during prohibition. Charlie was making raviolis and had the grocery store and he would also deliver groceries to his customers. He bought a new black panel truck which was very similar to the police paddy wagons. He didn't have time to have the sign advertising the store painted on the truck when he had to deliver some groceries to a lady customer. He pulled up in front of the house, rang the doorbell and had to wait quite a few minutes before the lady answered the door. When she finally answered, she looked at him and said, "Damn you Charlie! When did you get a new truck?" She had seen the black truck drive up and was afraid it was the police. She had been making gin in her bathtub so she ran and pulled the drain so that the gin would go down and then she found out it was Charlie. All that gin gone to waste.

Now getting back to 1938 and Charlie and Lee's first vacation in 11 years. The Buick they bought was a four-door sedan and there was room between the front and back seats to place a steamer trunk in that space. Then they put blankets on top of this and made a bed and play area for Carlo who was 3 1/2 years old. By this time they had sold the store but kept the ravioli factory. They put a cousin in charge of running the factory as they planned to be away for about five to six months. They drove down to San Bernardino first to say goodbye to Lee's aunt and cousins, then across the United States to Vandergrift, Pennsylvania, to see more of Lee's aunts and cousins, and ended up in New York loading their car on board the ocean liner REX and sailing across the Atlantic. The REX was the ocean liner which won the blue ribbon for crossing the Atlantic Ocean in the least amount of days. After eight days they came into the port of Genoa. The roads in Italy were a bit narrow of course because there weren't many American cars on the roads at that time. Charlie was just happy to be back to show people in his home town that he amounted to something. Before he went into the Navy he had a girlfriend but her mother didn't want her to go with Charlie because he was poor and came from such a big family he would never amount to anything. Well, he showed them! Coincidentally, there was a man from San Francisco who was also from the same area as Charlie and he also had a 1938 black Buick. People told this gentleman that there was another car just like his and he couldn't believe it so he drove to Pontinvrea to see for himself who came from America with the same type car.

This gentleman was Luigi Piombo who was in construction and had built the Union Square Garage in San Francisco, the Yerba Buena Tunnel and also part of the Bayshore Hiway from San Mateo to the San Francisco Airport. Charlie and Mr. Piombo had quite a visit.

Charlie's father was still living and he was so proud to sit in the front seat of the car whenever they traveled around, and they did quite a bit of traveling. When people found out that Charlie and Lee were going to Italy, they would give them envelopes with money such as $10 or $20 and asked them to please go see their parents, siblings, or relatives and bring them the money. They had a long list of people to see and bring news of the relatives here in America. While in Italy, they also went to Bologna and purchased a machine to make tortellini. They are similar in shape to small doughnuts and filled with a meat filling. The machine would cut out pasta dough in the shape and size of an egg. Then it would fill the dough with the filling, twist it around to form a ring and press the ends together. Three tortellinis would be made at a time. There was a dehydrator that came with the machine also to dry the tortellini and they were placed in bags much like the dry pasta we buy today. Charlie bought the machine and had it shipped to San Francisco making this the second machine on the west coast of California. They left Italy in October aboard the Conte di Savoia.

When they returned from Italy Charlie also had the idea of cooking raviolis, putting a dozen of them in a cellophane bag, adding a ladle of spaghetti sauce and freezing the bag. Then a customer could buy the bags of frozen raviolis and drop them in boiling water, heating them up for a meal that would be ready in minutes. The only problem was that many stores at that time didn't have as much freezer space as they do now. They had small freezers for ice cream and perhaps a few packages of vegetables. Also the cellophane bags gave off a smell of petroleum so the Dupont Company worked with Charlie to develop a bag that could be used for placing food in it. It worked fine then but Charlie was too far ahead of time because the market was not quite ready for this. However, he was plenty busy with making raviolis and tortellini.

In 1940 Charlie moved the ravioli factory to Visitation Valley in San Francisco and again opened up a grocery store next to it. They were really busy, especially during the war with tokens, stamps and rationing. Carlo attended St. Joan of Arc Catholic School in the Bayview district and would catch the city bus to go to school. St. Joan of Arc School was taught by nuns from France so it was only natural that they taught the children French. If the students wanted to learn the language it was another 1/2 hour of schooling at the end of the regular curriculum. They also offered piano lessons for an extra charge. Carlo took piano lessons for two years.

Charlie was also an air raid warden during the war for the neighborhood where they lived. One time he was out delivering raviolis and the air raid sirens sounded so he had to park the truck because of "lights out" and walk the rest of the way home. He was thankful that he was not too far from home. Carlo said that he enjoyed the baked potatoes his mother would cook during the air raids because the oven didn't give off a light and they could eat something for dinner.

Charlie and Lee worked very hard in the store and factory so Carlo was a big help to them by being the cook on Saturdays. When he was nine or ten years old, he would go to the butcher with the red stamps for meat and would cook up the same meal every Saturday — breaded veal cutlets and raviolis.

There were two other clerks working in the store along with Lee and in the factory there was one or two other workers with Charlie. One incident that was costly to Charlie was that one of the workers didn't wash the spinach for the filling in the raviolis or he didn't wash it well as he was in a hurry. Another worker mixed all the ingredients together. When Charlie tasted the filling he tasted the sand that wasn't washed away. He had to throw the entire batch of filling away and couldn't fill the orders of raviolis for the stores.

In 1943 Charlie bought property on San Antonio Road and Alma between Palo Alto and Mountain View. He bought 10 acres for $1,000 an acre for a total of $10,000. On the property there was a large house, a small house, a big barn, a corral with a blacksmith shop and all the equipment in it. The barn had four stalls for horses and all the tack for the horses, a tank house which still had the water tank on top and an outdoor oven shaped like a big clay turtle for baking bread and meats. About 100 years ago this had been a working Spanish Rancho. Later an Italian family sold it to Carlo's parents and they thought they really pulled it over on Charlie by selling it for so much money. When the land was developed later, the sellers claimed that Charlie "stole" the property for such a cheap selling price.

Charlie and Lee sold the store in San Francisco in 1945 and moved to Palo Alto in 1946. Carlo attended St. Clare's Catholic School in Santa Clara and would commute on the Greyhound Bus from Palo Alto to Santa Clara.

When Carlo's family moved to Palo Alto, there was a huge amount of "stuff" to clean up. They hired someone to clear the

barn and to remodel the big house. The house didn't have a bathroom. The rooms were rearranged so that they ended up with two
bedrooms, one and a half bathrooms, a living room, dining room
with a fireplace, a kitchen, laundry room and an enclosed porch.
The house also had a full basement. Clearing out the barn consisted of getting rid of things that today would be an antique
dealer's delight. There was also farm machinery such as old culti-
vators, big rakes, wheat cutters, etc. Charlie bought a pinto mare
for Carlo and she was called Queenie. Carlo would sometimes ride
into Mtn. View on the horse but some people delighted in scaring
the horse by honking the car horns. After the remodeling, things
settled down especially since the war was over so Charlie and Lee
decided to go to Italy again in 1948. This would be the second
vacation in 10 years. They asked a single gentleman friend to stay
on the property and take care of the horse and other animals. In
addition to the horse, they had pigeons, a dog, pheasants, ducks
and chickens. When Carlo got out of school for the summer of
1948 they again drove across the United States but this time they
stored the car in a garage in New York and flew to Rome. They
bought a car in Rome, the dealership filled the car with gas and
gave them an extra large container full of gas as there was a strike of
the gas truck drivers. The first night they stopped when it got dark
and they slept in the car by the side of the road. When they awoke
the next morning they really didn't know how far it was before they
could get gas again and they saw two men on bicycles and asked
where they could get more gas. Because of the truckers' strike no
gas was being delivered to gas stations. The men said to follow
them and they would take them where they could probably get gas.
They were led to a huge enclosed field of army trucks, tanks, and
other vehicles used in the war. One of the men knew the man who
was guarding the place. He let them siphon the gas from the military vehicles. Charlie wanted to pay them but they wouldn't take
any money but they asked if he had cigarettes, which he did and

they were happy. To this day, people in Italy are happy to help you and more so if you speak the language.

While there in Pontinvrea, Carlo made friends with the young people his age and when his parents said they were going to visit relatives or other people out of town, he was just happy to stay there and also to go fishing in the river that ran through the town.

There was a young girl who was probably a couple of years younger than Carlo whom we still see when we go back and she always says how she was smitten with Carlo and cried when he left to return to the U.S.

While in Italy, Charlie and Lee visited a glass factory near Pontinvrea and ordered stemmed wine glasses which had a design etched on them and he ordered them etched with the "Marenco" name also. He ordered four dozen glasses and gave one of his brothers a dozen. We still have about thirty of these glasses today as some were broken when they lived in Palo Alto. They lived across the street from the train tracks and during the first few months, whenever the train passed, it would shake the house a bit and if the glasses were stored touching each other, they would chip or crack because of the shaking. Lee then learned to store them a bit apart.

The return trip was by airplane also but this time it was a bumpy ride with stops in Geneva, Paris and Shannon, Ireland. Charlie swore he would never fly again, but that phase passed after a few years.

While in Italy Carlo's parents bought an accordion for him as he had taken lessons for three years before the trip. When they went through customs in New York, the agent asked who the accordion was for, and when told it was Carlo's the agent asked him to prove that he could play it. So Carlo had to take the accordion out and play it right there.

When they returned, Carlo started Bellarmine College Prep and he would catch the train near their home in Palo Alto and there was a train stop behind the baseball field on the campus.

In 1949-1950 Charlie, along with a group of Italians decided that it would be nice to have a club where they could socialize, have dinners, play bocce ball or play cards so they formed a club paying $100.00 each. Then the members took out a loan to purchase about five acres of land and build a building on Escuela Street in Mtn. View. The building had a full basement where the dining hall and kitchen were and on the main floor was the big hall for dancing with a stage and a long bar. There were also four bocce alleys and a space with tables where people could play cards. At the very back of the property were picnic tables and huge barbecue pits. This club was called the Sunnyview Family Club and was the site of many fun picnics or parties there. The seating downstairs could hold about 500 people seated at long tables. The service was usually family style. The Club would have dinner and dances on Saturday nights and dinners also for the Club members on Sunday for a price of usually $5.00. This is the same Club where Carlo and I were married.

The picnics which were held during the summer were good family get togethers. There was plenty of food, plenty of parking and fun games. One I remember was that about 4 or 5 salamis were hung from a cross beam and then for about $1.00 you could get five chances of throwing pieces of raw potatoes, which were cut into four or six pieces at the salamis. If you hit a salami, you won it. Then there were other games for young children and also wheels of chance. Someone would always bring an accordion and there was always plenty of singing.

On the property where Carlo's family lived in Palo Alto, there was a gasoline pump to fuel the trucks, tractors, etc. which were used on the five acres which they owned. They purchased the gasoline from Valley Oil and Charlie was approached by the Mobile

Gas Company to build a service station on the corner of their property. They did this and leased the station to Mobile and Carlo got
a job there right after high school. Charlie couldn't sit still for long
and in 1955 he decided to build a nursery next to the gas station
facing San Antonio Avenue. The nursery opened up in October,
1955 and was a beautiful place with flowers, plants and trees and a
lot of work. The nursery was open 6 days a week and closed on
Tuesdays. Charlie was happy among all this beauty and he loved
being out in the open spaces instead of living in a city with homes
being right next to each other. He loved to get up in the mornings,
go outside, sing songs in Italian and just enjoy being out among
nature. He still knew songs word for word in Italian and many
times he would also recite poems he learned in school in Italy.

This brings me up to the time I met Carlo and we got married.

When we got married we rented an apartment about a half mile
from the nursery. Carlo worked at the nursery and I also helped on
weekends and learned a lot about plants and flowers. We lived
there for about six months and we were looking to buy a house.
Instead of a house we found a six-unit apartment building in Sunnyvale near the store my parents owned. We decided to buy it and
moved into one of the units. Around March of 1960 I became
pregnant and when Charlie and Lee found out, they mentioned
that we should go to Italy to meet the relatives as we probably
wouldn't be able to go once we had children. They offered to pay
for our trip so we made plans to go in the summer of 1960. When
my grandmother in Italy found out we were coming, her first reaction was to say, "Why is Rose coming back, she didn't like it when
she came in '53 and now she is coming with a husband who probably doesn't speak Italian." They were not looking forward to my
visit.

When Carlo and I went to Italy in July my mother of course was
very apprehensive since I was pregnant but I never had morning
sickness and the doctor gave me a clean bill of health. We left San

Francisco with stops in Los Angeles, Montreal, Paris and arrived in Rome at noon Italian time the next day. We went to the hotel and decided to rest as we were tired. It was hot in Rome and Carlo lay on the bed "au natural" and I decided to take a bath. I am very curious when it comes to touching things before finding out what they are. There was a string hanging down from the ceiling over the bathtub. I pulled it and nothing happened — I thought. When I came out of the bath, Carlo was a bit upset with me. It seems that the string was a call for help. The maid came, knocked on the outer door and said "Permesso?" which means, may I enter? Then there is a space where people put their shoes to be shined or clothes to be cleaned, etc. and then an inner door. She didn't hear anything so she knocked on the inner door and asked again "Permesso?" Carlo was half asleep so she entered the room and seeing Carlo in the buff quickly excused herself and then he realized that I had touched something I shouldn't have. He explained to her that it was probably his wife and she left the room. Sadly I still haven't learned not to touch things I shouldn't.

We were three days in Rome and saw the Borghese Palace, the Pantheon, St. Peter's Cathedral, the Colosseum, the Fountain of Trevi and the Tomb of the Unknown Soldier. I almost passed out at the Borghese Palace because of the stuffiness in the room and the humidity of the weather. But that was the only time I ever felt sick. We also visited the catacombs of Rome, something I didn't care for.

We left Rome aboard Alitalia Airlines for Torino and went to my Zio Pino and Zia Francesca's house. We left the next day for the cascina in Quargnento. The taxi driver who was my mother's friend came to pick us up. When we arrived at the cascina, my apprehensive grandmother found out that Carlo spoke perfect Italian and I now had a smile upon my face. My great aunt who lived in the other half of the cascina immediately latched on to Carlo when she learned that his family had a nursery and wanted him to see all of her beautiful flowers and asked him if we had the same flowers in America. I sensed that my grandmother was a bit jealous when my great aunt took him away to her side because she said, "Look at that — look at her, now she wants him to pay attention to her." I couldn't help but laugh to myself at all this, but to them, relatives coming all the way from California was a big thing.

At the cascina there were all the people from the first time I visited except for my great grandmother. Carlo took an immediate liking to my nonno because he was not just a farmer. He read the Readers' Digest in Italian and asked questions constantly so that he could learn something about America. He asked Carlo if it was true that some day soon there would be men going to the moon or into outer space. When Carlo told him it was true he said that if he was younger he would love to do that. He was 84 years old at the time.

Carlo made plans with the taxi driver, Pino to go to Alessandria to rent a car. Pino told him he could also buy a used car, use it for as long as we needed and then sell it back to the dealer which sounded good to us. No one had a car at the cascina. We decided to do this and wrote a check for the car which was about $1,200.00. When we talked to my father during the next phone call, he told us to leave the car with my Zio Evasio and he would reimburse us. My zii and nonni had already been hosts for three trips that my parents and I had made and stayed with them with this being the fourth time they had to put up with someone from our family.

My nonna was always ready to go somewhere with the car. She told us one day, "Since you have the car, could you take us to Alessandria to have a studio picture taken of your nonno and me so that we have a good photo for our funeral and to put on our crypt?

Maternal grandparents, Rosa Zeppa & Domenico Stanchi 1960

The next time she asked for a ride was when Carlo and I had to run an errand and we were going to Alessandria. My nonna asked if we could drop her and nonno along with another relative off at the cemetery so they could visit the loved ones who passed away and they would walk back to Quargnento and we could pick them up on our way back. They would stay with the relative. My nonno hearing that we were going already had a plan in mind, and he got ready with his suit, tie and hat, which is what he always wore when he went into town. When he was younger, he used to bicycle into Alessandria, which is about five miles away, so he didn't get to this town very often any more. When we made our rounds at the cemetery, Carlo told nonna that we were going to leave and we would meet them back in Quargnento. As we started heading to the car, nonno was walking along with us. Upon seeing this, nonna said, "Nonno, they are going to Alessandria, you are staying here with us." He didn't pay any attention to her, it was as if he was deaf. He told Carlo to keep walking. She repeated her demand and Carlo realized that nonno wanted to have an outing with us. Carlo turned and told nonna, "Don't worry, he will be fine with us." She answered back, "Don't let him out of the car, he will get lost." We really had a laugh with this part as he had planned to go and see a friend who owned a sporting goods store and he hadn't seen him in many years. He was sitting on the edge of his seat in back with his hands holding on to our seat and just enjoying his ride so much.

Alessandria is abut the size of San Jose and nonno was directing Carlo where to go and led him right to the store. Carlo dropped me off to run my errand and then Carlo and nonno went to the sporting goods store. Carlo said it was great to see my nonno and his friend meet after so many years. They were like two young men reliving their past times.

The next day we left for Genova to meet Carlo's relatives. Charlie's brother, Edoardo and his wife Aurelia lived in Murta and Carlo had never been there. We found the exit from the main highway before reaching Genova and followed the winding road up the mountain toward Murta. We reached the piazza where the church was located and started to follow the only road up further. The road or path was extremely narrow and just abut 300 yards past the church a man came out of his doorway as we passed and I told Carlo that I thought the man was his uncle. We backed down and sure enough it was Zio Edoardo. There was nowhere to park there so he directed us to park in the piazza by the church. So this was my first meeting with Carlo's wonderful and kind uncle. He was like a big fuzzy bear whom everyone loved, the town's Jack of all trades, who never seemed to raise his voice or lose his temper. I immediately took a liking to him. We arrived in time for dinner and then it seemed as if the heavens broke lose with thunder, rain and lightning. It seemed as if the world was going to crash down on us. During the night it was almost impossible to sleep as we had to get used to the church clock ringing every fifteen minutes. It would ring the time, such as twelve and then at 12:15 it would ring twelve and a pause and then once. At 12:30 it would ring twelve times, pause and then twice and at 12;45 it would ring twelve times, pause and then three times more. You surely knew what time it was but you didn't have time to fall asleep. In the church tower there was a carillon also and on Sundays sometimes someone would play the bells. I loved listening to them.

The next day was Sunday and Zio Edoardo's son, Bruno, along with his wife, Adelia and daughter, Maura, wanted us to go along with them and zio to Pontinvrea, Carlo's father's home town and of course also zio's. It took us about an hour to get there and it was a winding road after we got off the main road near the coast. Zia Aurelia told me to watch zio so that he didn't drink too much wine because of his high glucose. I didn't like to be put "in charge" of watching someone's diet but I said I would watch him. We ate lunch at one of the local restaurants where everyone knew everyone and zio had two small glasses of wine and as he did so he winked at me. Driving back to Murta I experienced some sharp pains and I almost panicked. What if these pains were labor pains, what if I had to go to a doctor. I didn't like going to Pontinvrea, especially with the winding road. When we got back to Murta, I voiced my concerns to Carlo and he calmed me down and told me not to worry and that we would just take it easy for a few days. Also when we returned zia asked if zio drank wine and I said he only had a small glass. She seemed satisfied and he had a big grin on his face.

While we were there, Carlo went into Genova to register at the American Consulate as he was still in the Naval Reserve and had worked on a classified or secure base while on active duty. We took a small side trip driving to Portofino and Santa Margherita which were really beautiful. After about a week we went again to Pontinvrea with zio, zia and a cousin Rosanna Marenco. Zio Edoardo went every summer for a month or so but since he was retired from working for the railroad, a government job, he and his wife could travel for nothing, but since we had the car the five of us piled in. Zio Edoardo was a big man and the car was not very large. He also wanted to bring along a demijohn of wine (about 5 gallons). Everytime we hit a pothole or a bump, he car springs would hit bottom. We held our breath all the way to Pontinvrea. Zia hated Pontinvrea and also Rosanna never really liked it, so zia just stayed a couple of days and then returned via the train to Murta. Zio would always call Pontinvrea "The Garden of Italy."

There was nothing to do in Pontinvrea other than take walks, visit, go fishing in the river and just enjoy the fresh air. Many city residents go to Pontinvrea during the summer and increase the population tenfold. While zio and I were sitting outside one day a man came riding by on his horse. He had beautiful leather riding boots and the horse was a beautiful chestnut color. The man was handsome with a mustache and jet black hair. He seemed to be a stranger and zio said he was with the gypsies who were camped about a half mile past the house near the river. They had their little trailers parked down there. The next day we were sitting again outside and a gypsy lady came by, entered the yard without asking and was trying to sell sewing supplies from a small basket which she carried. She was barefoot and when my uncle told her to leave that we didn't want anything, she turned and stepped into a chicken dropping. She said some choice words, wiped her foot on the ground and left. But I had heard some stories about the gypsies who would try to gain entry in the houses and steal items. Since we were outside she didn't get a chance to enter.

One day zio left the house early and when he returned with his shotgun he had a squirrel in his hand. I asked what he was going to do with it. He said it was dinner. I thought "Yuck!" Well, it was that or nothing. He started to make polenta and when he was finished with that, he cleaned the squirrel and cooked it with tomatoes, wine, mushrooms, and other spices. I thought, "How is that little squirrel going to feed three of us?" plus a friend stopped by before dinner and was asked to join so it was four adults. Well, I have to confess, the squirrel tasted just like chicken and Carlo said he never saw me eat so much before and was very surprised. As they say, I guess I was eating for two.

11

MUSICAL HOUSES

After our family moved from San Jose to Sunnyvale we played a sort of "musical houses" much like musical chairs. I'll explain. The first house we lived in was in the living quarters above the store on Maude Ave. in Sunnyvale. I loved that house. We lived there almost three years before the new store was built right next door to the old one. A subdivision of homes was also being built right behind the store so my dad had to opportunity to buy one of the first homes. Since it was directly behind the new building and although all the homes were going to be with a one car garage, he was able to order ours with a two car garage. Not that we had two cars but he was already thinking to use one half of the garage for warehouse for the store so we could buy in bigger quantities for a better price. We were able to move into our new house around the same time as opening the new store. In 1951 my brother Louis got married to Betty Rakowski and moved about two blocks away.

In 1956 my dad saw a beautiful custom house and decided to buy a lot across town near St. Martin's School and have the house built on this property. When the house was finished my father suggested that Louis move into the house that we were occupying behind the store as he now had two children and his house had only two bedrooms. So in November of 1956, my parents and I moved in the new house on Carlyn Court, Louis moved behind the store. I had just met Carlo and we were not married yet.

In 1959 Carlo and I got married and we lived in an apartment in Mtn. View for six months and then moved to Sunnyvale in an apartment.

Then in 1961 my parents along with my brother Louis bought property on Columbia Avenue and decided to build a 15 unit apartment house. When it was finished, my parents moved into the large manager's unit of the apartment building. Louis and family moved into my parent's house on Carlyn Court since his children were going to St. Martin's School and Carlo and I with our six-month old daughter, Marina Lee, moved into the house behind the store on Arbor Ave. Carlo's parents asked if he wanted to take over the nursery business and my father and brother also asked Carlo if he wanted to go into the grocery business with them. After weighing all the facts, Carlo decided to go into the grocery business. The nursery business is hard work and open on weekends. The grocery business is open seven days a week but Louis and Carlo took turns having Sundays off. We felt it was better that someone be near the business and since my dad owned the house on Arbor Ave. it was also cheap rent. We lived there for seven years and it was really enjoyable. The neighborhood was great and we knew almost everyone because they were customers of ours. We also had a shortcut "path" between our house and the one next door so that people wouldn't have to go all the way to the end of the street and then back to the store. They just walked between the two homes and up through the parking lot. It was very convenient.

So in 1961 Carlo's parents closed the nursery and took off for Italy, again driving across the United States with a 1960 Thunderbird with air conditioning. They again took the car on the ship and returned in December of 1961. They drove the return trip along the southern route of the U.S. and hit such snow storms in New Mexico that Lee didn't think were possible. It was also the winter we had snow in Sunnyvale but I don't remember in which month. All I remember is that Marina was barely standing along the window sill and looking outside but she had a cold so I wouldn't let her go outside in the snow.

During the time we lived in the house behind the store our second child was born. Marco Stefano was born two years and one month after Marina. I wanted to name him Mark Steven after our two fathers and Carlo wanted the traditional Italian name. When the pediatrician asked what we were going to name the baby, I told him of the difference of opinion and he immediately took Carlo's side by saying that we should stick to the traditional Italian since we had an Italian surname. So Carlo won.

In 1967 we decided to look for a house near St. Martin's also and found one on Maxine Court which was right next to Carlyn Court where my brother lived. My mother was not enjoying living in the apartment building. Everything made her nervous such as if someone was playing the stereo too loud, she worried that it was bothering the other tenants. She was becoming very nervous and when we said we would be moving from behind the store, she said she wanted to move back in that house. So back they went to square one. We all enjoyed the house behind the store. We had a buzzer set up that we could buzz from the store to the house if we wanted someone to pick up that phone extension. If the phone rang and if the call was for someone who was at the house we would buzz once. If we needed help in the store we would just buzz twice or more and that meant "Come up, we need help."

My parents only lived in the house behind the store two years when a large chain store moved in on Mathilda and Maude Avenues and made a difference in our business. Our butcher also announced that he would be leaving our store, so my father, brother and Carlo decided to sell the business.

We had been in the grocery business in Sunnyvale for 21 years when we sold and it was a bit emotional. Our customers were really friends, not just customers. Years later whenever we saw our old customers they would always say how they missed our store. The new owners had it only one year before they closed for good.

I don't think the possibility of playing "musical houses" would have worked if our family did not get along so well. We did not have a deadline to move everything out of our houses. In fact I still had wedding presents in my mother's house for a while after we got married as I didn't have room in our apartment or in the house behind the store when we moved there. Only when we moved near St. Martin's School did we have room to get all the china, crystal, etc. that comes with a large wedding.

Now I will tell you a bit about the neighborhoods we lived in. We moved to the house behind the store when Marina was a little more than six months old. Since we were so close to the store, Marina got a lot of attention from the grandparents, uncle and aunt and employees. My father, Nonno Steve, had already started a routine with my brother's children by bringing them to the bank with him when he did the daily banking. He was always so proud of his grandchildren. So when Marina began walking, it was her turn to go to the bank with nonno. The bank teller at the merchant's window knew our children more than they knew me. I think I needed Marina for identification. Marina was also very headstrong and wanted to be important by carrying the bag of coins with her nonno. He told her it was too heavy as it was about twenty pounds. She insisted so he put the bag on the floor in the bank. She tried to lift it and of course she couldn't. He said it was very funny to see her tugging at the bag and stamping her feet as she tried to lift it. So they went back to the teller and she was given a small cloth bag with four rolls of pennies in it.

When she started talking, we tried to teach her the Italian language. It was a bit of a chore for us to try to use Italian in our everyday routine and it was especially hard for me as I had used the Piemontese dialect before I met Carlo. Well, Marina began using and understanding Italian words before she was two years old and whenever we went to the Sunnyview Club or to the Sons of Italy Lodge the members loved to hear her talk. The drawback was that my sister-in-law did not speak the language nor did Marina's cousins so when they played together it was a bit confusing and when my sister-in-law babysat she said it was hard to communicate with Marina.

Other than the cousins, there weren't many young children in our neighborhood as most of the children were already in their teen years when we moved there. When Marina was three we decided to put her in a nursery school two mornings a week so that she could get used to playing with other children. By this time Marco was one year old. At nursery school Marina decided that the other children didn't understand her so she stopped speaking Italian and converted to English. When Marina began kindergarten we enrolled her at Bishop Elementary School right across the street from the store. We also found that there were three girls about a block or two away from our house who were in the same class as Marina and used the shortcut next to our house to go to school so Marina had some friends. She was terribly independent however, and when I told her I would be waiting for her at the end of the first day, she informed me that I shouldn't pick her up, she knew how to walk home by herself. I did go and was waiting for her by the door along with other mothers. As soon as she came out the door she saw me and said "Why did you come, I told you not to." The other mothers looked at me with a look of pity on their faces. Oh, the rejection by a 5-year old!

When Marina started kindergarten, Marco started nursery school. He was not too keen on going the two mornings to school. He didn't talk as much as Marina had at this age and when I questioned the doctor, he said Marco didn't have any reason to talk as Marina was doing all the talking for him. Marco was happy running up and down the sidewalk, bent over his Tonka truck and pushing it. He would stop by braking with his toes and he would wear holes in his shoes within three or four months. One thing Marco did was to communicate with the grownups. As I said, the neighborhood didn't have too many children so Marco made friends with the older people. He had a friend Mr. Pate who lived two houses down and had no children. He usually had his garage door open and would be working on some project. Marco had a pedal tractor which he also loved and when he used it so much the metal seat broke and came loose, he of course told Mr. Pate about it. Mr. Pate drilled holes in a piece of plywood and attached the wood to the seat and it was as good as new. The neighbor on one side of our house was an employee of our store and he had moved there from McCloud so he was also a good friend. The neighbor Gil had a heart attack when Marco was about three years old and he recuperated for about three months at home. Gil's wife, Irene had a ladies' dress shop next to the store so she was close by if Gil needed anything. Irene would also close the shop for an hour at lunch time, fix lunch for Gil and set him up with dessert such as canned fruit. Marco was treated to the dessert also if he was there. Soon Marco would run next door every day to see Gil and it was always around lunch time. I told Gil to send Marco home as he was probably a bother. Both Gil and Irene assured me that Marco was such company that Gil enjoyed having him come over. Marco also learned the license plates and telephone numbers of all the employees so Gil would quiz him on these facts and was always playing the memory game with Marco.

When Marco started nursery school, the cook was an Italian lady so Marco loved running in to school, greeting Zelinda in Italian and saying a few other words to her, but he didn't like nursery school as Marina did so he dropped out after about six months. Since he had another year before kindergarten, we took him out and then re-enrolled him in nursery school the following year. He was much happier then.

We moved to Maxine Court after Marina started first grade at St. Martin's Schol. She took the school bus for two months and the bus stop was about a block from our house. When we moved near the school in November, she only had to walk across the school field. Our court had 10 children among six houses. The next court over where my brother lived had 34 children among 8 houses so there were always a lot of children running around and a lot of games being played such as hide and seek, kick the can, baseball on the school field, flying kites, etc. During the summer, on nice warm evenings, the adults would sit outside at the end of our court next to the school field and we would just talk or barbecue and let the children run around playing. Sometimes it would be almost ten or eleven o'clock before we would to in as we were all having such a good time. Nowadays when we see some of the former neighbors, we reminisce about the fun times we had on Carlyn and Maxine Courts.

12

OUR DOG LIGHTNING

When we moved to our home on Maxine Ave. the children were 6 and 4 years of age and had been wanting a dog. Now that we had a bigger house and larger yard, we gave in to their request. Carlo took the children down to the Humane Society to see if there was a dog available. Sure enough there was one they loved right away, however, since he was brought in just the day before, they had to wait four days and if no one claimed him, they could go back and buy him. He was a cute chihuahua/terrier mix with huge black eyes. He was a bit bigger than a chihuahua, the same color, a tail that had been cut to about 3 inches and a white spot on his forehead. Marina said the spot on his forehead looked like a lightning strike so she called him Lightning. The dog was spoiled immediately with Marina and Marco holding him and all the other children in the neighborhood

coming to see our newest member of the family.
Everyone in the neighborhood already had animals so
the children really felt as if they now belonged.

We had Lightning just for about a week when he started developing some sort of mucous around his eyes so we took him to a vet.
When the vet checked him out, he said it seemed that the dog had
distemper and asked if he had been vaccinated. We replied that we
picked him up at the Humane Society. He said since he was so
young, he probably didn't get that shot and picked up distemper at
the dog pound. He said he had a 50-50 chance of surviving. He
instructed me to boil some hamburger meat and rice every day, it
would help the dog and also he gave us some capsules to give him
every day. He did warn us that if the dog started to run around in a
circle and foaming at the mouth it meant that it was near the end
and to bring him in so he could be put down. We thought we hid
the capsules very well in his food but every once in a while we
found them around the yard. I fixed his special food every day for
about 30 days and it seemed that he got better. I had called the
humane Society to tell them that the dog got sick shortly after getting him but we were going to keep him. After a few days, the
people who lost the dog checked with the Humane Society and
were given our phone number in case we wanted to give him back.
The lady said that Lightning had a twin brother and they still had
him but wanted to get Lightning back and wondered if I wanted to
give him up. I said that our children were now attached to Lightning and we would keep him.

Lightning never barked and we thought he was not a very good
watch dog. One day I was in the enclosed patio room that had
siding glass doors between the family room and the patio room.
He saw his reflection in the door and started to growl and bark. It
was so funny I had to laugh at this little "big watch dog."

Carlo constructed a big dog house for him with a hinged roof so that it could be cleaned out and it was situated on the side yard next to the school field of St. Martin's Elementary. On a Tuesday, which was the delivery day of the Culligan Man with the water softener tank, I forgot to unlock the gate. The service man just went around on the school field and jumped the fence into our yard. Boy did Lightning bark. Another time, an eighth grader lost a ball into our yard, jumped the fence and because I heard the noise, I opened the door to see the student scared as can be at seeing the size of the dog house hurrying as fast as he could to jump back. He must have thought the dog was as big as a German shepherd instead of as small as he was.

Lightning loved to run in the school yard when he was loose and he was as fast as his name. There were many squirrels in the yard as it was surrounded by pine trees and he loved to chase them. A couple of years after we moved to Maxine Ave., which was actually a court, the church installed a chain link fence between the school yard and the court. One day Lightning was out and saw the squirrels running around and took off at top speed to catch them. He ran straight for the yard and CRASH!! — smack into the fence. A bit dazed, he wondered "What happened?"

We always took Lightning to Lake Tahoe when we went there and he would love to sit atop the luggage and boxes in his dog bed. When we were loading up the car we usually had the garage door open, and perhaps the gate was open, etc, Lightning would be running around. One time, when we called him, he came slowly through the school field and when Carlo picked him up to place him in the car, he snapped at Carlo and yelped. Carlo felt his body and right at his ribs, it seemed as if someone had kicked him. All the way up to the lake, he didn't move and when we got there he also didn't move from his bed. Another time that we were getting ready to go up it seemed as if he got into a fight with another dog. Although we couldn't immediately see any wounds, we found a couple of bite marks on his back haunch or hip. It was always when we were ready to go on vacation so we did not take the time to bring him to the vet. This time, Carlo put antiseptic on his wounds and again he recovered.

A strange thing happened soon after we got Lightning. Marina was receiving her First Holy Communion and we were all busy getting ready for early mass at St. Martin's and somehow someone left the gate open and we didn't realize it until we returned home after a few hours. Marine went outside to see the dog and came running saying, "Lightning's gone! He is nowhere!" We looked around the neighborhood and I promised to check with the dog pound the next day. Meanwhile, my brother and his son David went to visit my parents who now lived on

east Arbor Avenue where we lived before moving to Maxine. The dog had never been to that house. While driving on East Arbor Ave. about a half block from my parents house, David said, "Dad, isn't that Lightning? See, it doesn't have a tail." My brother stopped and called out to the dog. The dog ran and jumped into the car. I think it was so strange that of all the streets in Sunnyvale, he happened to be on the one where we had lived for eight years and he had never been there before.

Another time, on a Saturday, a young lady rang our doorbell and she was crying. She blurted out, "I just killed your dog." I was stunned and replied, "I don't think so, he is in the back yard." She insisted that she did and said she accidentally hit him with her car on the cross street and he was lying in the street. I went outside with her and Marina was mowing my mother's lawn next door. I asked Marina, "Marina, where is Lightning?" She replied, "Oh, he is around here." Then we looked up and here was Lightning staggering like a drunken animal, bleeding from the top of his head and heading for home. The lady was shocked but happy he was still alive. She knew we would have to take him to the vet so she handed me a $100 bill and said it was to pay for his bill. I declined the money and just told her to stop by in a few days to see how the dog was. We took him to Palo Alto as our normal vet's office was closed. We were told to come back in the early evening to pick him up. When we went back to pick him up it seemed as if the effects of the tranquilizer were still working on him because when he was picked up and placed on the linoleum, all four legs spread out from under him. We felt sorry for him, but it was funny seeing him not being able to stand. The young lady did stop by after a few days to see how the dog was doing. We did spoil him by letting him stay in the house near the fireplace for about a month. After that it was back in his dog house. Speaking of his dog house, he kept all his bones in it. When we moved to our present home, his house was right below our bedroom window and sometimes we could hear him gnawing on the bones during the night.

We had Lightning for 14 years. We lost him one evening when we were at Lake Tahoe. Carlo's mother who lived with us did not want to go to the lake so she stayed home. That weekend, we had terrible weather in Sunnyvale. It was raining and the wind was blowing hard and an electrical wire came down in our back yard and was arcing and sparking. The wind blew the gate open and Lightning ran out. The next morning Lee called us to say she couldn't find Lightning any where. When we got home we checked with the Humane Society for a few days and also checked the list of DOA animals and their descriptions and put an ad in the paper but we had no luck. I guess Lightning used up his last life as he survived so many other close calls and he is now in doggie heaven.

13

HOLIDAY DINNERS AND GILROY

After Carlo's parents returned from Italy in December, 1961, they decided to sell the property and the nursery on San Antonio Road in Palo Alto. During the year of 1962 was when I became pregnant with Marco. Charlie began selling off the remainder of the inventory of the nursery and clearing out the barn, etc. We started to reminisce about the good times at the house and the space they had surrounding the house.

My brother Louis and his wife Betty already had three children when we got married. My mother's sister, Adriana and her husband, Angelo had two children at that time. Holiday dinners were held at random places by the time we got married but then it sort of came down to a fixed routine for many years. In 1961, Easter was held at Charlie and Lee's home with my parents, my brother's family and my aunt's family all attending. Charlie and Lee were great cooks and Charlie especially liked to barbecue. He had a large outdoor brick barbecue and cooked two legs of lamb and a small ham in case someone didn't like the lamb. The ham was left-over as everyone including the young children loved the barbecued lamb. It was a beautiful warm day so we set up a long picnic table and benches outside beneath a huge pepper tree. Another dish Lee was famous for making was beef tongue with tuna sauce and I was very surprised when two of the young children asked for seconds. In fact in the years following one of them would always ask just before Easter, "Is Lee going to make tongue and is Charlie going to barbecue lamb again?" Before the meal we had an Easter egg hunt in the grassy area near the house. We had plenty of empty space to look for eggs and the five children had so much fun looking for eggs. We spray painted a plastic egg gold and placed a $2.00 bill inside and we just had to remember where we placed it. Marina was just a baby so she didn't partake in the hunt. The following year was different with her tottering after her cousins looking for the special egg. Some years later was the only time the Easter egg hunt got rained out. It wasn't really pouring down rain but was wet enough that we had to hide the eggs in the barn. I guess you could say we were like chickens hiding them in the barn.

For Thanksgiving we got into the habit of going to Zia Adriana's house in San Martin. I'll tell you about Adriana. Adriana was my mother's sister born in Italy thirteen years after my mother. When she was 25 years old in 1950 my mom asked Adriana if she wanted to come to California for a visit. She jumped at the chance. She had been living on the farm with my grandparents and one brother. When she came for her vacation my parents would accompany her to the Sunnyview Family Club for their dances on Saturdays or Sundays and she could meet Italian speaking young people. Of course, older Italians would meet Adriana and would try to fix her up with some single Italian young men. Well, she met Angelo Robba, an orchardist in San Martin. Angelo raised prunes and between he and his father had 90 acres of prune trees. Angelo asked Adriana to marry him and they set the date for July, 1951 and my brother at that time also asked Betty to marry him and they set their wedding date for August, 1951. So we were quite busy during the two months with two weddings taking place.

Zia Adriana moved to the "country" of San Martin and after I got married, she began having Thanksgiving dinners down there. It was always beautiful with fall colors and being outdoors in the fall atmosphere. Zia was also a good cook and of course we always ate too much. One of the Thanksgiving dinners I will never forget was in 1974. One of our cousins from New York on my mother's and Zia's side came out to California with her daughter Wanda. The mother, Ada, had never been to California and she said she was worried because she knew that California had earthquakes quite often. I assured her that it didn't happen that often so she need not worry. A little while after she voiced her concern, a rumbling noise could be heard, the chandelier began tinkling, and the table and chairs started to shake. Henry, Adriana's son dove under the table. Ada looked at me with a puzzled look and I tried to remain calm. Most of us just sat in our places and the earthquake was over in less than a minute. We then told Ada and Wanda that California was welcoming them and they had just experienced their first earthquake.

After Adriana and Angelo had been married for a few years, Angelo pulled out all the prune trees and they planted pickling cucumbers. They also planted flowers for seed for the Ferry-Morse Seed Company such as zinnias and asters. The zinnias were so colorful and the asters with their many hues of pinks and violets were gorgeous. With the flowers, they just had to plant them and of course nurture them and then Ferry-Morse would come in and harvest the dried flowers for seed. With the asters, however, they could not plant them in the same spot more than one year. It seems as if the asters would take too much out of the soil so they only planted them for a couple of years before going into something else.

The biggest crop they went into was squash of all types, such as Danish, turban, spaghetti squash, butternut, kabocha, etc. They were selling to a big wholesale outfit in Los Angeles called Frieda's Fine Foods and big 18-wheel trucks would come to their farm to pick up the boxes of squash. Thanksgiving was the time of year when all the squash would be ready for harvest so we always got treated to different dishes prepared by my aunt using what she raised.

Christmas dinners were usually the responsibility of either my brother, Louis or myself. One of us would have Christmas eve and the other would have Christmas day. The following year would be just the reverse. By the time we had Marco there were usually 17 people at our table. Then Betty's brother and his family joined our family gatherings and there were an additional 12 people so we started to split up into two events with one of us getting everyone together for dessert.

In 1963 when Charlie and Lee sold the nursery to a developer for townhouses, they moved to Gilroy. They bought a house on Miller Avenue and a 10-acre parcel on south Monterey Highway south of the city limits of Gilroy. The property went from the highway all the way back to the railroad tracks. On the property there was a restaurant at the front of the property and land used for row crops such as tomatoes in the back. Within a year Charlie had a building constructed on the property which had two rentals on the bottom and two apartments on the second story. He decided to make one of the rentals on the bottom into a liquor store which he would operate and then he and Lee moved into one of the second story apartments. He was still the type that couldn't just retire and do nothing. Also he loved being on the property instead of living in town in a neighborhood. While he was living on the ten acres, he planted two or three of every kind of fruit tree such as apples, peaches, nectarines, apricots, cherries and of course we benefited from his harvests. The children also loved being out there, they would take long walks to explore the fields going to the railroad tracks, putting pennies on the tracks to get flattened by the trains. They also discovered a hobo living in a cardboard box among the blackberry bushes near the tracks and ran as if he were chasing them back to the house.

The years of Carlo's parents living in Gilroy were fun times for us, especially the children. When Carlo had every other Sunday off from the store we usually went to Gilroy. At that time there was no freeway past San Jose and we had to go down the old Monterey Highway. Traffic was always a bear going down and then driving home after dinner. It always took at least an hour. Marina and Marco always played the alphabet game which consisted of finding the alphabet in order on their side of the street. One would usually choose the left side because there was a winery in Morgan Hill that contained the letter "Z" in the name so they were sure to be able to get that letter in that city if not before. Lee and charlie also loved having the children come down and stay for a few days with them. Marina didn't do it very often but Marco loved to go down there. Sometimes he was allowed to take along one of his friends. The boys would go out into the garden with Charlie or around the barn to putter around and "fix" things. The barn was a paradise with tools and all kinds of places to explore. On the workbench in the barn there was a regular sized vise which Charlie used and there was a very small vise next to it. Well, Marco figured that this vise was his since it was small. Charlie removed it one day because he didn't use it very often. The next time Marco went down to Gilroy, he went into the barn, came running out of it and up the stairs and demanded, "All right, where is it? Who took it? Who did it?" Lee had to chuckle because he was acting as if the bank had been robbed. Needless to say, Charlie had to replace the vise on the workbench.

When my father sold the grocery store in January of 1969, Carlo said we should take a trip to Italy with the children because if he settled down with a job, we didn't know when we would be able to go. He did get a job for the next six months so that we could still have the medical insurance with the Retail Clerks Union. We contacted an Italian friend who was a travel agent in San Francisco and he gave us great advice as to what to do when traveling with the children. At the time they were 8 and 6. Besides going to Italy he suggested we visit London and Copenhagen but to take only one tour as the children would get bored or tired and he set us up with a stay in Rome for three days and also a stay in Venice for three days. The remainder of the time was spent with relatives. Carlo's parents also decided to go to Italy and they went a month before us and would mostly stay in Pontinvrea instead of touring around. You could say they wanted to show off the grandchildren to the relatives and friends.

14

TRIP TO ITALY 1969

We first went to London and took one tour and also went to a movie where the film was "Chitty Chitty Bang Bang". We also saw the changing of the guard at Buckingham Palace. The next stop was Copenhagen and we stayed in a hotel which was on the main street within walking distance to Tivoli Gardens. Our hotel was also next to the river which had a drawbridge over it. Marina and Marco loved looking out the window to watch all the cars and many bicyclists stop for the bridge to go up and the boats go through the opening. Marco also did just like me in touching things he shouldn't touch and pushed the button for the room steward. The steward came and asked if we needed something and with red faces we had to say, "Sorry, our son touched the button." We took a tour which was partly on the water and partly on land. We saw Hans Christian Anderson's home and we took pictures of the statue of The Little Mermaid. We also saw the palace of the Queen and took pictures next to the royal guard whom the children tried to make talk but he wouldn't even smile.

On to Italy, we went first to Torino to see my aunt who had been in America and left in 1932. She now had three adult children. We also went to visit my mother's brother, Zio Pino, who owned the latteria (dairy product store). They were all so happy to see the children. Then we went to the cascina which by now had running water and electricity which was installed two years prior. A nice bathroom was made upstairs next to Rosita's room at the top of the landing.

My Zio Evasio was really happy to have the children and would always take them out in the field and he would let them ride on the tractor or on the hay rake. Marco always sat next to Zio Evasio at the dinner table as he was his buddy.

One day zii were getting a shipment of 300 young chicks and had to transfer the 300 they already had from one pen into cages. My Zia Pina would catch the chickens and hand them to Carlo or Zio Evasio four at a time (two in each hand). They would hold them by the legs and bring them from one end of the cascina to the other and put them in cages. Marina wanted to help also so she carried them two at a time (one in each hand) but the chickens would start flapping their wings until Zia Pina told her to hold them next to each other and they would stop. She quickly learned and wasn't afraid. I asked Marco if he wanted to help also but he said — "Oh no! They might poop on me". He didn't want any part of that.

Marina and Marco loved Rosita and the fact that she had a little FIAT 500 car which she used to go to work in Casale at a firm that made and printed boxes for cereal. She could speak German and

English besides her native Italian so she worked in the office as a translator. She would arrive home around 7:00 and the children could hear her car buzzing up the road. They would run down the road for the last 500 feet before the incline to the cascina. They would wait for Rosita, she would stop for them to get into her car and then she would gun the motor to get up the hill. They thought it was great fun especially in the tiny car which seemed like a toy.

When we went to Pontinvrea to be with Carlo's parents, the children found two Italian bicycles waiting for them. Charlie thought they would be bored in Pontinvrea so he bought a folding bicycle for Marina and a small replica of a racing bicycle for Marco. Marco, especially was always on the bicycle racing up and down the side streets. He got quite a few flat tires on the bicycle and he would bring the bike to the only gas station in town. It was owned by a Venetian who had married one of Charlie's cousins. Marco would quickly go to Ivo and would make a gesture with both hands going down and saying "Ivo, poof!" Ivo knew right away what had happened and being the nice man he is, would change the flat tire. There were a few children in Pontinvrea and Marina and Marco made friends with them even though there was a lot of hand waving and pointing and asking us to translate. One word they learned very quickly was "gelato." There was also a small stream going through Pontinvrea and Marina and Marco went there almost every day. Marina would fish but Marco would mainly throw rocks much to the dismay of Marina. There was also a place where some of the women would come to wash their clothes in the river. They would use a large flat rock which was half way in the water. They would rub the clothes with soap on this rock and then rinse them in the cold running water.

We would eat our three meals a day at the local restaurant where we knew the owner. The owner was the young girl who was smitten with Carlo when he went in 1948. Our breakfast was usually coffee and milk and focaccia. The children were also given this meal but of course it was more like 2/3 milk and 1/3 coffee. The focaccia was the best we had ever eaten, hot from the oven with the oil brushed over it and sprinkled with salt. Marco to this day still talks about this focaccia. Carlo has learned to make it and Marco says he almost has it down pat.

After about a week in Pontinvrea we went to have lunch at another cousin's home and Marco seemed a bit listless. I felt his forehead and he was burning up. We went back to the apartment where we were staying and put him to bed. The next morning he had a few red spots around his ears and neck so Carlo went to call the doctor who had an office in the main part of town. The town is very small so the main street is only about a block long. At the time there weren't many phones in town either. When Carlo was walking under the porticos, the green grocer, who had a public telephone in his store, told Carlo that there had been a call from America for us and to be there at 9:00 when the caller would call again. That really made us anxious as we expected very bad news. When we received the call, it was my father calling and between the static and breaking up we understood that Charlie and Lee's apartment in Gilroy had been broken into and he needed to know something. Being unable to hear all he was saying I asked the operator if she could repeat what he was saying. She said she could not legally do that but suggested we go to another bigger city and go to the public telephone office and call him back.

So we left Marco with Carlo's parents and we headed down to Savona which is on the riviera and about 30 minutes away. We found the telephone office where there were about 15 phone booths. The office was full of people as it was a Sunday and there were many service men calling home. One had to tell the receptionist who they wanted to call and when the connection went through she told you which booth to go into and you could speak to the one you called. We finally found out that my parents had gone to check the property for Carlo's parents and they found the

window in the apartment had been broken. The sheriff had been
called but he wanted to know if there were any guns or firearms in
the house. My father didn't know the answer. We told them there
were firearms and told him where to look as they were hidden.
Later when we talked to him again, he said the burglars had not
found them. The burglars had taken small appliances, the radio,
mantle clock and other items and probably went to the flea market
to sell them.

When we got back to Pontinvrea we had to cancel our flight to
Rome and reschedule it for a later time as the doctor said Marco
had a slight case of measles so he was confined for a few days in the
apartment.

We flew from Genova to Rome and when we landed we had to
take the bus to the main terminal in the center of Rome. The travel
agent had booked us in the Hilton Hotel because he said that the
children would be able to order hamburgers and french fries and
also to swim in the pool there. Of course Carlo said while shaking
his head, "We travel 5,000 miles to Italy, which has some of the
finest food in the world and the children want hamburgers and
french fries." The Hilton was not in the center of Rome but up on
a little hill and there was a shuttle bus which came by every hour
from the Central Terminal. It would be a few minutes before the
shuttle came so I started looking for a restroom for myself and the
children. It was at the far end of the terminal. Carlo stood with the
luggage while we headed for the restroom. The shuttle came and
Carlo told the driver where we were. He loaded the luggage on and
told Carlo he couldn't wait too long as he was blocking traffic.
Carlo looked in our direction, saw us and motioned for us to
hurry. Now if you have ever travelled with children in Italy, you
will agree that people there love children. They will do anything
for them. The carabiniere (policeman) was telling the bus driver to
get moving. The bus driver was barely inching the bus along and
telling the policeman that he was moving — really! We arrived and

Carlo all but lifted us into the bus. The bus driver, instead of being angry or frustrated gave us a big smile and welcomed us aboard and waved to the carabiniere. We were very lucky.

Our stay at the Hilton was memorable. The best thing was that Fred Astaire and Robert Wagner were also staying there as they were in Rome to film the TV series "To Catch a Thief." The next day at poolside Robert Wagner was allowing people to take photos of him with young people but we were too bashful to do so. The children did get an autograph from Fred Asaire and he was very gracious to them, especially when they told him they had seen Finnian's Rainbow and how much they enjoyed it.

We took one tour of the Tivoli Fountains and it was in the early evening. We had decided to go in the evening because the weather was very hot and humid during the day. It was a bit of a distance by bus but it was beautiful as the fountains were all lit up. When the tour was over it was almost midnight. The children fell asleep on the bus, Marina waking up when we went to catch the bus for the Hilton but Marco was asleep in Carlo's arms.

When we got back to Pontinvrea we decided to go to Venice with Charlie and Lee. A few days before we left was when the first landing on the moon occurred. There weren't TVs in the homes in Pontinvrea, but there was one in the restaurants or bars. Many of us gathered in front of a rather small TV (compared to the huge TV's of today) and watched as the first men walked on the moon. Some of the people, knowing we were Americans clapped and yelled "Bravi!!" They shook our hands or patted us on the back. They were happy for the United States and we were very proud.

We drove to Venice and the car was a bit tight with three of us in the back seat and Marco sitting on Nonno Charlie's lap in front so we didn't go all the way in one day. We stopped in the town of Brescia which is a large city noted for making firearms. There was also a big zoo not too far from our pensione. We didn't have reservations in Brescia but Charlie would just ask a local such as a service station man or the like. He directed us to a pensione which he said was clean and the food was good. He was right but Marco will never let us forget that it was just a "one star" pensione. This meant that we had to share a bathroom down the hall. Our son was not used to that and complained a lot. We visited the zoo and the next day we continued to Venice. In Venice we visited the island of Murano where the glass blowing is done. We went by speed boat or taxi and took a tour of the factory. The children were treated to a glass figurine of their choosing. Since it was my birthday I picked a birthday present which Carlo bought for me. It was two beautiful birds and a rather heavy dark blue vase and two round heavy ashtrays. The factory would pack them and insure and mail them.

On the way back to the main part of Venice our water taxi came upon a gondola with a young couple in it and the gondolier was having trouble navigating the rather open water and wind of the main canal. Our taxi driver asked us for permission to help them and we said, "Of course." Our driver threw a line to them and started to tow them in. I don't think the young couple was too happy to be towed in, it wasn't romantic.

Our hotel was situated right on the Grand Canal not far from St. Mark's Square and exactly opposite from the church Santa Maria Della Salute. Only three years ago I found a beautiful water color painting which was painted as if the artist was viewing the church from our hotel so I purchased it and I enjoy looking at it and reminiscing. We stayed two nights in Venice and we did some of the touristy things such as feeding the pigeons in St. Mark's Square, taking a gondola ride, etc.

On the drive back to Pontinvrea, we stopped overnight in Verona which is the home of Romeo and Juliet. Again we had no reservations and we almost didn't find a place to stay. This was the time of year when the open-air operas are held in Verona and they have a huge arena shaped like the Coliseum in Rome. The opera that evening was "Aida". We walked around the outside and we could see part of the huge sets used for the opera. We asked around and finally found a motel a few miles out of town. We also found a restaurant which had delicious food served under a grape arbor. Again the weather was very hot and humid. We also met an American couple staying at our motel who was traveling from Turkey to Avelino in Italy. The gentleman was in the Air Force and Avelino is the base where he was to be stationed.

I think it is very interesting to talk to people when we travel and it is so true that it is a small world because we always seem to run into Americans or just really interesting people.

When we returned to Pontinvrea the town was having the Feast of San Lorenzo who is the patron saint of the town. The towns-people had booths set up with goodies for sale and they also served a barbecue of sausages. A competition was held for the children of different age groups competing in sack races, egg race where the children held a tablespoon between their teeth with an egg in the spoon and they had to hurry along without dropping the egg. They also had a high jump competition and a very slow bicycle race, this one being "how slow can you ride the bicycle without falling off. Marina was the only girl in the high jump competition and won second place. She and Marco came in first in the sack race. Marco won first in the egg in the spoon race and also won first in the slow bicycle race. To this day whenever we go to Pontinvrea and talk to people, they remember when we were there in 1969 and our American children won almost all the prizes. I don't think they were too happy.

A few days after this festival we left to return to the States. We had all planned to return by ship, "The Michelangelo." We went to the port of Genova and many of our cousins were already there to see us off. Rosanna and her husband Dalmo, Rosita, Zia Maria and her sons, Piero and Mario, Carlo's cousins, Giovanni, his wife Rina, Bruno, Aldo and Luigi were all there. They were able to come on board and we all had champagne in the grand ballroom. When they sounded the whistle for visitors to disembark, we all said "good-bye" and went on deck so we could wave to them below on the pier. Since Marco was only six years old he could barely see over the bulkhead. He was very quiet and we were all chattering and waving to the relatives. When I realized that Marco wasn't talking and just being very quiet, I looked down and saw that he had tears in his eyes. I asked what was wrong and he said, "You know how you feel when you like someone and you know you won't see them again? I feel sad because I won't see Rosita again." Of course, we all had lumps in our throats when we heard this. I assured him that we would see her again sometime. Since that time 41 years ago he has seen Rosita only twice, once when she visited us here in California and once when he and his wife Kristen visited her in 2001.

Our trip on the ship was wonderful. We had the early seating because of the children and then in the evening we played Bingo in the grand ballroom. The numbers were called in Italian first and then in English. Marco, Marina and Carlo each won money. Marco called out Bingo after only eight numbers and since he was so young, the game official told everyone not to move their markers as he thought Marco didn't know the numbers. Well, it was a good Bingo. Altogether, Marco won about $70.00. Again, the children were spoiled on the ship. At meals, we had the waiter, the assistant, the drink waiter and they told me to enjoy my meal and they would help the children with cutting their meat, etc. Whatever the children wanted, they would get it immediately. One day we took a tour of the ship and went through the kitchen. When we saw the cooks preparing pizza, Marco was really happy but found out when he ordered it, the waiter said it was for a party in first class. The next day for lunch, our table had pizza.

After leaving Genova, we went to Cannes, France to pick up passengers, then to Naples for a day to pick up passengers also.

Since we had time to take a tour, we disembarked to take a bus tour of the city. We really wanted to go to Pompei but that day was Ferragosto, a national holiday, and many of the sites were closed. The entire month of August is vacation time in Italy and many shops and businesses are closed. The 15th of August is similar to our Labor Day.

It was on board the Michelangelo that Marco learned to swim. He didn't want to go in the wading pool because he said it was only for little children. He wanted to go in the big pool which was at least 8 feet deep all over. He wanted to go down the slide so Carlo let him go down and caught him when he landed in the water. He went down a few times and then Carlo did not catch him after that. He started swimming on his own over to the edge when he realized that there was no "safety net." The water in the pool was salt water and would be drained every evening. Along the coast of Africa the water was very warm.

From Naples we then sailed to Algicires or Gibralter, to pick up more passengers but it was during the night and we did not pull into port. People were brought out to the ship and boarded out at sea. For the next few days, we didn't see land. We had a safety drill and a talk on hints on landing in New York, how to deal with customs, etc. The children attended a party with baloons, hats, games, etc.

On the seventh day of our crossing, I awoke at 4:30 a.m. and heard cabin doors opening and closing. I wondered what was happening, so I dressed and went out of our cabin and up on deck. The Verazzano Bridge was about 15 or 20 minutes way. I hurriedly went back down to the cabin and woke everyone and made them come up on deck. When we went under the bridge, everyone was wondering if the ship would clear the bridge. Of course it did, but the ship was so tall it seemed as if the smokestacks would hit it. Also, in the early morning light the Statue of Liberty was such an

awesome sight I could only imagine what it was like for the immi-
grants who came to this country many, many years ago.

When we landed, we had to assemble in a cavernous warehouse
and gather up our luggage and assemble under the letter of our last
names. We had to get our luggage and place it near us and then
wait for a customs office to come and check us out. We found all of
our baggage, including the two bicycles and waited patiently.
Some people would tug at the sleeve of the customs officer and
that was when he would ignore them. So we waited very quietly.
When he came to us, he opened every bag, even going through my
purse but he did not open the suitcase where we had all the things
that we had purchased. I had packed all the goodies in one suitcase
and put it under the bunk on the ship so that we wouldn't have to
move it as the space was at a premium. As he was asking questions
about how much we had in goods, Marina kept tugging at me and
saying, "What about all the gloves you bought in Rome?' I had purchased about 10 pairs of leather gloves in Rome and they were all
worked with embroidered cut work and I had planned to use them
as gifts. I had to give her a stern look to keep quiet. Whether the
customs officer heard her or not, he did not open the lone suitcase
with all the gifts. We went to our hotel in downtown New York
and later that afternoon my cousin Wanda, who worked at the Citi-
bank on Wall Street, came to visit us before going home on Long
Island.

The next day, Carlo's parents returned to California and we
took a tour of New York and then took a Circle Line boat tour
around Manhatten.

We returned home a day later and were so happy to be home
again. It was a memorable vacation and Marina and Marco still talk
about it. With the fact that there are no longer any crossings of the
Atlantic by ship this was truly something to remember.

When we returned from our trip to Italy in 1969 after selling the
supermarket, Carlo went to work as a wine salesman for Pellegrini

Brothers Winery. Not long after that, he became district manager with eight salesmen under him. One of the salesmen had a stroke and when he recuperated, Carlo wanted to treat him to lunch at a restaurant. He picked a restaurant in Palo Alto which was next to the Palo Alto Lumber Yard and we just happened to know the owner of the lumber yard. Carlo parked in the parking lot in the very last spot just before the driveway goes into the lumber yard. While Carlo and Les were eating lunch a big lumber truck was making a delivery to the yard and as he tried to turn left, he couldn't swing wide enough to clear Carlo's car. The owner called the restaurant and had them announce the problem and ask if anyone with the certain car with the certain license place could please move their car. Since Carlo was driving the company car, he didn't recognize the license number so the car didn't get moved.

The owner of the lumber yard, Bill Gretz, waited but no one came out of the restaurant. The next best thing he thought of doing was to move the car with the fork lift. He drove the fork lift and had the truck driver look under the car to be sure they didn't hit anything vital on the car. Well, he lifted the car up and moved it and so far, so good. Then he moved the fork lift down and out and oh, oh, somehow the gas tank got punctured. Gas started to pour out of the tank and all over the parking lot. Bill called the fire department and they came to wash the gasoline away. Carlo and Les were still inside the restaurant, oblivious to what was going on outside.

Finally Carlo and Les finished their lunch, came outside to see the fire department there and his car had been moved. When Bill saw Carlo he couldn't believe it. He said,"Carlo, don't tell me this is your car." Carlo explained that actually it was the company car. Bill felt so bad, but Carlo said to him, "Well, at least you know me and you know I'm not going to be upset."

Bill and Carlo saw where the puncture was on the tank and figured there was at least a tiny bit of gas (or fumes) to go about 1/2 block to a gas station to get the tank replaced, so Carlo started the car and keeping his fingers crossed, went out of the parking lot, turned left on the El Camino Real, and down the block to the light to make a U-turn and into a gas station. He barely made the U-turn and had to jump out of the car to push it off the street into the gas station. Then he called me to come and pick him up as he was stranded.

Many times when the Gretz's and we are together at a gathering, Bill will recall the time he tried to move Carlo's car with the fork lift. He still feels bad about it.

15

THE MCCLOUD
REUNIONS

My father always liked visiting people, especially the people of McCloud. When we lived in McCloud, Sunday afternoons were for visiting friends whether they lived in McCloud, Mt. Shasta, or Dunsmuir. Then we moved to San Jose in 1946 but my parents always kept in touch with the friends. If they found out that someone was moving in our area my father immediately got in touch with them. He also helped some of them get a job if they didn't have one yet.

When we moved to Sunnyvale and opened the big store, two people came from McCloud and were hired by my father. While in Sunnyvale, my father learned of a picnic which was sort of a reunion for former McCloudites. He and my mom attended the picnic which was held in Sacramento, and he talked about this great picnic for days. Then he came up with the idea of having a reunion of McCloudites in our area of Santa Clara County instead of going up to Sacramento. He obtained the list of addresses from the committee in Sacramento and we compiled a list of our own and obtained more names from people in our area. We had a committee of about six or eight people and had several meetings before sending out about 500 letters. We held our first McCloud Reunion on October 20, 1962 at the Sunnyview Family Club with 361 people in attendance. The price of the dinner was $5.00. Most of the people were former McCloud residents living in the area. Many were living in South San Francisco, Sacramento, Santa Clara, etc. Everyone had such a good time visiting and seeing old friends it was especially gratifying to my father.

Two years later in October we had our second McCloud Reunion. Since we were experienced in having the first event and knowing the expenses, we again had the reunion at the Sunnyview Family Club, again charged $5.00, gave the people two free drinks at the bar, had about 10 door prizes and this time we had 512 people attending. We also were bursting at the seams as the Club normally held only 500 diners. We also gave out souvenirs such as soft plastic coin holders which had the information of the Reunion printed on them and book matches with the information on them. I still run into people who talk about these Reunions and they pull out the souvenir coin holders to show me they still have them and love them after all these years.

The third reunion at the Sunnyview Club was the last one held there as it had 523 people attending and that was almost too much. We also had a gentleman in McCloud, Charlie "Chino" Haines, who organized a bus load of people who wanted to attend the Reunion. He was a railroad company employee so he was the "conductor" of the busload. Our dinner tickets were still $5.00 and the bus far was $15.00 per person. They stayed at the Holiday Inn in Mtn. View. We were informed by the Sunnyview Club that they had quite a few roasted chickens left over so before the bus left the next morning, we brought a big box of roasted chickens, bread and drinks to the motel so the people wouldn't have to stop at a restaurant during the six-hour trip home. They could stop at a rest stop along Highway 5 and enjoy the food and do some additional reminiscing.

Since we had outgrown the Sunnyview Club, the fourth and fifth reunions were held at the Bold Knight Restaurant in Sunnyvale and the prices went up to $6.00 and $7.50. Another bus load of people was added since the word had spread that this was such a fun time and such a wonderful time was had by people seeing friends who had moved away from McCloud. Many of the McCloudites wanted us to hold the reunion in McCloud but if the 500 plus people wanted to go to McCloud, there wasn't enough lodging in those years to house all of them. The dance hall was large enough to handle the crowd but there weren't enough hotels or motels right in McCloud.

The extra money we made on these events went into the checking account and we were always able to buy quite a few door prizes such as a T.V., electronics such as radios, coffee pots, hair dryers, etc. We were not a for-profit organization, we were giving back to the attendees.

In February of 1973 my father had a very big heart attack while we were up at Lake Tahoe. He lived through it but was mostly confined to a wheel chair as it was difficult for him to walk around. We had a reunion at the Little New Yorker in Santa Clara in October of that year and my dad was in his glory with everyone coming up to him and telling him how they loved coming to the reunions that he had started. This one was the last one he attended as he died in 1975.

The next reunion was held at Lou's Village in San Jose and it was our biggest yet. They claimed to be able to seat 700 but at 623 we were very crowded. We also began giving away commemorative glasses with a drawing of Mt. Shasta on them. These glasses were prized as if they were gold. Again two buses came down from McCloud. We always had a four-piece band for dancing after the dinners.

I was usually in charge of the tickets with people writing in on forms sent out with the letters as to how many tickets they wanted, etc. I was also at the door when the people came in. During the last week before the dinner we would have some cancellations and also requests for more tickets even though the deadline had passed to get tickets. My father would always give in to the ones wanting more tickets, some requests coming right at the door. I would be more cold hearted and wanted to say "No" but my father would always override me saying that there would always be cancellations at the last minute. He was so right and it would always come very close to the number we told the restaurant to cook for but it made for some nervous times before we would settle down to dinner.

After the huge reunion at Lou's Village, we began to hold them at the Holiday Inn at Park Center Plaza in San Jose. McCloudites occupied three floors of the hotel and we had people coming from all parts of the United States. In 1980 we charged $15.00 per person and in 1996 at the last one at the Holiday Inn we charged $25.00 per person. I don't think that was such an outrageous price for a dinner-dance, wine with dinner, door prizes, etc. and especially a great time. When the orchestra folded usually at 12:00 people didn't want to go home. There was usually a crowd of half the attendees talking and visiting on the dance floor. The last three reunions had a golf tournament held on the day before the reunion and were well attended. The last two also had a decline in attendance. One had just over 350 people and the very last one had less than 200. This was not due to lack of enthusiasm but due to the fact that many of the people were getting older, many of the ones that remembered McCloud had died and the younger population didn't know the people that were left. The one good thing with the smaller reunion was that everyone got a chance to visit with everyone.

After we had our last reunion, someone in McCloud called me to ask if they could have the list of names and addresses. By this time it was nearing 1,200 different addresses. A centennial was going to be held in McCloud in 1998 and it was going to be a three-day affair. The first day on Friday was going to be a dinner on the dinner train going from McCloud to Mt. Shasta. The next day, Saturday, was going to be a barbecue held at the park where I used to play on the monkey bars. These events were held in conjunction with the Heritage Days usually held in August. There were booths on the main street such as our art and wine festivals. All the events were wonderful, well planned out and we had countless memories when we left McCloud. Carlo's mom and my mom also attended this weekend. One of the best memories I had was that I encountered a teacher who taught my brother in elementary school. I recognized her name and began talking to her and telling her who I was. I didn't have her but she remembered my brother's class. She asked if I knew one of the classmates of my brother who was now living in Atascadero and if he was in attendance. I said I knew he was there and would go looking for him. The teacher was now in her late eighties. I walked around the park and found Dino Boneso and brought him to Mrs. Ives. When he saw her, he began to get tears inn his eyes and said she was the best teacher he had and she taught him so much. It was so heartwarming for me to witness this, especially since this man was very successful in his life. Unfortunately he passed away a few years after attending this weekend.

This proves that reunions aren't just for classes of schools attended or family reunions, they are also for towns, but we always did consider McCloud as a big family.

16

VACATIONS

During the next few years after our trip to Italy with the children our vacations included a house boat vacation on Lake Shasta for four days. This happened on a Labor Day weekend, which was a drought year and the water was exceptionally low at Lake Shasta. It was just the four of us with my parents joining us the day after we got there. The owner of the houseboat ran us through all the basic instructions and we took the boat out to find a sheltered cove for the night. We started having trouble right away with the motor and it would not start. After working with it for a while, Carlo was able to get it to a cove and we spent one night on it. It was supposed to be a six sleeper but we realized it was a bit tight and wondered where we would put my parents on this boat. The next morning we started out to fish and had more trouble with the boat so we contacted the marina and the owner said he would exchange the houseboat for us. He upgraded the boat to a 40 foot, 8 sleeper houseboat for no extra money so we thought it was great. We picked up my parents thinking we would be just fine. My mother was a person who worried about everything and thought everyone worried also so she immediately wanted to phone my brother to tell him they arrived at the lake in fine condition without any problems. So she wanted to make a telephone call back to Sunnyvale and she forgot to buy a few things for the "camping trip". This year was before cell phones so Carlo knew there was a marina nearby so he headed for it. Since the water level was down the area for the marina was very narrow and the wind was blowing quite hard. Carlo managed to get the houseboat in a slip and we went to make the phone call and buy a few items from the store. On backing the very long houseboat out of the marina, the wind swung the boat a bit and Carlo was not experienced in handling such a long boat. My father was not used to boats at all, so as a consequence we had an accident because the back of the boat was swung into the rocks and we broke the propeller. This of course elicited some choice words. We called the marina from whom we rented the boat and they came out with a new motor and a hefty bill for us to pay. So this was one of the more memorable but not so pleasant vacations.

The following year we went on a camping trip with our neighbors at New Hogan Reservoir which included the children and Carlo learning how to waterski behind our neighbor's boat. Our neighbors were Bobbi and Bill Seyfried and their son and daughter, Scott and Rene. Bobbi and I slept in the camper and the rest slept out in sleeping bags. Rene did not come with us and Scott had a school friend. We went twice to New Hogan, the second time with the Seyfrieds, Paul Bacon and his sister-in-law, Ethel, plus their large German Shepherd dog named Klaus. Ethel, Bobbi and I slept in the camper again and everyone else outside. Mornings were beautiful but the quietness was disturbed by the friendly, tiny woodpeckers busily pecking and poking their heads out of holes in the trees. We felt especially silly and while opening champagne bottles for breakfast, aimed the corks at the woodpeckers. After missing them with two of the corks we decided to stop that. One evening while we were sitting in a row facing the lake and enjoying the campfire at sunset, a family of skunks crossed in front of us. We were especially fortunate that we didn't get sprayed as we stayed as still as statues and remained quiet.

One year in winter we decided to rent a cabin at South Lake Tahoe near Myers. My brother Louis and family and his brother-in-law and family all came with us for the weekend. We had quite a bit of snow around the cabin and we drove about five minutes away to find a nice sloping area where the children could ride their saucers or inflated inner tubes down the hill. We really had a great time and we began thinking how nice it would be to buy a cabin or property to build a cabin so we could enjoy our vacations in the Lake Tahoe area. The following summer we went up to Lake Tahoe again and drove all around the area looking at lots or cabins for sale. A friend of ours in Sunnyvale had purchased a cabin on the west side of Lake Tahoe in Homewood and told us to go around the lake and see the place which they had purchased. It was a nice cabin or I should say "house." We also noticed that the lot behind their property was for sale. We returned home and didn't think too much about this idea again.

The following February we decided to spend the Presidents' birthday week at South Lake Tahoe and rented a friend's apartment at South Shore. We invited my father and mother to join us as my father always liked to go to the casinos to gamble. We were there about three days, going to an area with the children where there was a nice hill and many youngsters sliding down on saucers, inner tubes, etc. My father would be dropped off at the casinos. We also took the children to Heavenly Valley to take lessons in skiing. That year, 1973, there wasn't a huge amount of snow and we had to take a tram up to a level where there was some snow for Marina and Marco to take lessons. The wind was really blowing that day and it was knocking Marco off his skis. They learned enough to make them want to ski more. That evening when we picked up my father from gambling, he was complaining of a pain in his back and thought it was from the flu that he had ten days prior and felt this was a residual effect on his body. During the night he had chest pains and took his nitro glycerine tablets, not wanting to bother us. The next morning my mother told me he had the pains and still didn't feel well, and felt they should go home but not wanting us to cut our vacation short, she said they would take the bus home. My father didn't seem to be suffering so instead of going to a hospital or calling an ambulance, we decided to go home. We packed up and were out of there in an hour and we were home by 5:00. My father still didn't say he was in pain. After about two hours, he called my brother and asked to be taken to the hospital and then we found out that he had had a heart attack. He was in the hospital about a week before he came home but he suffered for the next two years without ever really recovering from this heart attack. He died in March of 1975 at the age of 69.

When we realized my father was stable and we could go away for a few days, our friends who had a cabin at Homewood at Lake Tahoe invited us up for a weekend. Their place was right across he street from the Tahoe Ski Bowl area and all they had to do was walk to the place and we could enjoy watching them aki down the face of the mountain from the cabin. The first day we all awoke early, it was snowing lightly but the visibility was only fair. Our friends had five children and they had all learned to ski. Ours were willing but not that experienced on skis. Well, we got them suited up and off to the ski areas. Marina has always been very independent and willing to try anything. The grownups stayed a bit to watch them and they seemed to be doing well, so we headed back to the cabin. On our way back we heard someone shouting,"Mom! Mom! That's Marina up there!" Looking up to the face of the mountain, we could see a skier down in the snow, her wool yellow hat and crossed skis next to her. My Lord! What happened? We ran as fast as we could to the ski patrol office to wait for her. The ski patrollers informed us that she hurt her leg and they didn't know how bad and told us to take her to the hospital, 22 miles away in Truckee. So we drove in this bad weather and it took us about 45 minutes to get there. When they were ready to see her, and there were many injured people there, they asked "Where were you skiing?" The tone of voice was like "Why were you so crazy to be skiing in this weather?" Well, it turned out that she just wrenched her knee and had to use crutches for a week, so it could have been worse.

That weekend did turn out well besides the wrenched knee. We inquired about the lot behind our friend's cabin and bought it for $6,000 with the idea of constructing our cabin on it as this was the ideal area to build. We were right across from the ski area, we were within walking distance to the lake, there was a grocery store within walking distance also and it was just ideal for everything. The following year we built our cabin.

17

LAKE TAHOE

After buying the lot to build our cabin at Lake Tahoe, we began looking through magazines for plans for building. Our friend's cabin was ideal with three bedrooms on the first floor and the living area on the second floor. This might sound funny but when the snow is 6 to 8 feet high in the winter, you can't see out of the windows on the first floor. So, we found similar plans in a magazine and sent for them. We lined up a contractor in Fremont who was recommended to us and he gave us quote to build. He gave us a starting date of March of 1974. The weekend we were to meet him at Lake Tahoe so that he could measure everything off on the lot was a nasty weekend. He called us and said he couldn't come up so that weekend was signed off as bad. A few weeks later work was started with 6 feet of snow on the ground. The contractor Merv cleared the snow away where the house would sit and started building. The neighbors who lived there year round thought he was crazy. He had a trailer set up on the street for his men and they worked every day. On Friday nights he would take them to the south shore of Lake Tahoe and treat them all to the buffet dinner at The Sahara. He kept his men happy and willing to work. By June the cabin was finished.

When Marina and Marco started their summer vacation, Carlo asked for a week's vacation and with the help of our good friend Bob Garcia and my brother Louis we planned to move furniture and "stuff" up to the cabin. Bob was an independent produce man and had a good-sized truck we could use. Bob, Lou, and Marco rode in the truck and Carlo, Marina, and I following in our car which was stuffed to the gills. We were able to bring up hand-me-downs of twin beds from Lou and Betty, chest of drawers from the apartment house, our old queen-sized bed so we could buy a king-sized one and the old hide-a-bed which we had. Our stove top and oven went up there and we got new ones for our house. Our old dishwasher was going up to Tahoe and Carlo decided to run it once more just to be sure it was running all right and smoke came out of it and it died. So we had to buy one for Tahoe and one for Sunnyvale. During the night before the trip, I kept hearing a funny noise from the kitchen as if the motor of the refrigerator was cycling on and off. I awoke Carlo and he said something was happening to the compressor. We pulled the plug and the next morning we brought whatever was in the refrigerator to my mother's and left her in charge of seeing what a repairman would say about it. We left for Tahoe and later found out that the compressor died and we would have to buy a new refrigerator. I think Murphy was after us (Murphy's Law).

We arrived around noon at the cabin and started moving in. When we were finished, Bob and Lou rested for a bit but they wanted to go back home as soon as they could. We had no electricity or hot water as Carlo had to go in person to apply for service. This was a Saturday so he couldn't go until Monday. We knew we wouldn't have electricity so we brought along our camp stove and lantern. Cold showers were another story.

We stayed a week getting used to the beauty and peacefulness of the area. Marina and Marco absolutely loved it. Our street was a dead-end street and at the end there was a marsh area with a path in it to connect to another street. Marina loved to go there and pick all the wildflowers she could find and bring them home to put in a vase. She has always loved nature.

The private beach area for our neighborhood was a mile walk down to Chamberlands Beach and Mountain Club. From the windows in our living room to the back, you could see the face of Tahoe Ski Bowl and in winter we would be able to see the skiers coming down the face of the mountain without having to drive to a ski resort. Our family could come home for lunch by just skiing home. We truly made a wise decision when we bought the lot behind our friends.

During our first week, my sister-in-law Betty, along with her daughter Betty Lou, was visiting our friends at south shore. The friend Rena and her daughter Julie and another friend Peggy all decided to come visit us and go out to dinner at Sunnyside Resort. The nine of us went to Sunnyside which was famous for their deep-fried zucchini sticks. It was the first time we had them and they were so delicious. Marco remembers this dinner because there was a young boy bussing the table and filling glasses with water. The boy was paying attention to the three young girls and Marco said he could have died of thirst before the boy would give him any water. When we got back to the darkened cabin, we lit the kerosene lamp and sat for only a few minutes before we heard a car honking in front of the house. Looking out the window we recognized our friends, Bobbi and Bill Seyfried. They had decided to surprise us by showing up unannounced. Well, they would have to put up with no electricity and no hot water. That night we played with the Ouiji Board. It was spooky with no lights, just dark shadows on the wall and asking spooky questions. But we had a lot of fun.

Around 11:00 the gang from south shore left to go back and we settled down with candles in the bedrooms for light. Funny how this reminded me of the cascina in Italy back in 1953.

On Monday Carlo went to Nevada to get our electricity turned on and then he had to go to another office for the gas as the two companies are not combined as they are here with PG&E but finally we did get these two important utilities turned on.

A few weeks later in July, we asked two other families to join us at Tahoe for a weekend. We called it the July birthday club as my birthday is in July and the two other couples have one person whose birthday is in July. We were six adults and nine children. The adults took the bedrooms and the children all slept wherever in sleeping bags. We had a screened-in-porch next to the kitchen upstairs and they seemed to love that. During the day we went to the beach to lay in the sun or swim out to the raft in that frigid water. We also celebrated the anniversary of one couple Dianna and Doug Mahre. The other couple was Jackie and Bob Isola. All in all it was a fun-filled weekend except that on Sunday just as we were getting ready to come home, one of the kids accidently broke a bedroom window. The fathers had to go to Tahoe City to get a replacement glass and fix the window. You could say the cabin was now fully christened.

The year after we finished the cabin, our friends Bill and Bobbi asked if we wanted to go camping again at Hogan's Reservoir. We told them that since we had the cabin we didn't feel like going camping which meant sleeping on the ground or on cots in

sleeping bags. We offered to take them to our cabin for a week and
they could bring their boat for water skiing and we would have to
rough it. They said they had already asked their neighbors who
had two children to go camping and they had agreed. We suggested that the neighbors were welcome at our cabin also. So, we
met their neighbors, Sam and June Winklebleck and their children,
Sam Jr. and Beth who were just a year or two older than ours.

Bill was a United Airlines Captain and had been an usher in our
wedding and he and Bobbi had two children also a few years older
than our children. Sam worked for the Wall Street Journal in Palo
Alto and was a quiet man who enjoyed bicycling and nature.
During the week we were there, the men and the children went out
each day water skiing and one day went rafting down the Truckee
River from Tahoe City toward Truckee. The women went gambling or shopping and relaxed. It was a great week with good
friends. Sam decided not to shave and grew a very thick black
beard. To this day, he has not shaved it off, just keeps it trimmed
and with his horn-rimmed glasses looks very professorial. When
the week was up, Bill said it was a good idea to go camping at Lake
Tahoe instead of Hogan's and they really enjoyed our "tent." From
then on, the name of the cabin was "The Tent." We also keep a
loose-leaf binder at the cabin and invite people to write in it sharing
their experiences there. We have writings from people from Chicago, Italy, Pennsylvania, New York, Los Angeles and Canada. We
usually write in it also as to who was there and what was done while
there. We have many memories in this binder.

Our summers there have always been very enjoyable and our
winters have been enjoyable also although sometimes the snow has
been a bit much. Marina survived the winters of 1981-1982 which
saw record amounts of snow. She had decided to take a quarter off
from college and was a volunteer for the ski patrol at Tahoe Ski
Bowl. She got free skiing because of this. Sometimes she could not
get out of her driveway to go to the store so she would hitchhike,

which made me very nervous. She assured me that everyone knew everyone there and they all helped each other out.

The next big snowfall for us came in 1994 and we had invited a friend with his girlfriend and her daughter. We arrived on a Monday and Carlo went skiing. The company arrived in the late afternoon after they had stopped somewhere to ski. It began to snow and Carlo plowed the driveway with the snow blower. The next morning the snow was coming down full force and Carlo couldn't keep up with keeping the driveway clear so we just watched from the windows as it kept piling up. On Wednesday, we looked out the garage door and our guest's car was completely buried in snow. They wanted to leave to go home and were worried that the roads were closed. So we played a "wait and see" game. The snow was piling up on the deck also and soon we couldn't see out of the sliding glass doors. I stood on a chair to see if I could look over the snow and I could barely see the ski bowl. It wouldn't be long before I couldn't see anything out of the doors and windows. In the late afternoon we heard the county plow go by so our guests decided to get out while the getting was good. They left and promised to call when they were over the summit. We also decided to go to town just to stock up on more food and gas as we would be there until Saturday. When we got to Tahoe City, the line of cars at the only gas station that had gas was at least 25 cars long. At the Lucky store the shelves were empty of milk, bread, meats and poultry and vegetables. The trucks had not been able to get through from the valley or from Reno. So we turned around and went back to the cabin, not really worried because we had enough food and gas, we just wanted to top off. We heard from our guests when they reached Sacramento that evening.

The snow plows did not come again until Saturday and that is when we left Tahoe on a beautifully sunny clear day. There is nothing as beautiful as a sunny day after a heavy snowfall. Everything is white, glistening and pristine.

Marina and Marco learned how to ski right away and became quite adept. Carlo waited about five years before the ski bug bit him. He was about 45 years old and of course being the worry wart I am I worried about him breaking some bones. He loved being out there skiing and not having to go very far and I could usually see him when he decided to come home in the afternoon. It seemed as if something told me he was on the face of the mountain coming down from that last run. Usually I couldn't see them as they skied on the back side of the resort. Carlo wanted me to try to ski and he also bought a beautiful ski outfit for me so that I would be warm and look good. Well, I took lessons, I was warm but I was such a chicken to go up on the lifts I never got off the bunny hills. I didn't like it and I never did go up on a lift. I have gone cross country skiing with the family, but once I fall down, I have a very hard time picking myself up so I said "Oh, what's the use?" So I have given up and am content to just watch from the windows.

Carlo was careful until about 15 years ago when we were up to celebrate Marco's birthday in January. Carlo and Marco went skiing all day and they didn't stop to eat lunch. I was home and soon Marco came running home and said he had to get the car and me and go to the ski bowl as Carlo broke his arm. Of course, it was the last run of the day and he fell and his arm got tangled up in the ski pole and he got a spiral break of the upper bone in his left arm.

We had reservations at a restaurant with Marina joining us and when I saw Carlo in the first aid hut, I said I would have Marina cancel the reservations. Carlo insisted not to cancel the dinner, that he would be all right. So after much discussion with Carlo, Marina and Marco, we decided to move the time to a later hour.

We drove Carlo into Tahoe City to the urgent care facility and they put a heavy cast on his arm and told him not to lie down. He would have to sit in a reclining chair to sleep so that the arm was weighted down by the cast. Also he could not have pain killers if we were going out to dinner and drinking wine. Well, what Italian doesn't drink wine with dinner? So we went out to eat and before dinner came, Marco looked at Carlo and he was white as a ghost, holding his head in his hand and looking as if he would pass out. I was ready to take him home, but he just sat quietly for a few minutes and regained his old self and insisted that he was all right. Well, he made it through dinner, we went home and he took his pain killers, suffered through the night and we returned to Sunny-vale the next day. Another saga in the story of Lake Tahoe, or I should say the saga of "The Tent."

About ten years ago Marina informed us that Bill's father Dick who lives in Canada would be out for a week or more. Bill is Marina's significant other. We decided to go to Lake Tahoe so that we could enjoy Dick's company again. We had been to Canada to visit him on Lake Muldrew, Ontario Canada. During the summer he lives in a cottage on a small island on the lake. Carlo, Marco, Marina, Bill and I went to visit Dick Smallfield one summer for a week. We drove from the airport in Toronto to the lake which took about 2 1/2 hours. When we arrived at the small pier near his cottage, we phoned Dick as the only way to his cottage was by boat. When Dick answered and we told him we were at the pier, he said he would be right there. Within two minutes we could hear the motor of the boat start up around the bend and whithin two minutes he was picking us up for the short trip to his cottage. While we were waiting the short time on the pier the mosquitoes began eating us alive as it was just about evening. We rushed into the cottage and were met by Bill's sister, Nancy and her two almost teenage children. We had already met Bill's father so it was very nice seeing him again. So, we were nine people staying in this one-bedroom cottage but here is how we managed. Dick graciously let Carlo and me use the bedroom, he also had two bunkhouses which were used by Marina and Bill and Nancy and her daughter. The son, Aaron used a gazebo outside and Marco used the hide-a-bed in the living room. Dick used a neighbor's house around the bend as the neighbor was on vacation.

The next morning when we awoke, it seemed as if we were on Golden Pond. It was beautiful and so serene and the loons were calling. We walked around the island which took all of 10 minutes. There wasn't much to do on the island except enjoy the company which came by to visit Dick. His sister had the Smallfield family cottage which was inherited from Dick's father and mother. His brother also had a summer cottage nearby and came to visit. A young man who went to school with Bill came by with his wife and stayed a couple of days so there was a lot of visiting and enjoying company and having a few beers. Very relaxing times. Oh, I forgot, they did do a bit of fishing but weren't able to catch that elusive big trout "Walter."

Bill's sister also knew of a spot where we could pick some black-berries so we got into the motor boat and went a short distance, then we climbed up over rocks to a small lake up above Lake Mul-drew. No luck though finding blackberries. We did see a very big blue heron at the upper lake.

Well, now on to the trip to Tahoe. When we got to Lake Tahoe, Marina and Bill said they wanted to go on a hike with Dick on a trail which was from Sugar Pine Point to Emerald Bay. It is a hike of 5 1/2 miles. Bill took Dick shopping for a pair of hiking boots as he is always barefooted in Canada. We dropped off one car near Emerald Bay and then drove to Sugar Pine Point. Dick had his shoes on but after about two miles, he couldn't stand them any longer so he put them into his backpack and went barefooted. This was on a trail covered with pine needles and whatever is there. In some places we hiked on rocks but he was fine and he was in his 70's at the time. The trail is about 30 feet up from the water and follows the shoreline. The views are beautiful. Along the trail we came across what was once an old wooden lighthouse. Rather small and run down but it was interesting. When we came to an area with huge rocks we found some large flat ones so we sat down to eat lunch.

Then we continued on and down to the edge of Emerald Bay. As we were there on the beach or shoreline one of the paddle boats that cruises around the lake came into the bay and tooted its horn. Then we climbed up the hill from the beach to the highway where we left the first car. I was a bit tired but I was amazed that I was not sore the next day. Dick who is 10 years older than Carlo and me was in great shape.

About two years later, Marina again suggested that we go on a hike. She doesn't like to see me idle and reading a book. She always says it will do me good to get out and walk. Since the first hike was 5 1/2 miles, she said this one was about 8 miles and mostly flat and there were beautiful wild flowers on the trail from Squaw Valley to Alpine Meadows. So, she talked us into going on this little jaunt. This was the end of September and we had to take the tram almost to the top of Squaw Valley. Then we had to walk to where the trail started. This is a small part of the Pacific Rim Trail. We walked up from the tram and there was still snow left over from the previous winter. Then we started walking. From the top of Squaw, we could see towards Chico and the Sierra Buttes. There were, as Marina said, many wildflowers and they were pretty. After a few hours of walking, I thought we must be near the end of the trail. How wrong I was! We came upon a sign and it said "You are at the half way point to Alpine Meadows." Oh my God! I couldn't believe we had come only half way. I was getting a blister on my foot but Marina always carries a package of moleskin with her so we stopped a bit for first aid. Then we sat and ate our lunches. After about an hour or so I started complaining and then Marina started to feel sorry for me. She said there were usually people with horses at the lakes before one got to Alpine and she would go ahead of us and get one to come back and pick us up. I teased her and said they would probably drape me over the back of the saddle like a dead body so, "No thanks." So then she suggested she could go on ahead of us to her friend's house in Alpine and get a bicycle so I could ride back. Again, I said "No, thanks." Finally, after a few more hours we got to the end of the trail and I was exhausted. Marina felt bad and guilty about making me go on this hike and I teased her all the more by saying that I was going to write her out of my will. When we returned to the cabin, I soaked in the tub and relaxed and I was surprised that again I was not sore the next day. Bill, who did not go on the hike said he was proud of me and the fact that I went and finished the hike. He gave me a lot of credit so I felt good.

When we built the Tahoe cabin in 1974 there was a pack of dogs running wild around the neighborhood and knocking down the garbage cans to get to the remnants inside. They would really make a mess. Most of the homes did not have fences surrounding the properties and a big majority of the homeowners were week-enders or second-home owners. Carlo made a small "garbage house" to contain the two garbage cans up off the ground about 2 1/2 feet, sitting on two steel poles, with doors on the front so that the dogs could not get to them. This worked fine until the bears moved in. As the population of people grew, so did the bear popu-lation which quickly learned that there was food in them thar gar-bage houses. One week I went to south shore with three other ladies and when we decided to return home to Sunnyvale, I decided to drive around the lake and show the ladies our cabin. Two of the ladies were from Chicago. As we drove up to our place I noticed the garbage house was bent down, doors open and gar-bage scattered on the ground. I thought, "Wow, the wind must have been strong to almost knock the garbage house over." As I cleaned around the place and closed the doors, I noticed a big paw print of a bear on the front of the shed. I told the ladies and they quickly said, "Well, we have seen it, now let's go home."

Another time, Marina was staying at the house, came home around 10:00 and saw what she thought was a huge rock near the driveway. When she turned the headlights on the "rock" she noticed it was a large bear sitting there eating remnants of someone's garbage. She honked the horn but it didn't budge. She waited in her car until the bear was finished and then moved on.

A few years ago we drove up to our place and arrived at 3:00 in the afternoon. I saw something moving across the street from our house and realized that it was a huge bear eating garbage on the ground. We drove up about 20 feet from it and since we had a very noisy diesel truck we thought it would make him go away. No, he was too intent on what he was doing. So we went up the driveway to our house, I went in and took photos from the second story deck. Carlo finally threw a rock at the bear and he ambled on among the homes nearby. He later came back to finish his job. Lately the bears have gotten so smart and bold that they will look into the homes and if they see a refrigerator, they recognize that it has food. They will break the windows and go into the house and trash it.

Our daughter called not long ago to say that they had forgotten to close the garage door in the evening and while they were watching TV they heard a loud noise in the garage. They ran downstairs and discovered that the handle on their freezer was broken off. It seems as if a bear had tried to open the freezer and since he was facing the side of the freezer, he broke the handle off. There was a two-gallon vinegar barrel on top of the freezer. The bear probably shook the freezer, the barrel fell on him and that scared him off. They are quite sure the barrel hit the bear because it didn't break apart and it didn't hit the car which was in front of the freezer. A few weeks after that they again forgot to shut the garage door and a bear opened the freezer and trashed the inside of the freezer and scattered the frozen food all around. They have since learned to shut the garage door.

Other wildlife we have seen at Tahoe are mountain lions and coyotes. One morning I was in the living room and looked out in the yard and saw a huge cat, more the size of a dog. When I told Carlo, he dismissed it by saying it was a dog. But this animal had a white muzzle and a very long tail that reached the ground. A few months later I saw another one near the side of the road as we went into town and he saw it also so he agreed that the first one was probably a mountain lion.

We have heard the coyotes howling and yipping several times in the evening and one morning during Christmas vacation, our daughter-in-law Kristen and I saw a pack of five coyotes trotting through our back yard. They had a very thick silver grey winter coat and big fluffy tails. They were really a beautiful sight to see, however I am glad we were inside rather than outside.

At one time there were three families living near us full time. One family was right next to us and we became good friends with them, especially Marco because they had six daughters. Mr. Nored was a big friendly Scandinavian and his wife was a jolly Hispanic lady. Since Mr. Nored didn't have any sons, he enjoyed Marco's company when there was a football game or baseball game on TV. Marco enjoyed his company also plus the fact that we did not have cable and could only get one channel on the TV. Mr. Nored worked for a company which installed chair lifts at the ski resorts and during the winter he did snow plowing on the west side of Lake Tahoe. It was handy having him next door as a neighbor because all we had to do if we were going up to Tahoe was to call and ask him to plow our driveway if it needed it. Our membership in the Chamberlands Beach and Mountain Club entitled us to entrance to the beach area and snowplowing of our driveway during the winter. Tom Nored was the contractor who did the plowing. Another neighbor behind us was a celebrity of sorts. He was Dean Martin's piano player, Ken Lane. He was single at the time, white haired, drove an army jeep and loved to ski. He was a very nice man. He later moved about two miles away to a lakefront home and has since died.

The wildlife we enjoy watching are the stellar jays who wait for me to put pieces of bread on the railing of the deck. They are so beautiful with their almost black pointy crests and dark blue bodies. They look like a blue cardinal. They are a noisy bunch up in the pine trees and descend on the railing to pick up the bread. Sometimes one of them doesn't want to share and will stuff as many pieces of bread in his beak as he can. He will go along hopping and picking up about six pieces and then flies back to the tree.

The Canadian geese have learned to put up with the harsh winters of Lake Tahoe and don't really migrate south. They usually enjoy Tahoe year round on the shores of the lake and Truckee River. Mallard ducks are also regular local residents.

After 36 years of spending time at this beautiful spot on earth, we have not gown tired of it and I am sure we will continue to enjoy it.

18

THE EARTHQUAKE OF 1989

How many of you can recall what you were doing and where you were during the 1989 earthquake? I'll bet all of you can do that.

I remember going to the store just a few blocks from home to buy something which I needed for dinner. Carlo's mother, who lived with us, was getting something ready for dinner and Carlo was in the lowest level of our house. This level is about four and a half feet below ground level and has a window facing our pool. He was sitting and working at the computer just a few feet from the window.

I had made my purchase and started the car and proceeded to back up and then pulled forward to exit the parking lot. The car began to feel as if I had a flat tire, so not wanting to be in the middle of a road I started to pull off to the side. A gentleman walked in front of me and made a motion to me to stop and mouthed the words "earthquake!" I looked around and saw the tall palm trees swaying and people began streaming out of the store with a look of terror on their faces. When the earth stopped rolling, I headed home and as I came down the street which led to our court, two of our neighbors were standing on the corner. I stopped to talk to them and they asked if I had been home yet. I replied that I had not been home and one of them reported that we had an earthquake and a lot of her dishes were broken. I could see a tremendous amount of water in the gutters of the street and I couldn't figure out where it was coming from as we didn't have a fire hydrant in our court. I hurried as fast as I could into the house and Lee was sitting at the table looking a bit white and began telling me what an awful feeling it was not to be able to walk to go out of the house. Carlo also had a story of how he was downstairs when the house began shaking and then a huge wave of water hit the window near where he was sitting. He said it seemed like a tidal wave. There were four houses in that part of the court which had pools and the rolling motion of the quake emptied them of about three to four feet of water and merged to go down the street like a river. Carlo said he looked out the front window and saw our neighbor walking towards our house and his feet were up to his ankles in water. His sunken patio near the pool had about a foot of water in it.

Somehow we escaped having damage at our house. We had one glass break about three days after the quake when we opened a cupboard and the glass had been leaning against the door. One object fell on the rug. It was a Galileo thermometer which is a glass cylinder filled with a liquid and it contains lead weights with markers and they rise and fall with the rising and falling of the temperature. Thank heaven it didn't break.

My mother was home alone, sitting at the kitchen table, and peeling apples to make a pie. She felt the earthquake but didn't pay too much attention to it. She was 77 at the time. She noticed the neighbor across the street was motioning to her to come outside. She didn't feel like changing her routine so she ignored him. Only after he motioned to her the third time did she go out and ask what he wanted. He asked her if everything was all right. When she assured him that she was fine after he tried to talk her into staying outside, did he relent and let her go back inside. She had no damage whatsoever. My brother instead, who lived on the next court, had his grandfather clock fall face down on the rug, just missing the dining room table. They also lost three or four Lladro porcelain figurines.

Our daughter living at Lake Tahoe called about an hour after the quake to see how we were. After her phone call, we were not able to use the phone. Our son was working as an airline mechanic for United Airlines on the swing shift at the airport and when the quake happened, all the electricity went off, just the emergency lights went on. They had been working on an airplane which was up on jacks and the shaking caused the plane to shift and have a jack go right through the wing. Since Marco used to take a van pool to work, the van wasn't there at that odd hour. The employees were sent home and he was able to catch a car ride with another employee who was coming toward San Jose. As they drove down Highway 280 they said all the cities were dark and there weren't any lights. He said it was a spooky feeling. When they came near Sunnyvale, the driver dropped him off on 280 and he walked home from there.

Of course, Carlo, ever the calm one, didn't think the quake was as bad as it was. He was taking a class at DeAnza College for real estate and decided he had better go to class. Of course all the signal lights from out house to the college were off and when he got there, he was told there was no class.

During the night, after finally getting to sleep, our phone rang at 3:00. It was one of our cousins from Italy. It was noon over there and she had seen the news about the quake and was worried about us. This cousin is such an excitable person that she was talking so rapidly I had to wait for her to breathe to get a word in edgewise.

she kept asking questions without giving me a chance to answer. Finally I had to just tell her to be quiet for a minute so I could tell her what I had to say. After reassuring her that we were all fine, I asked her to call the rest of the relatives to tell them that we were all fine.

Our good friends, Bob and Marge Garcia who lived in Corralitos which was very near the epicenter had a lot of damage to their home. The roof fell in and a stone wall in their living room came down. The house was red tagged but thank heaven no one was hurt. They slept in their truck on the front lawn the first night. Then a day or two later it rained and they had to move everything out of the house. It took about six months or more for the home to be repaired. Then a few months after they moved back in, there was another smaller quake in the same vicinity and Marge ran out of the house and up the hill behind their home. When her husband told her it was alright to go back in, she broke her ankle going down the hill into the house. She had to be operated on for a shattered ankle and had to have a cast and crutches. She didn't go live in the house until about three months after that episode. That was such a trying time for their family.

It was a shame that we no longer had our pet canary bird to warn us of these earthquakes. My mother-in-law Lee always had either a parakeet or canary as a pet. When we had the deli, Lee had an orange canary and it was such a good singer. One day while working at the deli, we had an earthquake which sent one of the ladies running out of the back door and going home as she was so frightened. The next day, Lee said her canary lost a lot of feathers and they were at the bottom of the cage. She connected this phenomenon to the earthquake. The next time she noticed feathers on the bottom of the cage, she told all of us at work that we would probably have an earthquake soon. Sure enough at 5:30 the next morning, as most of us were in bed, we had a good wake up call with the bed shaking and rolling. It didn't take much to convince the ladies that this bird was a very good predictor of quakes. He would even pull some of the long feathers from his wings and in all I think he predicted about four quakes before he died.

19

JACK OF ALL TRADES

I consider my husband Carlo, a Jack of all trades. I think he can do almost anything. When I tell him this, he says "Jack of all trades, master of none," which I don't think is true. He has always worked since he was about 8 or 9 years old when his parents had a ravioli factory. When he was this age he and another young school friend would fill up the ravioli boxes with 54 raviolis and close them and stack them up for distribution. During this time he would also roll up the pasta dough and feed the roll into a machine which would have a knife or cutter which came down and cut the pasta for tagliarini or noodles of different widths, depending on how it was set. Now Cal OSHA would have a fit if they saw such a young man doing this job. He would also grate the cheese and grind up the meat and vegetables for the ravioli filling. It was also his job to fix lunch on Saturdays because his parents were so busy. He said it was the same menu every Saturday, raviolis and breaded veal cutlets. He would also have to go to the butcher and buy the meat with the meat coupons.

When the family moved to Palo Alto, Carlo had a bit of a rest until his father developed the land and there was a gas station on the corner, he got a job pumping gas, so this was really close to home. He just had to walk a few hundred yards from home. During his two years at Menlo College he had a job cleaning the library in the morning and in the afternoon he worked in the snack bar as a soda jerk.

After going through Heald Radio and Television Technician Program Carlo got a job with HiFi Unlimited installing and repairing stereo sound systems until he went into the Navy and was stationed in Hawaii for two years. During the two years he was in Hawaii, he had spare time so he worked at a radio station KAHU in Waipahu as a radio engineer. Basically he was making sure that everything ran smoothly, made necessary announcements on the radio, station breaks, etc.

When he was discharged from the Navy, he returned home to work for his parents in the nursery and a few years later decided to go into business with my family in the super market. He was in the market for 8 years when it was decided to sell the market. That was in 1969 and we decided to go to Italy with the children. When we returned, my brother had already gotten a job as a wine salesman with Pellegrini Brothers Winery in South San Francisco. He told Carlo there was a job opening and he got the job. Carlo's sales route was the southern end of the city of San Mateo down to Redwood City. Every other week on Fridays he would have to go to Half Moon Bay. He loved this day because he would always have an abalone sandwich from a small coffee shop in Half Moon Bay which was located next to a fish stand where the owner went diving for fresh abalone and sold it to the coffee shop. He loved these sandwiches.

After two years as a salesman Carlo was approached to become District Manager for the area which had eight salesmen under his management. He held this position for six more years. The base pay was a bit better but along with this job were all the headaches and fires to be put out and problems smoothed over. A good salesman with good accounts could really take home some great commissions without any worries. Carlo was sometimes making less than the salesmen and had all the problems, if any. So it wasn't long before Carlo decided to quit and joined a company which sold fire suppressant systems to companies which had rooms with costly computers or machinery which had to be protected from fire. He was with this company for two years and in the meantime he was always looking for a business which he could own and run himself. Eight years after he started with Pellegrini Brothers Winery I was also ready to get a part time job as the children were in high school and I felt I could do something to keep me from getting bored.

Carlo beat me to the punch and came home one day and said he was thinking of opening up a fast food sandwich shop in an industrial area in Sunnyvale. Since he was on the road a lot, he noticed that these businesses were doing a great job in selling food to people who didn't have time to eat at restaurants or were too far from eating establishments, so they had to rely on catering trucks or at least have an hour for lunch or bring lunches from home which hardly any one does anymore.

It wasn't long before Carlo came home one day and said he found a building which had space for rent and wanted to open up a business selling food in an industrial area. This was on Hammerwood Avenue near the UPS facility in Sunnyvale. He quit his job

with Firemaster and began working in August to get the space
ready for occupancy.

Carlo's parents had been in Italy the winter of 1976/1977
building a house for themselves on a hill in Charlie's home town.
They lived in it for a few months and then returned in April of
1977. Their idea was to go to Italy for six months and then return
to California for six months every year. In September of 1977,
Charlie complained of pains one day and thought he had an attack
of kidney stones. He suffered for three days and the doctor visited
him at home and also thought it was kidney stones as he had them
years before. After three days, the doctor advised him to go to the
hospital to have a test to determine if it really was an attack of
kidney stones. Carlo brought him to the hospital along with Lee.
When they got Charlie settled in they said they would return that
evening and then he could probably go home. It was very strange
because Charlie shook his head and said he was not going home.

That afternoon Carlo received a call to come to the hospital
because his father was failing. We all returned to the hospital and
we got there too late to see him once more. He died of heart
failure, so I guess he had a premonition that he wouldn't make it.
He never did see the new business venture Carlo was going into.

Carlo did most of the work himself with the help of our two
United Airlines pilot friends, John DeCofano and Bill Seyfried.
Since they were home for days at a time and one was a great car-
penter, they really got so much work done such as cabinetry,
making tables out of electric cable spools, etc. Carlo would pour
liquid resin on the tables and then let the resin harden and then
buff them with a jewelers rouge to polish them. A metal table base
was attached to the wooden tops and soon we had tables to seat
100 people in our restaurant. Carlo then had the job of going to
different restaurant supply houses to get everything for the "deli."
We were not exactly a deli as you would see in the North Beach
area of San Francisco but we called it the Friendly Franciscan Deli

because Carlo was born in San Francisco. Our logo was a rather rotund Franciscan Friar. We served about 15 different sandwiches, soup, chili, salads in containers in addition to a salad bar. We served a hot special every day such as lasagne, stew, meat loaf, enchiladas and other hot "comfort" food. At first we bought the meat loaf but then decided to make our own. Sales took off and that was one of our good sellers. We served it with mashed potatoes and gravy. Our stew was also a good seller. In addition to all the soft drinks, we served beer on tap and wine.

We did not have a restaurant stove but we had a two burner commercial hot plate, a low-heat large oven, a large steam table and three microwaves. At first we were only open from 9:00 to 3:00 but soon people were asking us to open earlier and stay open later. So we soon started learning how to cook breakfasts in the microwaves. We offered egg sandwiches similar to the Egg McMuffins all done in the microwave. We also made a plate of Eggs Benedict and egg omelets in the divided paper plates. Most of the people who worked nearby had only 15 minutes for breaks and 30 minutes for a lunch break. Our deli was similar to a cafeteria where orders are placed at the counter and then checked out. When word got around that our deli was a good place for lunch it wasn't long before we had quite a crowd at lunchtime. I remember looking up and seeing a sea of faces and after that I just concentrated on the person I was waiting on. It was scary. We had five people making sandwiches or taking orders and two or three people at the cash registers and pouring beer or wine. It was hard getting help but soon we had five or six ladies who just wanted to work four or five hours a day and to be home when their children got home from school. This was ideal for them and us. We had one lady who was a retired manager of a school cafeteria who was recently widowed and she loved the job as it kept her busy and she worked in the food business again.

We had nicknames for some of our customers. There was "Mr. Mortadella" who always ordered a mortadella sandwich and there was "Mr. French Dip". Whenever we asked Mr. French Dip "How are you today?" he would always answer "Terrible." This was his standard answer every day and he always ordered the French Dip sandwich. One day when he was asked how he was, he answered "Fine." We were very busy and I took about five steps before I was aware of his answer. I turned around and said," What did you say?" He laughed and said he was just testing me to see if I was paying attention. We really had a lot of nice customers who came in day after day and bonded with the ladies who worked for us. We did have one that was a grouch from day one but we were determined to change him and we did. We killed him with kindness and he became one of our nicest and more caring customers.

Our counters where people ordered had to be built about five feet up from the ground and had a clear plastic shield to cover the food where we worked. Three of us were rather short, a little over five feet tall with one being under five feet tall. One day a young man came in, looked at us and since he could only see our heads, came over asking, "Are you ladies all standing in a ditch?" We did have some funny moments.

The UPS facility was just a block down the street and some of the workers who worked the graveyard shift would come in at 7:30 a.m. when they got off work. They would come in for breakfast or sandwiches and drinks and sit and talk before going home. Some people who worked a mile or two away also found out about us and would come in for lunch. Carlo and I got very friendly with some of the customers. Carlo's birthday is five days before Halloween and some of the customers who worked for Rolm brought in a big pumpkin with all their signatures on it and birthday greetings for Carlo. Another customer from Lockheed brought in a tie tack of the lunar module for Carlo. Carlo's mother also worked along with us in the kitchen and one day one of the office managers at UPS came in with a bouquet of flowers for her "just because." She was in her 70's when she worked there.

In the mid 80's after having the deli for eight years, some of the electronic establishments were closing, business was going down, we decided to sell the business. It had been ten years since Carlo's mother had been to Italy. The house she had built with Charlie was vacant, the car was sitting in the garage without being driven so we were anxious to go back to see if everything was still OK.

We sold the business and the three of us went back to Italy in July of 1986. Carlo's father had arranged for his friend to keep an eye on the house so he would go there every week, open it up to air it out and take care of things if needed. However, the car just sat in the garage for 10 years. Carlo's cousin said he might as well dump the car in the river as it probably wouldn't start. After about four hours of working on the car with a mechanic, the car started and it is now here in California with us. It is a 1973 FIAT 124 Sport Coupe and runs like a clock.

When we returned home, Carlo took some classes to become a realtor and got his realtor/brokers license. He hung his license with Coldwell Banker and worked from 1987 as a realtor. You could say he is"retired" but he keeps his license active and works from home if he gets a referral. Now Carlo has another calling — Chef Extraordinair of our kitchen and I think he enjoys this the best. He always looks up recipes and doesn't mind if they are long complicated ones. (I'm always looking for the easy short ones.) The best dish I feel he has cooked is Roasted Duck Breast in a Cherry Port Wine Sauce. This is an outstanding dish.

I am so lucky that Carlo is in my life — he is truly a Jack of All Trades and I think he can do anything he sets his mind to.

20

MORE VACATIONS

When my in-laws got married in 1927 the first vacation they took was ll years later in 1938 when they went to Italy with Carlo being 3 1/2 years old. They were there for about six months. The next vacation was ten years later in 1948 and they stayed almost three months.

My family had a similar life. We hardly ever took vacations. For one thing, we didn't have a car until 1938 and there was no bus or rail service from our town. We had to go 12 miles to Mount Shasta City to make any connections and frankly, we didn't have the money then for vacations. My father, however was very active in the Sons of Italy Lodge and was at the very first state convention in Stockton before he was married so as he continued being an active member his trips as a delegate to various yearly conventions were paid for by the Lodge. In 1939 he was a delegate to the convention in San Francisco and during this time there was the Golden Gate International Exposition in San Francisco on Treasure Island. My father took the family with him to see this and I still remember a few of the things I saw. One of the things which made an impression on me, though I don't know why this exhibit was there, was a girl in a stockade up on a platform. Perhaps since I was only four years old, I was told that this would happen to me if I didn't behave myself. I do remember beautiful fireworks in the evening and staying in a hotel. My mother kept us in the hotel room while my father attended convention meetings and this was boring and of course my brother and I would try to amuse ourselves.

The next trip I remember when I was about five years old was to Los Angeles to visit cousins. The two children were quite a bit older than my brother and I but I do remember two things. We had just eaten dinner at the cousin's house and I got up and touched the keys of the piano they had in the living room. The father looked up and said, "No, no, no, little monkey. Don't touch." He did not yell or say it loudly, but it was enough that I could still remember his words to this day. The other thing that happened was that we were outside and their front yard sloped slightly to the street. They had a small retaining wall of cement so that the lawn was at an even level. In the retaining wall, there were sprinkler heads imbedded in the cement. My dear brother turned the sprinklers on just a wee bit and told me to get a drink of water from them. Gullible me, I did as I was told. The minute I put my face down to get a drink, he turned the water on and got a good laugh. Well, it was hot in Los Angeles and I was wearing a sun suit so I dried off quickly.

The other memorable vacation we had was already written about regarding Klamath Falls on my cousin's farm. When I was young, our fun times were picnics while fishing in the rivers around McCloud or mushroom hunting in the woods or just visiting friends on Sundays. We never went camping because the woods were there right at our back door and we could go fishing or hiking in the woods and then come back to our house to sleep.

Carlo and I also were not the type that needed a vacation every year. We took a vacation the year after we got married and went to

Italy but then our next big vacation was nine years later when we sold the store and went with the children to Italy. We did take two or three days here and there to go on little trips but never for a week or two.

I remember one trip of four days where we went to McCloud with the children when we still had the store. We arrived in McCloud and had a sightseeing trip on the open car railroad train from McCloud to Mount Shasta City. There was a "hat" of clouds over the mountain so we couldn't see the splendor of this magnificent mountain. The next day we planned to go fishing and we awoke in our motel to a downpour. Well, we decided to go for a tour of the sawmill in McCloud. Being August it was closed down for vacation time. So we decided to go north to the town of Weed where my paternal grandparents and father lived for a few years but as you can guess, being August, the mill was shut down also. The motel where we stayed had a ping pong table and we spent a few hours playing ping pong. Then we went to visit an older couple who knew me when I was born and they were happy to see that I now had a family.

The next day we did try fishing in between rain showers but we weren't very lucky. Marina got her hook caught on something and called Carlo to help her unsnag it. When he jerked the line it came loose but he didn't realize that he hooked his neck with the hook. He didn't feel anything until he started to reel in and pulled his neck. He wanted me to either push the hook through or cut the hook at the barb and pull it back. I couldn't do it so we had to go to the emergency room at the hospital. Carlo walked in with his hand covering his "catch." The doctor jokingly said, "Wow, you sure caught a big one." This was a bit embarrassing. We left a day earlier than we had planned to come home. The rain followed us off and on all the way down and when we got to Sunnyvale it was pouring down rain and this was August. It seemed as if we were like the cartoon character Joe Piffleslick who always had a black cloud over his head.

We went to Disneyland when Marco was five and Marina was seven. Marina was the adventuresome child and wanted to go on the Matterhorn more than once. Marco wanted to go see the girls in the Small World Exhibit. He loved the music and the animated figures of each country so he and I rode the boat in this ride more than once and Marina and Carlo went a few times down the mountain.

From the 1969 trip to Italy until 1986 our vacations were mostly short trips to McCloud, Lake Tahoe, Disneyland, Bodega Bay to see where the movie "The Birds" was filmed or day trips to San Francisco. When we went to Bodega Bay we stayed in a motel in Santa Rosa and what a coincidence that evening as we turned on the TV. The movie "The Birds" just happened to be showing.

I should make a correction though. When we had the deli, most of the electronic manufacturing plants around us would close for the two weeks during the Christmas holidays. This was when we would also close the deli and escape to our cabin at Tahoe for a much needed rest. It usually was for a week or ten days.

One year on the day we were packing up to come back to Sunnyvale, we received a phone call from my brother who asked when we would be home. We said we were just about to leave and he said he was glad to hear it. He said the Sunnyvale Fire Department had been called to our deli because some one reported a liquid coming out from under our back door and since the building was in an industrial zone of the city, they didn't know if this was a hazardous material. Since we weren't home, the next emergency number they called was my brother. When he opened up, they found that the big water heater had broken and the deli was flooded. Doors were opened and water swept out and when we got home, we had to get a new water heater and deal with some of the case goods that got wet. At least this got done before we had to open after the holiday. Never a dull moment!

After we sold the deli, I have already told you about our trip to Italy in 1986 with Carlo's mother. In 1989 our son, Marco got a job as an airline mechanic with United Airlines in South San Francisco. This meant that we as his parents could fly on a space available ticket with his pass. So in 1991 we flew again to Italy. This was the first time we flew on his pass and I didn't know what to expect. Well, we went to the airport. We had our tickets checked but we couldn't check our luggage until our names were called which meant we could go on the plane. This was usually ten minutes before departure. I am usually the nervous one and this is a very trying time for me. I kept thinking we would have to turn around and go home and try the next day. As luck would have it, we were able to get on the flight to Frankfurt. We couldn't check our luggage all the way to Genova because we were on standby. In Frankfurt we waited for our luggage because they couldn't open the cargo doors on the plane. Finally after 1 1/2 hours we got our luggage and then had to wait again to see if we got on the plane. Well, we didn't have a problem. On the return flight we again stopped in Frankfurt and stayed over at the Sheraton Hotel which is right across the street from the airport. One just has to take the escalator up and then walk across the street on the enclosed footbridge to the hotel. It is very convenient. Since we had a little bit of time, we also caught the subway train which is under the airport and went to downtown Frankfurt and to the old section called Saxenhausen which was not bombed during the war. We ate in the plaza and enjoyed the warm summer weather.

In 1994 we again went to italy and stayed overnight in Frankfurt so we could rest before we went to see the relatives. We learned to do this because if we flew straight through to the relatives, we would talk so much when we got there we would be exhausted for a day or two after we arrived. It was during this trip that we almost didn't get on our flight home. Our young cousin from Sassello, Diego Assandri, asked if he could come back with us to the U.S. as we had invited him to do so a few times. He had about twelve days which he thought would be great to see a bit of California. Since we were traveling on a pass, he had to buy a ticket but we placed our name on the list for the flight on August 1 and were told there was plenty of space. We arrived at Milano's Malpensa Airport and Diego checked in. When we checked in with our tickets, the clerk said "I doubt if you will get on today." That was a shock to me as we had checked in by phone a few days earlier and they said "No problem." Immediately, my stomach did flip-flops. Then the waiting game began. They began boarding so we told Diego not to worry. He would be changing aircraft in Washington D.C. but if we didn't get on, Marco would be waiting in San Francisco for him. Diego did not speak English. The time for departure came and still they didn't call us and also a group of about 20 standbys. A ticket agent came up to all of us and asked for dates of employment, which our son was very junior on the list. There was a lady waiting with us who seemed to be a pilot's wife and she said she didn't think we were going to get on. After a few minutes we found out that TWA had overbooked their flight to the U.S. and United was helping them out by taking all the extra passengers. At the last minute the agent began calling names of the most senior people and after about 8 or 9 people, she called us. She told us we would have to hurry with our luggage and go through customs but to run down the hallway and check in at the gate. Carlo was pushing the luggage cart and he said I looked like a fullback going through the people to get to our gate. We got on and were able to be on business class and Diego was in the back in economy class. When we approached Washington D.C. Carlo asked the flight attendant if he could switch seats with Diego so that he could see the city. She said usually this wasn't approved but she would let him do this.

Diego came up front, enjoyed the business class setting while I pointed out different landmarks to him.

He was twenty years old when he came here and we did a whirl-wind tour of some of California. Of course, we took him to San Francisco, Carmel, Monterey, Santa Cruz, Big Basin Park to see the redwood trees and then Marco who had a pilot's license, flew him and Carlo to Columbia State Park where one can fly to the airport and walk to town and then they continued the flight to Lake Tahoe. They flew around the lake and landed at Truckee Airport. Meanwhile Carlo's mother and I drove up with the car and we all stayed a couple of days so Diego could meet Marina and Bill and do some gambling at the casinos in Reno. Diego turned 21 the night we went to the casinos. He also won $40 on the slot machines. He drove home with Lee and I so that he could see a different route from Tahoe and we stopped in Sacramento to see the capitol. We ate hotdogs from a vendor's cart parked next to the capitol building. When he was finished with this trip Diego said he felt like a spinning top but he said he would never forget this trip.

21

LA MARCIALONGA (THE LONG MARCH)

Our daughter and her then-husband went to Italy in 1986 and while there she saw a poster for a 70 K cross-country ski race which took place in northern Italy near the Dolomites. She asked our cousins about it and said then "I want to enter that race some day." Well, finally 15 years later she got her wish.

Marina called me up in October 2000 and announced that she had signed up to be in the Marcialonga in Italy which was taking place at the end of January 2001. Five other friends from Lake Tahoe were going. A few days later she called and said her friends were entered in two other races which were taking place before the Marcialonga and would I go with her since she was only entered in the one and didn't want to travel alone as she was going later than they were. I said, "No way! I'm not going to northern Italy in January where I will freeze — you know I hate to be cold." Now my daughter was 40 at the time but she pleaded, "Please, mom —

please go with me." My husband, Carlo also said "Why don't you go, you will both have fun and you will have some quality time together." All right, I finally conceded to go.

The Marcialonga is a 70K race and Marina had only done races of 50K in the Lake Tahoe area so she began practicing.

Marina had plans for us to take a train from Milano, change trains and then change to a bus as I didn't want to rent a car, especially in snow country. Well, I didn't like to think of going on the trains and bus with all the oversized luggage we had. I didn't have too much, one large suitcase because of bulky clothes to keep me warm, and a carryon, but Marina had skis, a huge duffel bag with ski boots, etc. and a carryon. She even had a kit with something like an iron to hot wax her skis every night. When I called my cousins in Torino and told them we would be there for the race, she said she and her husband would hook up with us and drive us to the town that was the start of the race. They would stay with us for the time we would be there. Whew, I felt better.

We went to the San Francisco Airport on January 21, 2001 with all our luggage and wearing warm clothes. One good thing about these oversized things was that when an employee at the airport saw us in line with the oversized luggage, he promptly brought us to the line for oversized luggage and we went ahead of everyone else. When we were on the plane I realized I left my folding umbrella in a leather case, which had been my father's, hanging on the back of a chair where we stopped to get a cup of coffee. I asked the attendant if I could get off. She gave me another boarding pass and I hurriedly got off the plane. Carlo saw me and asked,"What are you doing?" Then he helped me to look for the umbrella. It was gone. Well, back on the plane. I then started to get comfortable with the earphones and listen to some music. I couldn't get it to work and I was pressing buttons. Marina looked to see what I was doing but apparently I hadn't plugged something in. When she plugged it in, the volume came on so loud I almost jumped 10 feet in the air. Marina just shook her head and said — "This is going to be a long two weeks."

We landed at Milano's Malpensa Airport at 7:00 in the morning. My cousin Rosita was working in Milano and told us to call her when we got in. I bought a phone card to call her and I kept getting a busy signal. I asked the gentleman at the next phone if I was doing something wrong. He told me I had to tear off the corner of the card before inserting it in the phone. Then it worked. Rosita could not come to airport which was 40 minutes away so she instructed us to get on the express train downstairs at the airport. This train just goes to Milano and back with about four or five stops in between. We had about 10 minutes before the train was taking off. We started to board the train. Marina was inside and I was handing her the luggage. I had the biggest one still on the platform and she said she would get it and for me to get inside. I got in and the doors closed. Panic!! We didn't know how to open the doors. A nice young man came up and pushed a button on the side of the doors and they opened. Marina just rolled her eyes because I left the luggage on the platform and someone could have taken it or the train could have taken off. But we still had a few minutes to spare. It takes 40 minutes to get to the end of the line and we were to get off there and Rosita would be waiting. Rosita was there at the end of the line and then we stood in a line to try to get a taxi. One or two stopped but when they saw the long skis and other stuff, they shook their heads and took the next people waiting. Finally a cab came up and I could see he had a hatchback with a space in between the front seats. So we argued with him and he took us. Her apartment wasn't too far from the center of town. She got us settled in and then went to work. Before leaving she gave us instructions on how to take the trolley to the piazza with the duomo and the galleria shopping center. She would be home around 7:00 p.m. Marina and I took a short nap and then got up at 1:30, took the trolley to Piazza del Duomo where the cathedral is and headed for the galleria. The first thing she saw was a gelato store and I think it was about 30 degrees outside. She insisted and we had our gelatos inside the store and then headed out. Almost every woman we saw whether they were 19 or 90 had on a fur coat, usually of full length. This wasn't a fashion statement; it was a matter of keeping warm. We returned to my cousin's apartment around 6:30.

We went to bed early but hardly slept. The refrigerator which was in the kitchen next to our bedroom had something wrong with it and sounded like a train coming down the track every half hour. The next day, Marina went to the pharmacy to buy earplugs for us because we had one more night to stay there. After getting up from a sleepless night and awaking to an overcast and rainy day, we were happy to see our other cousin and husband, Rosanna and Dalmo. They had come to see us from Torino and took us downtown again. We went around a little on foot and then went to see the Castello Sforsesco which was now a museum. Dalmo had plans to take us to Lago di Como but the weather would not have permitted us to see much because of drizzle and fog, so we just went around in Milano. We enjoyed their company since we would not see them again that time.

That evening, we slept a bit better with the earplugs. The next morning, our cousin Marisa and Beppe (short for Giuseppe) came to pick us up to go to the race area. Beppe had converted his car to propane and the tank was held in the trunk. Beppe was prepared with a rack for the skis and other luggage but we were a bit crowded in his car. We stopped along the way at an autogrill — a restaurant just off the road but you don't have to get off the freeway. The food was really good and we had lasagne. We got to the Hotel Bellaria in Carano at 4:00. The town just down the hill is Cavalese and we decided to walk to it. On the way back it was raining quite hard, but we made it back just in time for dinner in the hotel. Marina's friends had not shown up yet. They were coming the next day and were staying at the same hotel. We were the only ones in the dining room that evening.

The next morning Beppe took us to an area where Marina could practice. It was called Lavaze and there was a race going on. Marina went and practiced and we walked around a bit. The temperature was 3 degrees Celcius or about 25 degrees Fahrenheit. Marina returned at 2:00 and we all ate at this resort. We returned to the hotel and then we went out to eat in the adjacent town. Beppe and Marina had pork shin, Marisa had venison, I had capriolo or small roe deer. We had salads, two desserts, a bottle of wine and our bill came to $70.00 for the four of us. Everything was outstanding. The next day, Beppe brought Marina to Lavaze again so she could practice. Marisa and I went shopping. Later when Beppe and Marina returned we went to a grappa distillery and bought a bottle of grappa to bring home.

There wasn't too much snow around the hotel and town of Cavalese but we awoke to a fresh fall of snow the next morning. We drove to Moena which would be the start of the race. Big trucks were bringing in snow to cover the streets that would be used for the race. There were a few outdoor booths with food such as sausages and coffee, etc. We walked around like the tourists that we were. We returned to the hotel, walked to the church for mass at 6:30 and they were praying for the victims of the tragedy three years prior when a United States military plane flying in the valley hit the cable of a gondola and killed 20 people. It was quite sad. We walked back to the hotel and had dinner with Marina's friends. The hotel restaurant had a table set up for nine people which was used by us for breakfast and dinner during our stay. The breakfasts consisted of a continental buffet with toast, cereal, yogurt, juice which was usually orange juice made from blood oranges. At first we didn't know what the reddish colored juice was. There was usually coffee cake or apple strudel and of course tea or coffee and milk. We had a great time discussing races, shopping, food, etc. That evening everyone retired early to get ready for the race.

The morning of the race Marina got up at 5:00. I got to sleep in for another hour. In the dining room the owner of the hotel had a light breakfast ready for us along with a soft boiled egg which she had also given to the skiers. We walked down to Carano and then caught a bus to Moena which was the start of the race. By accident we ran into Marina and were told she was in the third wave of skiers. There were 4,700 participants and each wave started 1/2 hour after the previous one. The participants were given a micro-chip to insert into their ski shoes to keep track of the skier and register times, etc. We heard the shot of the cannon and saw the skiers begin the race. It was a wave of 1,000 people gliding and poling on the snow tracks. When Marina's group was to start I took a photo just to do so and after examining it with a magnifying glass I found that I actually took her picture. We then took the bus to Canazei which would be the halfway mark but it would be about two or more hours before she would get there so we killed time by walking around and having coffee. We got to the half way mark just in time as we only waited about 20 minutes and happened to see Marina. I didn't have my camera on in time so all I got was the back of her but at least we were able to spur her on by yelling "Go, Marina, Go! We were also able to see her friend Elizabeth and Beppe also spurred her on with the Italian equivalent, "Forza, Eliza-betta, forza!" She loved that.

From there we took the bus back to the finish line at Cavalese. The bus ride took over an hour. We waited quite a while at the finish line but finally here she was coming down the track. I took the photo but she was behind the Cavit sign but there she was. She was just happy to have finished the race.   Then she had to get her belongings. The race was very organized. Before the race started the skiers were given a colored plastic garbage bag in which to put all their belongings. Each group of 1,000 had a color such as green, blue, red, orange and yellow. The bags were closed with a closure with a number and the skiers had a corresponding number. The bags were then transported to the finish area and hung on racks much like clothes racks. Then the skiers looked for their color and number.

Marina and her friends were tired but happy so they were going to celebrate in town after the race. We went back to the hotel for dinner.

The next morning we went to buy the newspaper to find the results of the race. Marina had taken five hours 21 minutes and came in number 2,112. Also in her classification of women from 40 to 49 she came in 18th which I thought was very good. Elizabeth had inserted her microchip a bit crooked so her results were not tabulated but she was very close to Marina so she just figured it was close to the same times.

We had the whole day to just relax or do some sightseeing so Beppe suggested we take the ski tram up the mountain. The top of the tram was at 2,400 meters or 7,315 feet. We took some photos and the scenery was beautiful. Beppe had been in this area before and had done mountain climbing all over the valleys and mountains and pointed to many of the peaks he had climbed. We walked up to a *refugio* or refuge. As long as we stayed on the edges of the ski runs we were all right as there were other people walking. The refuge was like a big restaurant and bar so we had pizza and beer. When we finished, Marina and Beppe wanted to walk to another refuge on the ridge a little ways away but of course I didn't, so Marisa and I waited for them. The views were spectacular. Outside the restaurant was an igloo with a man selling grappa by the shot glass. He had plain grappa and many flavored grappas. Marina wanted to try the grappa to finish the meal we had and when she asked for a shot of it, the man refused and said in Italian "No, no, not for the ladies. I will sell you the flavored one." Marina asked why he wouldn't sell her the regular one and he responded to

Beppe that the regular one was too strong and would cause the women to have stomach pains and thus pass gas. But the word for gas in Italian was understood by Marina and myself and we both laughed. He immediately started laughing when he caught on that we understood him. He still didn't sell her the regular one so she had to settle for the peach flavored grappa.

The next morning we started back and Beppe said we could swing by Lago di Garda. Poor Beppe, all he did was pack and unpack the car. We left at 9:30 and arrived at 1:00 at the lake. Many places were closed as the hotel and restaurant owners find this time of the year to go on vacation. We did find a small hotel and our unit was similar to what a family could rent in summer. A bedroom with a sitting area and a kitchen. We asked the people at the hotel where we could go for a nice meal and they suggested a few not too far but they also said they might be closed. We drove to an area he suggested, parked the car in a huge parking area next to the water and started looking around. It was a bit foggy and there was a lit lamp post in the middle of the parking area and very few cars. The scene reminded me of a murder mystery movie where someone is walking alone in the foggy area and suddenly something happens. Well, we walked a bit and then found two restaurants side by side and their lights were on. Hardly anyone was in the restaurants and the hosts were looking out at us through the windows while we read the menus and it seemed as if they were begging us to come in. We picked one and had a good meal.

The next morning we left at 9:30. Marina asked Beppe if it was possible to swing by my Zia Pina's house in Quargnento. He said of course but we should go to the hotel near Milano first where we would be staying near the airport. We would drop off all the luggage and then go to Zia Pina's place and Marisa's brother and sister-in-law would pick us up to bring us back to the hotel. This way we could see a few more relatives which we had not planned on seeing. After dropping off the luggage we got to Zia Pina's

(Rosita's mother) place around 2:30. Marisa's other brother Piero and wife, Vittorina had arrived from Torino to see us. It seems as if the telephone system works quite well, having been told by the other brother Mario. Zia had champagne, cookies, coffee and tea for us. Then Mario and Fulvia arrived also from Torino. Zia was so happy to have all the company and while we were there we called my mother and she was able to speak to everyone. We left Zia's house after an emotional goodbye and headed for the hotel in Oleggio. Mario had a big beautiful Mercedes and he asked me to sit up front with him. Soon it seemed we were going quite fast and I looked at the speedometer and saw that it was registering 150K. I tried not to sound too panicky by asking Mario how fast we were going in American miles. He calmly said "Oh, about 90 miles per hour." I then said that as his older cousin, would he please slow down because if anything happened to me or Marina, his aunt who was my mother, would kill him. They took us out to dinner before dropping us off and then again, another emotional goodbye.

The next morning the hotel shuttled us to the airport which was a 15 minute drive. The short ride goes along the river near the town of Oleggio and the airport. On the flight home the plane was about half empty so I had two seats and Marina had three seats to herself in the middle so we had a good rest. You could say we had a great, fun time even though it was cold!! But I survived and Marina triumphed.

22

BAGNA CAUDA

After selling the deli in 1986 and going on vacation to
Italy, I was bored and didn't want to stay home so I
applied at the Fremont Union High School District for a
part-time job for any clerical position. There was a two
hour job in the Maintenance and Transportation office
at the District. There was already a secretary who
worked eight hours but since the bus drivers usually
worked a split-shift they needed someone there to be in
contact with them for more than the normal eight hour
day. The students transported were special education
students. I was glad to be occupied for two hours a day.
After two years a position opened up at Cupertino High
School for a secretary in the Guidance Office and it was
for four hours a day. I really liked this job and the
teachers were great. There was also a Student Advocate
in our office and she was a licensed therapist or coun-

selor. There was an opening for this position and when it was filled, Phyllis, one of the teachers said, "Rose, you probably know the person since you have been living in this area for so long and this new person's family has lived around here also." When I asked what the therapist's name was Phyllis answered that her name was Kristen Popovich. I went to school with Gloria Popovich and her twin brother, George. So I waited until the young lady started the following week. In the meantime, Carlo was working as a realtor in Sunnyvale and the assistant manager of his office was Gloria Popovich Walker so I asked Carlo to check with Gloria to find out if her niece was a Marriage, Family and Child Counselor. Sure enough, the new employee was Gloria's niece. I also knew the lady that George married, Christie Sorenson.

Well, Kristen started work at Cupertino High School for four days a week and had a private practice for one day at her office. We immediately loved her and she was excellent with the students. Kristen noticed a photo of our family and asked about everyone in the photo and commented that our son was handsome. I kept this in the back of my mind, as any true matchmaker would do.

In February, I decided to have a dinner that is very regional to Piemonte in Italy. This dinner is called Bagna Calda or in the Piemontese dialect Bagna Cauda and it means "hot bath". It is a fondue type dip in which you dip raw vegetables and is made of oil, lots of garlic and lots of anchovies. When I make it at home, the neighbors can actually smell the odors if they are outside. We have never come across someone who doesn't like it. So, when I decided to have this dinner, we invited a couple who worked with Carlo in real estate, Kristen's aunt and uncle, my brother and sister-in-law, our mothers, our son Marco and then I asked Kristen if she would like to join us as her aunt and uncle would be there. I also asked the other teacher/counselor, Gregg as his wife was out of town and he would have to fix his own dinner. So I thought, this set up didn't look too obvious. When I told Marco that I would be having Bagna Cauda on Friday, he said he had better invite a female friend who loved it and would never forgive him if she wasn't able to come. I had to tell him, "No, don't invite her! I've invited someone I want you to meet." I didn't get any static which I was expecting. So far, so good.

Friday night came and when I introduced Marco and Kristen, one of our friends said you could see the sparks between the two. They hit it off immediately and now have been married nine years. The Bagna Cauda Dinner tradition started in the late 60's as a small New Year's dinner when we still had the supermarket and my brother hosted it. My mother made the dip and Louis prepared all the vegetables and set up the tables. In the beginning there were perhaps 20 people and they were the people who worked in the store and their spouses. The guest list grew as we kept thinking of more people who would like to attend and the date was fixed at the first Saturday in December. The guests included good friends, salesmen who called on us at the store and heard about the dinner and friends of Louis's children. Then we heard that people who had attended began saving the date in December in hopes of getting invited again. The list of invited guests at one time hit 54 and this was a sit down dinner. My brother was fortunate that his kitchen, family room, dining room, and play room were laid out that he had a long line of tables which formed a U-shape and everyone had a seat. It was a noisy, fun filled evening which had a strong odor of garlic and anchovies.

The dinner was quite a chore for my brother. To set it up he needed the long banquet tables and chairs. Then the dip was to be kept warm, but not as hot as a fondue pot, so long ago he discovered that the old popcorn poppers that had the heating element below the pot were the right appliance for this dinner. So, Louis had to find enough pots by using his and ours and then trying to find old pots at the Goodwill store or the Salvation Army stores. He placed one pot among six people, then had to run the cords down the legs of the tables and over to an electric plug. Then he had to tape all the electrical cords so no one would trip. At the beginning, he had a few circuit breakers trip with all that was hooked up. He actually had to draw up a schematic of where the cords could go.

One time our daughter did not attend the dinner as she was at a school dance. She didn't have a driver's license yet and had to be picked up when the dance was over. Our nephew, David said he would go to pick up Marina and her friend. Our, son, Marco went along for the ride. When Marina and her friend, Nancy got in the car, Nancy turned to Marina and asked, "What's that smell?" Marco and David snickered and let Marina explain the odor.

The vegetables which were used in this fondue were Savoy cabbage, celery, mushrooms, red bell peppers, Jerusalem artichokes, cauliflower and we also began putting small pieces of meat in this also. The guests began bringing desserts and then it seemed as if they all tried to outdo each other as to the most lavish or beautiful dessert.

At the time, mom and my step father were living on the next court from my brother, and we were making wine, many of the people wanted to see the wine making cellar and to do a bit of wine tasting. This was also a good time for the guests to walk off some of the food and for the ones left behind to clear the tables to get ready for dessert. My brother continued this tradition for about 30 years until his wife Betty had a heart attack.

We have had bagna cauda at Lake Tahoe during the Christmas holidays also as it is really appropriate in the winter. One New Year's Eve we had our cousin visiting from Italy. He was in his 70's at the time and just to prove how regional this dish is, he had never tasted it and lives in the very next region of Liguria. So we planned to have this dinner and Marina had a couple who wanted to stop by to wish us a Happy New Year as they were going to a party. The couple, Katie and John Joubert came around 9:30 and were dressed up for their party. I told them that they were probably going to absorb the odor of the bagna cauda in their clothes but they weren't worried. John and Katie tasted the dip and they loved it. They kept eating and the time passed. Soon it was midnight and they were still at our house. John loved it so much he said he wanted to have this dinner for his birthday. His birthday was in July. They left at 12:15 to go to the other party.

Another year, we had a bagna cauda and four of Marco's friends were invited. One of them, Joe Gorman said that he hated anchovies but would attend to enjoy the company. He tasted it and then kept eating. He remarked that he never thought he would be eating anchovies as he disliked them, but here he was eating them.

The following July, Katie kept the promise to give John his bagna cauda birthday party but it just isn't the same in the summer. For one thing, some of the vegetables aren't available in summer, but we still had a good time. I am sure it is more the friendship and good food and wine.

My brother's son, David loved the bagna cauda and he and Marco were always the last two standing while eating. David passed away in September of 2004 after an illness of a few years. The dinner has been revived again by relatives at different homes in honor of David. They are not as large in number of guests but they are just as much fun and with a special meaning.

23

MAKING WINE

I mentioned earlier in my book that my dad made wine. However, he didn't really make good wine. It was drinkable but I remembered that he used to ferment it for too many days in the fermentation tank. Of course, he was limited to when he could draw the wine off the must and press the must as he had to wait his turn for the wine press.

Well, after my father died, my mother married an Italian man whose family was friends with our family. This man, Giulio (Pete) Picollo was born near Asti in Italy which is a center of great wines in the Piemonte region. Pete lost his wife a few months after my father died. The first year after he married my mom, Pete didn't make wine so Carlo asked if he had given up making it. He was surprised that Carlo was interested so he decided to teach Carlo how to make it his way. Pete had given some of the equipment away to friends so he told Carlo he needed a wine press or they would have to borrow one.

One day Carlo was driving down Old San Francisco Road and there were still some farm houses and farm land. Carlo saw a sign that advertised some farm items for sale and the name on the mailbox was Italian. Carlo turned into the driveway and asked if the rancher had a wine press. Sure enough, he had one so Carlo bought it and Pete was thrilled. Pete had contacts with grape growers where he could buy grapes or he knew growers who would let you go and pick the grapes off the vines. Pete usually bought the grapes already picked but once or twice he picked them in Gilroy and Carlo and Louis went along to help and they helped Pete with the crushing and pressing.

In 1986 Pete died of cancer and then Carlo and I went to Italy during the summer. When we returned, my mom said that some friends of ours had purchased land in Gilroy and they had a few acres of grape vines and although it was already September, there were still grapes on the vines and the friends would let us pick them. So that was the first year Carlo and Louis made wine on their own following Pete's guidelines. The following year, 1987, we found out that there was a land owner who owned about 20 acres of grapes in Calistoga, but they were abandoned. The owner told us we could pick anything we found on the vines because he was not tending to it. There were weeds, the harvest was slim and there were raspberry bushes growing next to the creek and into the vines. We also found out later that there were rattlesnakes near the creek. That made me nervous. The first year we left at 6:00 in the morning and it turned out to be a very hot day with the temperature in the 100's. The crew consisted of Carlo and myself, my mom, Carlo's mom, my brother, Louis and his wife Betty, their daughter, Betty Lou and her husband, David, Louis' son, David and his girlfriend Michele, Marco and his friend, Joe Bailey, Marina and her friend Katy and her husband, John. We picked until around 12:30 and we decided to stop to eat lunch but my mother wanted to keep going. She kept saying, "I just want to finish filling this bucket." We kept insisting that she stop as the temperature was so hot and we were afraid she would get heat stroke. My mother was 75 at the time and Lee was 79. Finally, my mom stopped but it was because she went down on her knees and felt nauseous. She was having an attack of heatstroke. Stubborn Italian!! When we stopped for lunch, I had brought cold cuts of lunch meat, bread, potato salad and cold drinks and fruit for everyone. Our chairs were either the tailgates of pickups or cars or the upended 5-gallon buckets we used to pick the grapes. After lunch we picked a few more buckets of grapes and then we started for home. We had more than a ton of grapes. We had picked 50 fruit boxes which hold about 40 pounds each of grapes and we picked some extra buckets.

A funny thing happened on the way home. My mother was riding with Louis and he stopped for gas and then told her he wanted something really cold like a popsicle so he was going to find a store where he could buy just one popsicle. He stopped in the town of Calistoga and told her to sit under a tree that was shady and it had a small wall under it, and to wait for him that he would not be long. He went to two or three stores but they wouldn't break up a box. Finally he found a place where he could buy just one popsicle. Meanwhile my mother was waiting and waiting. She really got panicky and thought he had forgotten her and abandoned her. When he got back and she told him about her fears he really laughed and up until the day she died, we would tease her about the time she thought she was left behind by the side of the road.

When we got back to the house, we unloaded the boxes of grapes and crushed them by dumping them in the electric grape crusher which was on the top of the fermentation tank. The tank held the entire ton of grapes. This process took about an hour. By this time it was about 6:00 and I cooked a spaghetti and sausage dinner for everyone. The next morning, we had to wash all the buckets we had used for picking and store them back behind the workshop and now Carlo had his work cut out for the next week or two. Pete taught Carlo to take readings of the alcohol content twice a day. He would punch down the grapes in the tank and he would fill a large vial with the juice from the tank. Then he had a hydrometer which he put into the vial and it would measure the sugar content or "brix" of the wine. When the number got down to zero it meant that the alcohol content was about 12 or 13% so it was time to draw off the juice and put it into the barrels and then press the must or the rest of the grapes. If the weather was very warm, it would take about 4 or 5 days. If the weather was cool, it took longer for the grapes to ferment.

When he drew off the juice into the barrels he would seal the barrels with an air lock which would keep bubbling because it was still fermenting. When the bubbling stopped, then he would seal the barrel and let the wine sit for a year or two.

We picked grapes in Calistoga for two years. The second year we picked there we had a great announcement after dinner from David and Michele as they announced their engagement. We celebrated with some bubbly champagne and being tired I think all of us slept well that night.

In 1989 we were talking to our friends, John and Velma Ferrero, in Lodi and they said their son-in-law's father owned vineyards in Clements on Hiway 88 east of Lodi in the foothills. He said he was sure he would let us pick grapes. We asked and he said yes. So that year was the first year we picked in Clements. The son-in-law, Jeff Myers was actually in the farmland appraisal business but he and his brother Randy helped the father with the vineyard. Jeff marked off so many rows so that we could pick grapes. The first year, he gave the grapes to us because they were the second picking but this is hard work because you really have to search for the little bunches of grapes that weren't picked at the first picking. He had a contract with a winery for the first pick.

The hydrometer that Carlo uses to measure the alcohol or sugar content of the wine is also used before we pick the grapes. About the time when we figure the grapes are almost ripe enough, Carlo goes to Lodi to see the vineyard and he picks two or three bunches of grapes, squeezes them with his hands, pours the juice into the vial and measures the sugar content with the hydrometer. He likes the reading to be close to 24 or 25. If it is 21 or 22, he keeps an eye on the weather and keeps in touch with Jeff and waits a week or so but when it reaches 24 or 25 we try to go to pick. Now Jeff usually checks the sugar content for us and now Carlo has a refractometer which only needs the juice of one little berry from the bunch of grapes.

The second year we picked we told Jeff we wanted to pay for the grapes if we could have a first pick. Jeff again marked off some rows for us and the grapes were beautiful. We also kept recruiting people to pick, but we weren't actively doing so. Two of the pickers, Armand and Lilly Lambert were in our Aquarobics class at Nautilus and when they heard we picked grapes to make wine, they said they wanted to help us. They are a lovely couple who were born in Belgium and came to the United States in the mid 50's. A few times, their son Edward and his wife and their daughter Helen and friend John have also joined us. Another couple we met was Laura and Ralph Babcock and we met them at a Christmas party at our neighbor's home. In the course of the evening Ralph and Carlo began talking about wine and Carlo mentioned that he made wine. Ralph immediately said he would love to help pick grapes and see the process for making wine. Of course Carlo and I thought — "Right, he wants to get up early, pick grapes most of the day for nothing other than lunch and dinner and he is a stranger to us." Well, about six months later Carlo and I were taking an early morning walk and we encountered Ralph doing the same and he asked if we were going to pick grapes in the fall. When we said we were, he reminded us to please call him to help. He was serious so when August and September rolled around and we had a date for picking, we called Ralph and Laura and they came to help us pick. They enjoyed it so much, they still come and pick with us every year we make wine. In 2007 we didn't make wine as we went to Italy during harvest season. With so many hands picking, we always finish before noon.

Our lunchtime buffet has gotten away from just sandwiches. Some of the ladies bring potluck and we try to bring different salads such as broccoli salad, five-bean salad, fiesta salad, fruit salad and we try to keep it healthy. Of course, we often bring dessert too and the gooier the better.

One year, Carlo was selling a house for a couple in Sunnyvale and in the course of talking, he mentioned making wine and the seller said his neighbor was into making wine. This lady had broken a hip years before and while she was immobilized, she began reading about making wine at home so with the help of her two grown daughters, she started doing so on a very small scale. The seller of the property, Dave and his wife Lynn said they were sure Nola would love to go in with us to make wine. Dave and Lynn also wanted to go so now we had five more pickers plus Nola's granddaughter, Jessica, and someone who wanted to split the harvest with us. So, actually we could pick more than our usual one ton of grapes and we would also have more wine. We pick Zinfandel grapes and Petite Sirah grapes on Jeff's property.

Just to prove that this is such a small world, Dave Heltman once mentioned that there was a neighbor on his street where he lived now who had connections with people in McCloud where I was born. Remember that McCloud was a small town of 2,300 people. One year he brought this couple to help us pick grapes. Lo and behold, I recognized this couple as someone who used to attend the McCloud Reunions in San Jose when I was one of the organizers. So we discussed many of the people she was related to. They came back to Sunnyvale with us for the spaghetti dinner. Since my mom no longer came to pick, but came to our dinners, she really enjoyed seeing these people.

After the second or third time we picked in Clements, Jeff told his wife, Michele, and his in-laws about the great spread we put out at lunch time, plus we had a beautiful oak tree to sit under, unlike the place in Calistoga. Michele told Jeff that the next time we went, they would like to join us and they would add to the food. They wanted to visit with us since we only see each other two or three times a year.

One year, my mother-in-law's first cousin, Katie from San Jose joined us. She was also in her 70's and she came for about five years. Then Katie's brother Jack and his wife Thelma from Vandergrift, Pennsylvania wanted to come out to help pick. So, they scheduled their vacation to our harvest and came out and picked grapes. John and Velma from Lodi also had two visitors from Lodi, Italy come out and visit us when we harvested.

The highlight of course, is the lunchtime buffet with fresh picked tomatoes from Lilly and Armand's garden which they sliced and marinated with oil and vinegar. There is always a fruit salad and many other salads. The spaghetti dinner with sausages in Sunnyvale is usually the home made sausage made by the group in Lodi and us, but that is another story.

24

ORCHIDS

When my in-laws had the nursery in Palo Alto, they had many beautiful plants and one of the plants they began to carry was cymbidium orchids. When they decided to sell the nursery at the beginning of 1963, everything was put on sale so I grabbed one of the pots of orchids to see what I could do with it. Anything that was left over after the final sale was taken to Gilroy on the property my in-laws bought. Some of the larger plants were put into wooden boxes and many of the fruit trees were planted in the ground. For instance, if one apple tree was good, three were better. There were different varieties of almost every fruit tree such as cherries, apricots, peaches, pears, apples. Charlie had a lemon tree and two orange trees in large wooden containers. He also had a kumquat tree in a container and when they were ripe, Marina and Carlo loved eating them, skin and all.

Well, I went home with my prize orchid and babied it for the next few years. Cymbidium orchids are not hard to raise nor are they very delicate. They like morning sun or filtered shade and they will withstand neglect and still reward you with beautiful flowers that last for about three months on the stalk after opening. If the flower stalk is picked to place in a vase of water, it will last for about a month. My first plant was very pale cream color with a bit of burgundy in the center. The flowers usually bloom from February to May so when the plant bloomed the following year, I made corsages for Mothers' Day for my mother, Carlo's mother, myself and my sister-in-law. I arranged two flowers with netting and ribbon and I do have to say that they looked quite professional. A few years after I had the plant, it outgrew its pot and we placed it in a wooden tub. Orchids like to be crowded in their containers. It wasn't long before we had to split the plant and make three out of the one plant and it kept doing beautifully. At our home on Arbor Avenue, we didn't have much shade. The backyard was all cement with a fig tree in the corner so we placed the orchid underneath the fig. When we moved to Maxine Avenue, it was also very sunny in the backyard and it was about three or four years before Carlo built a lath covered patio. Now at our present home, Carlo built a large lath-covered area so the orchids would have filtered shade. When he was in the process of doing this, all the orchids had to be moved to a spot in the yard where they would be out of the way. At the time, I had about 40 or 50 plants. Marco was grumbling as I made him move the pots and he kept saying — "Give some away, give some away." He didn't realize that I had already started giving some away because we kept splitting them and repotting them and making three or more out of one pot.

After my first plant, Carlo realized that I loved cymbidium orchids and I had not killed any yet. He came home for Mothers' Day with a gorgeous pink orchid plant and the next year I can truly say it was a blooming fool. It had 13 long stems on it with 13 or 14 flowers on each stem. This started the invasion of the orchid plants. From then on, whenever we went to the orchid growers in South San Francisco, I wanted a new color of cymbidium orchid. Carlo also bought two hanging pots of orchids, one green, one burgundy. I soon had orchids in green, yellow, salmon, white, burgundy, a cinnamon color, and various shades of pink. Two ladies working for us at the Deli gave me a burgundy one called Red Duke when I had an operation and to this day, it is one of my favorites. But with Red Duke I have had the plant for over 20 years and I have only been able to split it once into three plants. One of the ladies that gave me the burgundy one said she had a few orchid plants but they wouldn't bloom. I offered to babysit one of her plants to see what was wrong. I found that she had planted her orchid too deep in the soil in the pot. All I did was remove some of the soil around the plant and the very next spring it was blooming. I told her she could have it back but she didn't want it. So I acquired another plant. Two or three years later, the plant broke the sides of the pot and it was a thick plastic pot. I call this plant and all the ones that have been split from it "Jane's orchid" after the lady who gave it to me. The pink and cream colored ones are the ones that grow the fastest and I have split them numerous time. To prove how many times I have split them, I have given away 38 orchids that I have split beginning with three plants. With the two hanging baskets of orchids, I have split and given away 12 baskets, more of the burgundy one than the green. One year a burgundy hanging orchid had 31 hanging stalks of orchids and the flowers are very small, about the size of a quarter.

In 1990 we were at Lake Tahoe in January and we had a hard freeze in Santa Clara Valley. It lasted for about five days with temperatures below 30 degrees. Well, I came home to orchid stalks that were burned and drooping. I lost all the stalks but I only lost two plants. Our avocado tree also had a lot of damage. We must have had over 200 avocados on the ground and we just had to pick them up and throw them away. I really felt like crying.

Among my photos I have pictures of baby doves which hatched when the female dove made a nest in one of the orchid baskets. The female dove made the nest three different times and each time I had to be careful how I watered the basket. Two eggs would normally hatch after about two weeks of being laid. The mother dove got very used to us passing within a foot of the basket as it hung on our deck very close to the door that went into the kitchen.

Of the special orchids I have given away, a Red Duke, a cinnamon tobacco colored one and a salmon one are among the nicest colors. The ones in a shade of green do not multiply very easily so I haven't been able to split them yet. I enjoy people telling me that they think about me when their orchids started blooming and they seemed pleased.

25

SIBLINGS

Why is it that siblings don't appreciate each other until they are grown up? I guess when they are young, they like to pick on each other.

I remember when I was young and four and a half years younger than my brother, I guess I was the little obnoxious sister, always bugging my brother especially when he was with his buddies. One of my brother's chores was to bring in the wood for the wood stove upon which my mother cooked. We had a big box on the porch and it was his job to fill it with wood from the woodshed. Well, my mother would be ready to begin cooking the evening's meal and there was hardly any wood. She would say to me, "Rose, go find Louis and tell him to come home." I would run out and look around the neighborhood, find him and I would start nagging him by saying, "Louis, mom wants you to come home." He would answer, "Yeah, yeah." But he wouldn't move. I would stand around a few minutes and then repeat my nagging. He would keep ignoring me and keep playing. Very seldom would he come right away, most times it would be after 15 or 20 minutes.

One time I found a letter a girl had written to him so with that knowledge when I had to go and call him to come home, he again ignored me so I used this to make him come home. He was with his friends and when he wouldn't come I said, "If you don't come home right now, I'll tell your friends you got a letter from Sally." Boy did he jump up right away and started to chase me home. Well, I got him to move all right.

Other times, he would twist my arm behind my back to make me say "uncle." Of course since he was bigger than I, it didn't take much for me to say "uncle."

He also liked to scare me at night. He would go outside of my bedroom window and make noises as if there was a bear outside. Since there were bears in the woods and we were the second house from the end near the forest, I always assumed there was a bear outside. I would scream and he would be outside laughing because he scared me.

As we got older we started to care for each other more and more. When he was 16 and working at a theater in San Jose, he bought a watch and one of the first ball point pens for me for graduating from the sixth grade. He also would take me to the theater to see the movies and let me sit in the loge section. I thought this was the big time. He also took me to the classic California Fox Theater in San Jose and introduced me to the manager as his "little" sister and Mr. Saso let us both in to see the movie. Lou worked at the Mission Theater and this one, the California, and the Padre Theater all belonged to the chain of Fox West Coast Theaters.

Lou also taught me to drive a car at the age of 14. Laws were a bit different then with not as many restrictions as there are now. We were living in Sunnyvale at the time and we would cruise up and down First Street in San Jose. If you saw us, it looked a bit funny because I would be driving, Lou would be in the middle and a girl friend of mine would be on the passenger side. Lou sat in the middle in case he had to grab the wheel if I did something stupid.

Lou and his family live only three miles from us and we see each other quite often. When we see each other, it seems as if we run out of time to say everything we want to talk about. When we were living on the next court from Lou, he came over to talk to Carlo about something. After a while when he was ready to leave, I said goodbye to him and said I was going to take a shower. Carlo continued to see him out the door but they started talking on the porch with the door open. I took my shower, finished and got ready to go to bed, looked for Carlo and there he was still talking to Lou on the front porch. I guess Italians have too much to talk about.

When our children were growing up, it seemed as if Marina and Marco were always fighting as Lou and I were. Marina is the older of the two by two years and she was always the more aggressive one. Sometimes she would give Marco a smack on the back. Marco would want to hit her back and would raise a fist with threatening words such as, "Marina, I'm going to smack you." Yet, he never would carry out the threat. Perhaps it was because he heard that you don't hit girls or it was just his nature to not hit his sister, so I think she took advantage of that. Now Marina and Marco talk on the phone quite often and get along well together. I guess it just takes time for siblings to grow up and appreciate each other.

26

UNFORGETTABLE PEOPLE

The decade of the 50's was a decade in which some unforgettable people were born and also when I met some people I will never forget.

I'll start off with my brother's first born, my parent's first grandchild, Steven. He was born in 1952 and a sweetheart. Of course, we all doted on him as he was cute and smart and the first grandchild. My father started with taking him to the bank and showing him off as he was so proud. I enjoyed babysitting him whenever Lou and Betty went out. Steven also spent some time in our store and my mother made a small green apron for him with his name embroidered on the bib. He was about three or four and he was given a feather duster and he felt important dusting off the canned goods. One thing I will never forget was that when I purchased my very first car, a new 1957 Oldsmobile convertible, I took Steven and my father for a ride, Steven was standing up in the middle of the front seat, seat belts were not mandatory then. Padded dashboards were fairly new also and I think the smell of the leather or vinyl intrigued him and he bit down hard on the dashboard. The imprint of his tiny teeth were still on it when I sold the car years later.

The year after Steven was born was when I went to Italy with my mother and met my grandfather for the first time. Nonno Domenico Stanchi was 77 years old. I always marveled at his wisdom and patience and also his quest for knowledge. I was doubly happy that Carlo was able to meet him seven years later in 1960. Nonno fought in World War I in the Dolomites. He was still working out in the fields with the big rake pulled by the horse or going into town with the horse and buggy to do the shopping for my grandmother and aunt. He would always put on his suit to go into town. He never went with his work clothes.

In 1955 my brother's second child David was born. This young boy was a charmer just with his quietness and caring but he also managed to get into trouble. One thing that happened was also with my car. I came out once or twice to get into my car and saw the front windshield was all messy with a streaky substance that had dried. I couldn't figure out what it was. Then I also saw footprints going up the back of the car and on the convertible top. One day, I came out in time to see David kneeling on the top and looking down in the window. He was also a drooler and when he drooled on the window, he would move the wipers across it and it would make a mess. Of course, I yelled and got him down and then he started to cry and really sobbing because I had scolded him. Then I felt bad so I had to hug him to calm him down.

When I went to Hawaii to see Carlo who was in the Navy, David came to the airport to see me and my mom off. When he returned home, he went to his room and wouldn't eat lunch because he was waiting for his Auntie Rose and he began to cry as he thought I wasn't coming back. Again, when Carlo and I went to Italy in 1960 he just sat on the loading dock of the store and watched the planes landing at Moffett Field and said he was waiting for his Auntie Rose. When I worked at the store and David was little, he was told one time that I was his godmother for baptism. From then on, he would come up and just watch me and stare at me. I really think he was waiting for me to wave my magic wand as any good fairy godmother would do.

One time at the age of four, David decided to take a walk around the block without telling anyone. He went all around the block and came back and when he heard everyone calling his name and looking for him he figured he was in trouble so he hid behind some bushes and remained quiet. It was about an hour before he turned himself in. Everyone was so worried and I think he felt good that everyone seemed to miss him.

David loved to wear uniforms. He was in the Cub Scouts and wore his uniform whenever he could. He also played little league baseball and also loved that uniform. In adult life, he became a Sunnyvale Public Safety Officer and was very good in his profession. He was instrumental in the capture of some narcotics dealers but in so doing, his partner on a motorcycle and David both crashed into a car which resulted in his partner being paralyzed from the waist down for life and David being injured also. David died in 2004 at the age of 49 of a brain aneurysm and we all think of him often.

Lou and Betty had a third child in 1957, a girl named Betty Lou. She was the third grandchild my father took to the bank. My dad always had a small compact car such as a Hillman or an Opel to do errands in addition to the family car. The children nicknamed the car "The Putt Putt." Betty loved to go to the bank or wherever with nonno in his "putt putt." She also had the misfortune to look like me when she grew up. She worked for us at the deli during the school vacations and many of the customers thought she was our daughter. One year when she was on vacation in the gold country, she went into a shop in Jamestown. The shopkeeper struck up a conversation with her and asked where she was from. When she answered, "Sunnyvale," he replied that he also was from Sunnyvale and graduated from Fremont High School. Betty Lou said, "My aunt also went to Fremont." The shopkeeper looked at her face and immediately said, "Rose Bo!" She was dumbfounded. Then she began to believe that she looked a bit like me.

Another person who was special and whom I met was Carlo's uncle, Zio Edoardo. He was the 7th born of the Marenco siblings and just the nicest man. Everyone in Pontinvrea where he was born knew Edoardo. He actually lived in Murta, a suburb of Genova but he loved Pontinvrea and went there whenever he could. He often told me that Pontinvrea was the garden of Italy. His wife, Aurelia hated Pontinvrea, so he was often alone there. He was someone who could do almost anything. If something needed fixing, it was "go see Edoardo."

During World War II, everyone had a hard time just finding enough to eat, and Zio worked for the railroad inspecting the freight cars. He had a thin metal hollow rod that he could poke sacks of freight to see what was in them. He soon devised the rod with a sharp end and he would slip this up his sleeve. His wife made a little pouch at the other end of the rod and when he inspected sacks of wheat grain he poked them and got a little pouch of grain to take home. He devised a grinder that could grind the wheat grain and soon he had a bit of flour to make bread, but they had to be careful that the Germans wouldn't catch them baking the bread. One time, the Germans came to their house with a chicken they had confiscated and asked Zia Aurelia to cook it for them. She was an excellent cook and she cooked it. When the Germans left, they left the leftovers for them to eat.

27

THE LITTLE FIAT

When Carlo and I went to Italy with the children in 1969, he said he was going to buy only one souvenir. Well, he did and it was not a small one that we could put in a suitcase. It was a car, a FIAT 124 sport coupe. My cousin Dalmo worked for the Pinin Farina Company and he was able to help us order a car and have it shipped to California. Almost a year went by before we got it because of the color, etc. Dalmo also said that FIAT made an American model for export to the U.S. and another model just for California because of all the requirements for California such as smog, seat belts, etc. When we got it, it was the 1970 model. Carlo's dad saw it and immediately wanted one so when he went in 1974, he bought a 1973 FIAT and then had it shipped here. This was the year that Charlie and Lee started construction on the house in Italy up on the hill above the town of Pontinvrea. The property is called Bricco della Croce, or Hill of the Cross.

In 1976 Charlie and Lee returned to Italy as the construction on the house was just about completed. They also brought the FIAT back to Italy so they could leave it there and use it as they had planned to spend six months out of the year in Italy. When they returned to California, Charlie died about five months later. We had opened a business so it was impossible for us to return to Italy for nine years. In 1986 we sold the business and then we decided to go back to Italy with Lee to check on the property. We got there and the car was in the garage, not having been touched in nine years. Carlo and a mechanic worked on it for about three hours and got it going again. Every year we paid the registration on the FIAT and if we went to Italy we would put the stickers on it and we would also pay the insurance for a month or two when we got there, using a friend there who was an insurance salesman. When we went to Alessandria to shop we parked in a parking lot which had an attendant in a booth. He looked at our license plate from California and had a puzzled look on his face but didn't say anything. The next time we parked in the lot, he stopped us and asked, "Does it really pay for you to ship this car over here so that you don't have to rent a car?" We laughed and then explained that the car was stored in Italy and we just kept up the registration.

Another time, we were out sightseeing and the belt for the generator and water pump broke and we had to pull into a mechanic's shop. While it was being worked on an elderly gentleman was walking by, taking his daily stroll and passed by the car very slowly. Then he paced back and forth behind the car, looking at the California license plate. After about 15 minutes he got up the courage to talk to me and asked if we lived in California. When I replied that we did, he said he had a niece living in California. Well, since California is a bit larger than Italy, I could have just dismissed this but being curious as I am, I asked where in California, and he said Palo Alto. Then he said her last name was Germano. Well, I had heard that name before so I told him I was sure Carlo would know who he was talking about but he was inside paying the bill in the office. When Carlo came out and I told him of the conversation with the man, he said, of course he knew who the family was. The family was in partnership with the Rossi family in growing vegetables in Mtn. View. The Rossis are still good friends of ours. What a small world this is and all because of the California license plate.

In 1994 we tried to register the car here but they wanted proof of insurance and we would tell them where the car was kept and that we would get insurance there, but that didn't satisfy the DMV office so we couldn't get the sticker. After that we rented cars whenever we went to Italy.

When we went to Italy in 2001, we decided to bring the little FIAT back to California. By now it was a classic and was getting good mileage per gallon on the highway. One of my cousins had been in shipping, similar to FEDEX or UPS so he knew the ins and outs of shipping. Another cousin knew a towing company owner who could tow the car down to the port of Genova. Carlo and my cousin Mario drove down to Genova accompanied by the tow operator with the car on his truck and left the FIAT to be put into a container and shipped to Houston, Texas as it would be cheaper than sending it to San Francisco. Another funny coincidence, the towing company owner's last name was Piombo. Carlo's dad was friends with the man whose company paved some parts of Hiway 101, made the Union Square Garage in San Francisco and parts of the Bay bridge. The tow owner said it was his uncle and he was really happy to know that Carlo knew him. Also the uncle was the one who had the exact same Buick in 1938 and came to see Carlo's family in Pontinvrea.

Mario told me to check on the internet to see when the ship would be arriving in Houston, perhaps in a month's time. We had never been to Texas so we planned to drive to Houston, rent a car trailer and then drive back with the FIAT on the trailer. About a month after the car left Genova I checked on the internet and, oh, my gosh, the ship was arriving in Houston in about three days. If we didn't claim the container, they would charge us storage. We quickly made plans to drive down after getting information from the shipping company. We first called the shipping line and were informed that we had to go to a port nearest us, which was Long Beach and pay cash for the shipping. We left on a Wednesday driving down through Southern California, stopping in Long Beach, then stopping overnight in Palm Springs. Then we drove through Arizona and New Mexico. Through Arizona and New Mexico we kept seeing signs warning us not to pick up hitchhikers. I didn't understand this until we passed some signs informing us we were near a prison. There are quite a few prisons along this highway

We spent the next night in El Paso, Texas at the Holiday Inn. There were only two rooms left, both over $100.00 but it was around 9:00 at night and we were tired so we took it. It was a huge room with access to the special bar which was reserved for the people on the 2nd floor, however because of the late hour, it was closed. We were able to go down to the regular bar and have whatever we wanted on the house. The next morning we would be able to have a full breakfast in this 2nd floor bar and it was included in the price. We also had a fish bowl on the nightstand with a beautiful fish, a dark blue fish whose name was Georgie. It had a sign on the bowl that it was there to keep us company if we were lonely. We arrived in Houston on Friday, having driven all day across desert and sage brush and not too much to look at. The next morning we drove to the customs office and signed for the container and then drove to the port. The locked container was unlocked in our presence and there was the little FIAT. Carlo had also put a special cargo in the car's trunk. When we were in Italy, we bought about five boxes weighing about two kilos each of amaretti cookies from Sassello. These are the best macaroons we have ever eaten so now we had enough to give some as gifts and to eat to our heart's content. Since we were driving a truck, a Dodge Ram 2500, I felt comfortable driving it but I didn't like the idea of driving it and pulling a trailer. Since our son was still working for United and had passes, he flew to Houston so he could help drive back home. They drove me to the airport on Sunday and I was able to fly back home on his pass in first class which was not too shabby.

Relatives in Italy ask us if we still have the little FIAT and Carlo smiles and says "Of course." He loves driving his "toy" especially on the road when someone will honk their horn and give him a "thumbs up" sign.

28

SENIOR PRANKS

When June rolled around, I thought about graduation time for seniors and of course the senior pranks that sometimes happen. Our daughter, Marina, was one who committed a senior prank. She told us of her plans and at first I thought, "Horrors! Our little, sweet girl, who was a good student, was going to be doing a senior prank." All I could think of was that she would be caught and not be able to graduate. Well, she had thought about everything. She would not destroy anything, hurt anyone and in the end the school would benefit from what she did. Some of the pranks we had heard about was putting glue in the locks of all the classroom doors, resulting in many man hours to correct this and also at one of the local high schools one year students pushed one of the school trucks into the swimming pool damaging the pool and of course the truck.

She wanted to spray paint huge footprints going into the school campus and then dump a load of manure between two of the footprints. First, she made two huge stencil cutouts of footprints, one for the left foot and one for the right foot, which were more than two feet long. We had a 1955 Chevy dump truck which had been used by Carlo's parents when they had the nursery. We also were customers of Edelwiss Dairy while we had the deli business so she asked if Carlo could go and get a load of manure, which he did and it was given to us free of charge. Then on the night which she had chosen to carry out this prank, she and two of her friends, Katy Haggerty and Lorraine Escover, got up at two in the morning and drove with their load up to the school, St. Francis High School.

Becky McIntosh was supposed to join them but her mother wouldn't let her do it.

They drove onto the campus with the noisy, old dump truck and got off and started spraying the big feet in a line up to the quad area. Then they unloaded the manure, spray painted the last two feet on either side of the manure pile and planted a sign in the pile which said, "From the class that stomps hard."

Katy was squealing and saying nervously, "Hurry, hurry, hurry, we are going to get caught." The Brothers of the Holy Cross live on the campus so it was a miracle they did not hear them.

Meanwhile, Carlo and I were not able to sleep and we were worrying about them. We were so happy when we heard the sound of the truck pulling into our court about one and a half hours later. We did not hear sounds of sirens following them so we relaxed and heard all about it from Marina before we all dropped off to sleep.

That morning, some of the first students and faculty to arrive saw the prank and thought it was pretty funny. The custodians immediately began hosing off the footprints as it was water soluble paint. They carted off the manure which was a benefit to them as it was used around all the beautiful camellias which landscape the campus.

The dean of students, Father Bitterman, began asking around as to who could have committed this prank and he asked some boys, "Which boy committed this prank?" Someone who knew Marina did it replied, "What makes you think it was a boy?" Father Bitterman immediately put two and two together because he knew we had a dump truck. Although he figured out who did it, he didn't say anything until graduation.

On graduation day, Marina went up to receive her diploma, returned to her chair and opened her diploma. Oh, my gosh! There wasn't a diploma in the holder. Instead of a diploma, there was a piece of parchment with a big red footprint on it. It was signed, "Marina, I have your diploma, see me after the ceremony. From the Dean that stomps harder. Father Bitterman." Was she going to get her diploma? Was she going to be punished? All these thoughts were going around in her head. She could not imagine what was going to happen.

After the ceremony she found Father Bitterman and he handed her the real diploma and just wanted to let her know that he knew who did it and it was pretty clever without ruining anything. Katy also received the same red footprint as he figured that out but he did not know about Lorraine and she was jealous that she did not get the coveted red footprint.

Two years later our son Marco, not wanting to be outdone, also wanted to pull a senior prank, and we helped him also. He had me paint a sign on a piece of 4' x 8' piece of plywood. The sign read, "FOR SALE - SAINT FRANCIS HIGH SCHOOL Brothers of the Holy Cross Realty and the phone number." He also went in the dead of night to plant this sign in front of the school near the street. The school received a few phone calls before the sign was taken down.

Carlo and I are so glad that Marina and Marco thought about these pranks so that they would not damage property and hurt others and also for the fact that they talked to us first. I guess that's what communication is all about.

29

SO MANY TREASURED RELATIVES

Since I've written this story so that our descendants can somehow know a bit about our family, I will start with the Marenco side of the family, since that is the family name.

Carlo's paternal great grandparents were Giovanni Marenco and Caterina Baccino and that is all we know about them. Carlo's grandmother's parents were Antonio Gambetta and Caterina Zunino. I will write more about the Gambetta-Zunino side later on. His paternal grandparents were the ones that had 13 cildren, the last two which died as young children. So I will start with the ones I know. Carlo's grandfather was Antonio Marenco, born in 1854 and died on Christma Eve, 1939. His grandmother was Maria Gambetta, born in 1858 and died in 1932. Carlo remembers meeting his grandfather when he was three years old and in Italy.

His father had the big black Buick and his grandfather was so proud that his son was doing so well in America. Whenever they went somewhere, Antonio would be sitting in the front seat with his cane in front of him and his hands resting on the top of the cane.

The first child they had was Angelina Marenco, born in 1876 She had four children, Maria Luisa, Ivana, Valentina and Piero. We don't have any information on whom she married and when she died. She went to France and one of the cousins gave me the information we have. The second child was Maddalena Marenco, born in 1878 and married Carlo Lepra. Maddalena who was called "Manin" was called to come to San Francisco by the fourth born Pietro. She came over with the third born, Giuseppe Marenco in November 1912. Her daughter, Emma Lepra remained in Italy with her father until the following year and arrived in America on September 26, 1912. Emma was 12 years old. I met Emma in Santa Rosa when she was about 80 years old and she had a mind that was as sharp as a tack. Emma married Charlie Leiduano who had an automotive repair shop and later they had a resort/cottages on the Russian River in Guerneville. She and Charlie Leiduano had a daughter named Aida and when I met Emma she was a widow. She drove a car and she was still pruning the many rose bushes on her property along with many fruit trees. A person could learn many things from listening to Emma. She was always reading books from the library in Santa Rosa and she would get the books with large print. Emma's mother Manin died in San Francisco in 1928 and was buried in the Holy Cross Cemetery in Colma. Manin's husband Carlo Lepra returned to Italy and married Carolina Zunino, the washer woman in Pontinvrea who always had a bandana tied around her head. She lived across the river and we would access her property by traversing over a swaying wooden and rope bridge.

Pietro Marenco was the fourth child born in the Marenco family and was the first to come to America on March 20, 1907. Pietro was born in 1883 and married Rosin Rivera. They had three children, Josephone born in 1916, Pierina born in 1919 and Roy Marenco born in 1923.

We met Josephine in Fort Bragg along with her daughter and son-in-law, Jackie and Frank Bertoni. We also met Roy Marenco and his wife Virginia once in Gardenerville, Nevada. Roy has ten children (six girls and four boys). Of all these children and grandchildren, I think there are only two or three boys in this family to carry the Marenco name. Just recently for Thanksgiving 2009, we were able to spend Thanksgiving Day with much of Roy's family at their son's home in Gardenerville. We were invited along with Marina and Bill and there were 34 or us in all. It was a memorable day spent with relatives we had not met before.

Giovanni was the third child born in 1881 and came to America by himself in 1922 leaving his wife and four children behind in Italy. He died in 1937 and is buried with his sister, Manin, in the Holy Cross Cemetery. His children were Maria, Aurelio, Pierina and Gino. They were living in Murta, a suburb of Genova.

The fifth child born of Antonio and Maria Marenco was Teresa who was born in 1886 and later married Ignacio Biale. She was the sibling who had the most children, five. Our children remembered meeting her in 1969 in Pianbotello where she was for the summer. It was a hot day but she was next to the cast iron stove which was lit and she was bundled up in black clothes and a black shawl. We also met her oldest child during that visit who was Marie along with Marie's daughter, son-in-law and two grand children. Marie had gone to France and married Henri Mitteau. Their daughter Danielle, born in 1931, also married a Frenchman, Jacques Nugues, and they had two children then, Jean Philip and Didier. Later they had another boy, Michel. Jean Philip has three boys and Didier has one son and a daughter. I do not know if Michel has children. He was born in 1971. As long as Teresa was alive, the French part of the family would go every summer to Italy to be with relatives and that is when we met the French relatives in 1969.

Teresa then had Giovanni Biale, born in 1910 and married to
Rina Olcese. They had one son Franco Biale, born in 1938 and
married to Laura Barrozzi. Franco and Laura had one daughter,
Paola who was just two years old when we went to Italy with the
children in 1969. Didier, from France was also the same age then.
Paola is now married and has two daughters Camilla and Carlotta.
Giovanni was a great mushroom hunter. He would go into the
woods, stop and sniff the air and say "There are mushrooms near."
He also loved to fish for trout. Giovanni and Rina lived in Bolzaneto, a suburb of Genova but they would spend the entire summer
in Pontinvrea where they had their second home and he could
plant a beautiful vegetable garden and fish and hunt for mushrooms. His wife was a great cook and we had dinner with them
quite often. She would ask what we wanted and we would always
say that we loved their polenta and fresh porcini mushrooms.
They were embarrassed to serve us peasant food so in addition to
this filling feast, she would also make raviolis. Their son, Franco,
unfortunately died at the age of 67 a few years ago. We always
enjoyed visiting with him.

Teresa's third child is Luigi Biale, born in 1912 and married to
Lina Marini. Luigi is a kind, quiet, calm man and still living by himself in a suburb of Genova called Bolzaneto. He is now 98 years old
and has a daughter Maria Enrica married to Bruno Lantero and
they have a daughter Marta who was born in 1990. Luigi and his
wife Lina came to visit us in February 1981. We had the deli then
and I was calling the airlines to see if their plane was on time so we
could pick them up. It was supposed to get in around 9:00 p.m. in
San Francisco. When I checked and said the flight originated in
Milano with a connection in New York, I was told that the flight
arrived late in New York so they missed the connection. Neither
Luigi nor Lina spoke English and I was worried for them. I tried to
find out if they were on the next flight to San Francisco and I was
told that they could not give out that information. When I finally

explained the situation, they told me that they actually missed two flights and were on the third one to S.F. But, they told me that a Luigi Biale was on the flight accompanied by a Lina Marini. I didn't recognize the name at the time and wondered who he was traveling with. I did not realize that Italian ladies keep their maiden names for life. When we went to pick them up at the airport it was 1:00 in the morning. Luigi and Lina thought no one would be there to pick them up as they had missed the flights. When they saw us, they had tears in their eyes because they were so happy. They stayed with us for three weeks and we tried to show them a bit of California, such as San Francisco, Lake Tahoe, Carmel and Monterey. Lina died of an aneurysm a couple of years later and Luigi came again to visit when Carlo's mother celebrated her 80th birthday in 1988. That time Luigi stayed for three months.

Teresa's fourth child was Emma, born in 1914 and married to Paolo Lagana, a Neopolitan. They had one daughter Ivana married to Luigi Verdi. Ivana and Gigi have two children, Lorenzo and Elisa. Elisa is married and has two daughters, Alice and Serena. Lorenzo married in June 2008 and we attended the wedding.

Teresa's fifth child is Pierina, born in 1916 and she married someone by the last name of Morando. They had one daughter named Maria Teresa born in 1937. Mr. Morando served in the war and died during World War II. Then Pierina married Franco Ferrighetti. We met Franco and visited with him and Pierina numerous times. Franco was a very thin man who loved to smoke and he was always a lot of fun. He didn't eat much but he loved to eat salame. He later developed emphysema and died in 2002. Pierina's daughter, Maria Teresa has two sons, one is Luca who is a doctor of urology and Gian Pietro who is a sports writer for a sports newspaper. Maria Teresa's husband Pietro Timossi died in 2005.

The sixth child of Antonio and Maria Marenco was Giuseppe or Beppe Marenco. He also came to America in 1912. He married

Maria Drocco who was a widow and had three sons, Charlie, Eddie and John, so they didn't have any children from their union. They lived in Redwood City on Orchard Street and Carlo would spend some summer vacations with them when his parents were still in San Francisco.

The seventh child was Edoardo Marenco whom I met in Italy. He was a warm, kind, person and seemed like a gentle giant. At the time I met him, he and his wife Aurelia were living in Murta which was situated on a hill so if you stepped out of their doorway, you either had to go up or down. The only flat piece of land was the piazza in front of the church. Zio Edoardo said that if you had chickens, you had to put diapers on them so that the eggs wouldn't roll down the hill. Zio Edoardo was unofficially the town's "fixit" person. Everyone brought problems or broken items to be repaired to Edoardo. He had two sons, Bruno, a handsome man, born in 1921 and who died in 1985 of a brain tumor. Bruno had one daughter, Maura, a beautiful girl born in 1948 and died also of a brain tumor in 1995. Bruno, Maura, Carlo and our daughter Marina all have the "Marenco dark eyes". Edoardo also had another son, Aldo who had one daughter Rosanna. Aldo also died too young at the age of 58 in 1983 of a heart attack. His daughter Rosanna came to America for a visit in 1981 and we always enjoy her company when we go to Italy. Rosanna married Franco Zunino of Pontinvrea and they have one son, Marco who was born in 1991.

The eighth child of Antonio and Maria Marenco was Luigi Marenco, born in 1893 and he married Caterina Castagna and they had two sons, Roberto and Walter Marenco. Luigi went to Argentina with his family and he died there. We have not kept in touch with anyone of this family.

The ninth child was Caterina Marenco, born in 1895 who also went to France and married Francois Quillerou. They had no children and Caterina died in 1984.

The tenth child was my father-in-law Marco Marenco, born in 1898. He came to America in 1921 aboard the Arabia which landed in Boston so he did not go through Ellis Island. He married Lucresia Gillio in 1927 in San Francisco and they had one son, my husband Carlo born in 1934.

The eleventh child was Adolfo Marenco, born in 1900 and married to Santina. They had three children, Maria Rosa born in 1923 and died in 1945, Antonio born in 1925 and died in 2003, Tulio born in 1933 and died in a motorcycle accident in 2008 Maria Rosa was married to Francesco Margiocco and they had one child, Mario Margiocco, born in 1945. He was just a baby when his mother, Maria Rosa died so he was basically raised by his grandmother Santina until his father remarried. Everyone said that Maria Rosa was a beautiful, caring young lady. Mario, or Marino as we know him is a journalist for the "Il Sole, 24 Ore" newspaper in Milano. He has three children, Francesco, Silvia, and Marta. Francesco married in September of 2008 and had a child named Giovanni in 2009.

The last two children of Antonio and Maria Marenco were Ignacio born in 1902 and Marinin born in 1903. They both died in 1907.

There are no surviving children of Antonio and Maria, but there are many descendants in this family, both in America, Italy and France. When we go to Italy, we never have enough time to go and visit all of them, so we make it simple by asking them to meet us in a central location, such as a restaurant so that we can visit with all of them.

When we went in 2008 there were 14 of us and in 2009 there were only 10. We always manage to go to the restaurant "Arvigo" which is on a hilltop in Cremeno. This is our favorite place and the food is outstanding. Reservations are required. The restaurant is at the end of the winding road and sometimes you have to jocky for a parking place. The only other building besides the restaurant is a church. It is also the end of the bus line.

Now since I have written about the Marenco side of Carlo's family I have to write about his mother's side which is the Allera family. I don't know too much about the family, but this is what I have gathered. My mother-in-law, Lucresia Marenco's grandparents were Domenico Allera born in 1854 and died in 1917 and Lucrezia Enrico Allera born in 1864 and died in 1924 who were from Ivrea, Italy. On the ship's manifest, their home town was listed as Colbreto and most of the family arrived on Ellis Island on August 18, 1906 aboard La Touraine. They settled in Vandergrift, Pennsylvania. The ones listed are the father, Domenico Allera who was 42 years old. The oldest child was Rosa Allera, but she is not listed with them. The next one is Caterina Allera but she isn't listed either. The third child is my mother-in-law's mother, Maria Allera and she is listed as being 19 years old and arrived with most of the family. The next four children were Luigi, Jasper, Vittoria and Marco. Some came in 1906 but I have to do more research as to when some of them came as I haven't confirmed the records of the mother so she may have come with some of the children separately from the father.

Allera family circa 1907 — left to right: Caterina, Gaspare, Vittoria, Luigi, Maria and Rosa — Seated, Lucrezia, Marco and Domenico Allera

Well, I met just three of the seven children. I met the oldest child, Rose who was my mother-in-law's aunt. I first met her when Carlo and I were about to get married and his grandmother (Rose's sister) died. Rose was already in her 70's and still very spry and energetic. I had heard stories about her and how she started a lingerie factory and would drive across the United States to New York to sell her wares to the big department stores. Lee would say that Aunt Rose always sent many beautiful items to her and her sister, Teresa. She was really a business woman. She was married to a man named Ralph Vacco and they had five children, Fred, Teresa, Norine, Lynette and Bobby. They lived in San Bernardino and Carlo and I stopped once to see them in 1959. Bobby had already died of a heart attack at a young age. Uncle Ralph played the trumpet and he didn't especially like to get his hands dirty so he was the one who cut the patterns for the lingerie. Once when he and Aunt Rose were driving somewhere, they got a flat tire on the car. Uncle Ralph told Aunt Rose to cover him up on the back seat of the car with a blanket and stand near the car. Someone saw Aunt Rose and seeing the flat tire, stopped and helped her fix the tire. Uncle Ralph didn't have to do a thing, the good samaritan did all the work.

The next child was Aunt Catherine born in 1885 and we don't know too much about her except that she had a daughter named Mary. The third child was Carlo's grandmother, Maria Allera and she married Giacomo Gillio, born in 1874 in San Crato, Italy and died in 1944 in San Francisco. Maria was born in 1887 and she and Giacomo had three children, Teresa, Lucresia (Lee), and Joseph. Teresa died at the young age of 24 due to meningitis. She was married to Joseph Massara and they owned a small corner grocery store in San Francisco and they had no children. Joseph Massara later returned to Ivrea, Italy, remarried and had one daughter. Lee was born in 1908 and was named after her grandmother Lucrezia, but she hated the name so she was called Lee for most of her life. She died in February 2006 at the age of 97. Joseph was born in 1912 and died in 2002 at the age of 90. Joseph was married to Cesira (Jessie) Venturi and she died in March of 2010 after living in an assisted living facility for seven years. They had one daughter Sandra born in 1957 who was killed in an auto accident at the age of 18.

I have to insert a story now that we just learned about five years ago. We were sitting around the dinner table talking about family history when Lee related how her mother moved from Pennsylvania to San Francisco. She gathered up the three children and they were around the ages of 10 to 12 years of age and got on a train bound for San Francisco. The father, Giacomo was not with them. About halfway across the United States, another man whom they knew as Bartolomeo Rosetto joined up with them. He was from the same home town in Italy as Maria and he had been in Vandergrift also. So I guess this was about a wife and children leaving the husband and taking up with another man, but nothing was said in those days. They started life in San Francisco first on Francisco Street and Lee went to Daniel Webster School finishing the eighth grade. Neither she nor Teresa went to high school. They both got jobs in the laundry and then Teresa got married at a young age to Joe Massara.

The fourth child in the Allera family is Luigi born in 1889 and died in 1949 who had six children, Katy, Nora, Dominic, Mabel, Jack and Jim. Luigi married Rosina Quilico born in 1895 and she died in 1932 when Jack was 10 and Jim was 5 so their Aunt Vittoria took over the job of raising Jack and Jim. Katy was already married and the other three children were old enough to take care of themselves. Katy was married to John Bonessa and moved to San Jose from Pennsylvania and they had three children, Rosemary, Frank and Louis. We were very close to this family and still are. John and Katy are both dead. Rosemary lives in Elk Grove, married to Bill Crawford and they have two children, Ken and Nancy. Ken is married to Shannon and they have two boys, Colin and Cody. Frank was killed in a motorcycle accident and Louis is married to Sandy and they live in Morgan Hill. Louis and Sandy have two children, Susy who has two girls and Louis who has two boys. Sandy and Lou have owned Bonessa Brothers RV and Campers for many years. We always enjoy visiting with these cousins.

We met but never really visited much with four of Luigi's other children but we did meet Jack and his wife Thelma of Pennsylvania and got along so well from the very beginning, it seemed as if we had known them for years. It happened one year when Jack and Thelma were going to fly out to the Reno, Nevada area because their daughter and son were going to rent a cabin in the Lake Tahoe area for a ski week and they wanted to meet us. They said that they were going to rent a car and come to San Jose to stay with Jack's sister Katy. We suggested that we could go up to Tahoe where we had a cabin and we could get together with them, have them stay with us and then drive them to San Jose. We did so and Carlo and Jack skied together and it seemed as if we had known them for years. We really had a fun time. A few years later we went back to the East coast to a wedding and then stopped to see Jack and Thelma and stayed with them for the weekend. We also met Jim and his wife Lureen that weekend. Jack was still skiing at the age of 80 plus and died a few years later. He and Thelma had two children, Jackie and Randy.

The next sibling was Gaspare or Jasper born in 1891 and died in 1968 who married Mary. They had two daughters, Olga and Elda. Carlo and I met all of them except Elda. Lee always said many good things about Uncle Jasper and how he would always be so patient with the nieces and nephews and taught them many things, just common sense, everyday things.

The next sibling was Vittoria born in 1895 who married Pasquale Bella and they had two sons, Adolf and Domenic.

The last sibling was Mark, born in 1898 and married Eve who was of Polish descent. They did not have any children. Mark wasn't too proud of his Italian heritage and told nieces and nephews that when they saw him on the street, they were not to greet him and to please walk on the other side of the street. I guess Italians were too boisterous and loud for his liking, but that is how many of us are.

30

THE LAST THREE (SO FAR) TRIPS TO ITALY

In the spring of 2007 one of our friends who is a travel agent contacted us about going on a bus tour to the area south of Rome in Italy. Since we had never been to that part of Italy and we were planning to go that year, we decided to join this group for a two week bus tour in Southern Italy and Sicily. We decided to go two weeks ahead of the group so that we could spend time with our relatives. We began by flying from San Francisco to London and then on to Milano. We arrived in Milano around 6:00 p.m. on Thursday, August 30, and my cousin Rosanna and her husband Dalmo were there to meet us. We rented a car and then followed them to the cascina where I went with my mother for the first time to Italy more than 50 years ago. We arrived at the cascina around 8:30 p.m. and Rosita and her mother Zia Pina were there and also Rosanna's son Paolo, daughter Laura and son-in-law Marco were there waiting for us. They had a light dinner of soup, prosciutto and melon and salad waiting for us. It was a most welcome meal, but then we heard thunder rolling overhead. The thunder got very loud and crashing at times, lightning striking and rain started to come down in buckets. Oh, well, we were safe inside with nothing to worry. It thundered and rained all night. The next day, the sun came out and we were able to go into town as the road now has a covering of gravel. There were just a few spots of mud but we were able to go without any trouble. When we got back from town, two of my cousins from a city near Torino were there to welcome us to Italy. They are all retired so they took a ride out to the cascina to see us which really made us feel welcome. We would see them the following week at their home.

At the cascina living in the other half of the home were another cousin, age 88 and her daughter. They are at the cascina during the summer and they are company for my Zia Pina and Rosita.

On Saturday, we didn't do much and then Sunday morning we went to mass at the church in Quargnento. In the piazza of the church there was an auto show of the very old little FIAT 500 and also one of the FIAT Topolino cars. The Topolino was even smaller than the FIAT 500 and it was nice looking at these little cars. We met a cousin of mine on my father's side and he insisted we go to his house for an aperitif before lunch so we went for a quick visit as Rosanna and Dalmo were having us over for lunch at their house. We went to visit Gino Celerino and his wife and he showed us around his beautiful farm. He has all the latest John Deere tractors, some so huge I was amazed at the size. He also had huge round bales of hay stacked up and the courtyard of his farm was so neat it was beautiful. My cousin Dalmo said that Gino is the number one farmer in Quargnento and he has many holdings of land.

Monday was quiet and we just enjoyed visiting with my aunt and cousins. It was so peaceful at the cascina. We did have a threshing machine come to harvest the sunflower seeds that my cousin had planted so we watched that for a while. The machine looked like a combine and cut the stalks and separated the stalks from the heads of the sunflowers. The seeds went into a compartment and when the driver was finished he loaded the seeds into the back of a truck and that was driven into town to be weighed. Our cousin who lived in the other half of the cascina has a son-in-law who planted an expensive seed and his acreage yielded 4 1/2 times more than any other farmers in the area. He was on vacation so Rosita followed the truck into town. She didn't do as well with her acreage.

Tuesday we left the cascina for Torino around 3:00. It has been four days since it rained on Thursday evening. We went down the hill and made a left turn at the bottom and we saw my cousin Gino coming in his small Toyota pickup. The road is very narrow so we pulled over to the left side so he could pass us on our right. He waved and we started to go forward. Oh, oh, the car was stuck. The left front tire was mired in the mud which was covered by grass so we thought it was safe. Gino saw that we were stuck so he stopped and came back to help us. Gino and Carlo tried to push the front of the car back with me at the wheel. As soon as I stepped on the gas, the mud came up and splattered Carlo. What a mess and the car was still stuck. Gino said he would go up to the cascina and get a chain to pull us out with his truck. We tried that but it didn't work. Gino went back and asked my cousin Rosita to get the tractor and pull us out. Since there are no men at the cascina any more, Rosita has to do all the work that men would normally do so she got on the tractor and came to pull us out. This brought back memories of when I was there with my mother and after a rain, she and I had to walk about a mile and a half in the mud up to our ankles at 10:00 at night. It's strange how history repeats itself.

After getting the car unstuck, we went back to the cascina and Carlo got the hose out to clean the car a bit and also himself. We were only an hour late in leaving for Torino.

We arrived at another cousin's home just outside of Torino in Sangano. This cousin on my father's side is Marisa with her husband Beppe. These were the cousins that accompanied Marina and I when Marina was in the Marcialonga. They have a son, Luca and a daughter Elisabetta. That evening Marisa's two brothers, Mario and Piero and their spouses joined us. Also joining us were Piero's two sons Ricardo and Silvano and Silvano's girlfriend Gianna. Elisabetta's boyfriend Marco also joined us. There was quite a houseful of cousins and it was such fun with all the young people laughing, joking and just enjoying each other's company. It was one of our more enjoyable evenings.

The next day, Marisa and Beppe along with her brothers and spouses drove us up near the French border. It took two and a half hours to get to the town of Acceglio. I had never been there and it was where my and Marisa's grandparents came from. Marisa and Beppe had gone there two years ago and found where the original house was. I don't think the town has more than 100 people and is high up in the mountains. The air was cool but it was beautiful and clear. My grandmother had 3 sisters and a brother. The siblings would walk over the border into France to work. It was no easy task to walk because I couldn't see any civilization from where I was standing.

We talked to some of the locals and they remember the family name of Baralis so it was nice seeing the ancestral home which has been fixed up. We don't know of any other relatives remaining in the town and there was no one home so we couldn't see what the home was like inside but it was nice just to be able to know where it is.

While in Sangano we went to Torino to visit the Parco del Valentino and also the Egyptian Museum which is second only to the museum in Cairo. We only stayed there for a couple of hours. We also went up to see the Basilica of Superga where in 1946 a plane carrying the world champion soccer team of Italy crashed into the side of the basilica killing all aboard. The view from Superga is a 360 degree view of the city of Torino and the Alps to the north of the citty.

We stayed with Marisa and Beppe until Saturday and then we headed for Sassello where we would see Carlo's relatives.

Saturday we headed toward Sassello which is a small town northwest of Genova. Carlo's father was born just about 15 kilometers from Sassello in a town called Pontinvrea. In Sassello there is a cousin named Gianna who with her husband Rinaldo owns a water-driven grist mill which is about 400 years old. They grind all kinds of grains for such things as flour, cornmeal, etc. If there is not enough water in the river it does run by electricity. The stone ground cornmeal for polenta is the best we have tasted, especially when it is ground from freshly harvested corn. They also have a store which sells fertilizer, large bags of animal food for dogs, cats, goats, rabbits, etc. There are some groceries such as oils, vinegar, pasta, cookies, fruits and vegetables. Just the basics. Rinaldo drives to the province of Cuneo which is about two hours away at least once or twice a week to get large bins of fruits and vegetables. Also in Italy a person cannot go into a grocery store and help themselves to fruits and vegetables. The employees or owners have to serve them and weigh and bag the products and there is usually a sign telling people not to handle the fruits and vegetables. Needless to say, they are quite busy if there are 8 to 10 people waiting to be helped and all want to buy some fruits or vegetables. They are closed on Sunday and Thursday afternoons. This is a breather for Gianna and Rinaldo. Rinaldo's sister and husband who live in the coastal town of Albisola come up for the summer as she is a school teacher and they help them with the store. Since they had returned to their home because she went back to teaching, they let us use their apartment which is attached to Gianna's apartment so we were free to come and go as we pleased.

During the days we were in Sassello we visited with people we knew from our previous visits and we also went to Genova to see our many relatives - about 20 and we had a group lunch with them which is easier than visiting each family at their homes.

Sassello is famous for their amaretti cookies of which there are five factories. These are not like the amaretti cookies of Sarrono which are hard. The amaretti of Sassello are almond cookies which are softer, similar to macaroons. Years ago in the 1990s when Frank Sinatra visited Milano, he tasted these cookies and called the factory "Virginia" and told the owner he would send his limo driver for a large order of cookies. The owner immediately said, "Oh no, sir, we will be glad to deliver them ourselves to Milano to you." I am sure he wanted to meet Frank Sinatra himself.

One evening Rinaldo's sister, Rina and her husband, Luca, wanted to treat us to an all fish dinner in Albisola so the four of us met them and went out to dinner. When we got there the restaurant was empty and it was around 7:30. My thoughts were, "I wonder if this place is good?" I need not have worried because within an hour the restaurant was full and it was a Tuesday evening. Rina suggested that we order hors d'oeuvres first and then if we wanted more we could order more. All the antipasti were served on little platters of one or two dishes at a time and there were eleven of them. They were: focacciette which are little focaccias, mixture of vegetables, seafood salad, marinated sardines, fish fried in a marinade, mussels, carpaccio of smoked tuna, fritters with borage, little balls of fried calamari, stuffed calamari and also a frittata of little white fish which are no longer than three inches long. After these antipasti we were stuffed so we did not order anything else except, of course dessert. I had a macedonia which is a dish of fruit with gelato. Carlo and Rina had tiramisu, Gianna had fresh pineapple with gelato, Rinaldo had sorbeto and Luca had biscotti which in that restaurant were called cantucci.

Since we were being hosted so well Carlo said he would cook lunch for Gianna and Rinaldo one day. He went to the city of Savona and found all he needed for a dinner of roasted duck breast with Port wine and cherry sauce. Since I talk to Gianna almost every week, I often talk about Carlo's cooking and she said before our trip that when we got there he could do some cooking for her. So he was prepared with his recipe and dried cherries and was hoping he could find the duck breasts. There are now large super markets similar to Costco where one can find almost anything under the sun so he didn't have any trouble and the lunch turned out to be a delicious meal. Their son Diego and his girlfriend also joined us.

The next day we left Gianna and Rinaldo and drove to Genova to stay one night with another cousin who works for the newspaper "Il Sole 24 Ore", which is similar to our Wall Street Journal. We always enjoy visiting Mario and his wife Mariu as he is so interesting. We first met him when he was in the United States on a Fullbright scholarship at the University of New Mexico in Albuquerque in the early 70's and came to visit us during Easter break. The following year he went to Notre Dame in Indiana for one year so he speaks English very well and has a lovely family. Mario had been to the U.S. a few times to report on political topics and has visited us twice. The next morning we had to catch our flight to Rome from the Cristofero Colombo Airport in Genova. Mario drove ahead of us to show us the way and then we said our good-byes.

We arrived in Rome and met up with a representative of Insight Vacations who was gathering more of the people on the tour. We sat next to a couple from Vancouver while we waited for everyone to get together and immediately enjoyed their company. We already knew five of the other people on the tour because two of the ladies are Carlo's godparents' daughters and one is the travel agent. She organized a group of fifteen people all together to do this tour which would be all south of Rome and included Sicily. We were taken to our hotel, the Crown Plaza St. Peters. I thought since it mentioned St. Peters we would be near the Vatican — Wrong! It was just named that. It was actually about a mile from the Vatican, but that was OK as the traffic could be a bear. We all met around 5:00 for a cocktail party and were given information about where we would be going, etc. Then we all got on the bus to be taken out to dinner. The Insight Vacation buses are very large and have a lot of leg room as they have taken out ten seats from the normal fifty and have only forty seats. They are air-conditioned and very comfortable. The tour director or "guide" and the bus driver were with us for the entire two weeks. We had never been on a guided tour of this duration so we didn't know what to expect. Carlo was happy he didn't have to drive.

We were going to dinner at a large restaurant which seats 800 people, (600 outside under the olive trees and grape arbors.) This restaurant is called La Caravana was just a short distance from the hotel and it was a lovely evening with beautiful weather. We all left for dinner aboard the bus and the bus driver started to go down a narrow one-way street which he had done many times before but this time cars were parked on both sides of the street, which they were only supposed to park on one side. Oh, well, this was Italy and this happens. The driver went about half way down the street and stopped. The road was too narrow with some cars a few inches into the road. He stopped and then he could not back up because about 20 or 30 cars were already lined up behind the bus. I figured we would soon have many drivers honking their horns and waving their fists in the air. Instead, it was amazing. No one honked their horns and some of the drivers got out of their cars and came up to the driver to see what was wrong. When they saw the situation, they rolled up their sleeves and three or four men went to the front of the first car and some to the rear of the car and as if to pick up the car, counted as they bounced the car and on the count of three they moved the car about 6 inches toward the building. They did the same thing to four of the offending cars. Then the bus was able to move down the street. I keep thinking what the owners of the cars thought when they returned to their cars and found they couldn't get into their cars on the driver's side as they were too close to the buildings. Funny, it wasn't how they left their cars.

We arrived at the restaurant about a half hour later than our reservations but — no problem! We had a tour of the kitchen with two of the tourists (Carlo being one of them) given a chance to flip the big frying pan as the chef did. We had a delicious dinner and we were entertained by a trio of singers and musicians. On the way back to the hotel, the bus driver took us on a short tour of Rome at night to see the Coliseum, the Monument to Vittorio Emmaneul, the Forum and some other sights.

The next morning as during the duration of the tour we were given a wake-up call at 6:30. Our bags had to be out by 7:00 and we were on the bus by 8:00. We left for Alberobello which is in the region of Puglia. We stopped for 15 minutes for a break for coffee at one of the Auto Grills along the highway where you can buy food and drinks, use the restrooms, get gas, etc. Then we stopped again for lunch which was for 1/2 hour. We got to our hotel at 3:15 so it was a long ride during which time the tour director talked about the area and the history of the countryside and where we would be going for dinner that evening. The tour director looked like a Scandinavian, spoke English perfectly and also spoke Italian perfectly. I asked if she was Scandinavian, English or what and she replied that she was a native of New Zealand and had lived in Rome for the last five years. She also informed us that it was she and not the tour company who picked the restaurants we would be patronizing and she arranged the tours we would go on. So, it isn't that easy being a tour guide. They have to arrange everything and print out maps, instructions, etc. They also take care of the tipping of the hotel personnel when they handle our bags from the bus to the rooms and back again to the bus. She also was with us for the two weeks without a day off. The bus driver got a day off because that is the law in Italy. He was with us but didn't have to drive. A relief driver came on and drove for the day.

In Alberobello there are the homes known as Trulli. They seem like a beehive to me as they are all white on the bottom part and then the conical shaped roofs are made of stone without any mortar or cement holding the stones. I think they are so different, they are fascinating. It was said that the roofs are such because when the tax assessor came around, the people would dismantle the roofs and they would show the assessor that they didn't have a finished home so they couldn't tax them.

We took a short walking tour and then rested a bit before going out to dinner. Carlo felt that he was getting an attack of gout in his right hand.

That evening the bus took us to a farm house which had been run by an order of nuns, then sold and is now an agriturismo. This means that there are rooms for rent and most of the food is grown on the farm for the guests. We walked past the pens of pigs, sheep, chickens, ducks and we also saw a beautiful swimming pool.

We had another delicious dinner. For dessert we had macedonia which is mixed fruit and then a shot of Limoncello which was the beginning of having Limoncello at the end of most of our dinners. No wonder as there are huge groves of lemons and also olives in the southern part of Italy. Limoncello is a delicious liquor which can also be made at home.

The next day we went on a tour of Matera or "Sassi di Matera" which is the town of the cave dwellers or stone houses. The sassi are houses dug into the rock itself, known locally as "tufo" or limestone. This settlement is suspected to be the first human settlement in Italy. During the 1950's the premier of Italy, Di Gaspari, was horrified that there were people still living in caves like these in Italy. The residents were living in one-room houses along with perhaps a donkey, chickens, children. He ordered the government to forcefully relocate the population of the Sassi to areas of the developing modern city. However, the people continued to live in the Sassi. Mel Gibson's movie "The Passion" was filmed in Matera as it looks so much like old Jerusalem. In the afternoon we went to tour the white city known as Ostuni. It looks like a Greek City with the buildings painted white with blue doors and shutters. I was getting very tired from walking by the end of the day. That evening our group ate at the hotel restaurant and Carlo was really suffering with his gout.

The next morning one group went to see the caves but we decided not to go. The two tours the day before did us in so we slept in. Our bus would be leaving at 9:30 for Crotone. It was a six-hour drive to Crotone and there wasn't much to see there. It was just a stopover on our way to Sicily. However, our hotel was right near the ocean and our room overlooked the pool and the ocean. We had a buffet dinner in the hotel. We would be leaving for Sicily the next morning.

We left Wednesday morning for Sicily and arrived at the dock for the ferry at 11:30. The ferry took 20 minutes to go across the straits of Messina. Then the bus took us to a smaller bus so that we could go to the city of Taormina because our bus was too large. We took a short tour of an old Greek theater which is still being used for some events. Then we went back to the hotel and went to dinner in the hotel. The next morning we went up to Mt. Etna which is the volcano on the island of Sicily. Some of the people climbed up a little ways up the sides and peered into a crater. The lava was crumbly and slippery so I didn't go as I was not that steady on my feet. Carlo went and took some videos. There was a small eruption just a couple of weeks before we visited Etna and you could still see a lot of the ash lying around the cities. There were about three or four small restaurants where one could get some food and as it was lunch time of course we did so also. However, this time it would have been better if we hadn't.

We had a very dear Sicilian friend, John De Cofano for many years and he introduced us to a Sicilian food called "arancini" which means little oranges. The story was that he couldn't marry his love, Barbara, until she proved to have the right sized hand to make arancini. The way they are made is to boil some rice, place a small scoop of rice into the hand, make an indentation in the rice and place some spaghetti sauce in the indentation along with three cooked peas, a small cube of mozzarella cheese and then put some more rice on top and shape this into a small ball. Then the ball or "orange" would be rolled into beaten egg and coated with bread crumbs and then fried until it all turned a golden orange color. John would say that his wife Barbara had the perfect sized hand to make arancini so his father let them get married. We tasted these about 25 years ago. Well, there were many places that advertised arancini so we decided to try them again to see if they were as good as the ones Barbara made. Well, we were disappointed. The rice was very sticky and starchy and there wasn't any filling. Later that afternoon, I had heartburn and it was the only thing we ate for lunch.

That evening we went to a dinner at a restaurant called El Feudo or The feud. We had a delicious dinner of several antipasti, ravioli al pistachio, then chicken wrapped in lemon leaves, pork shin, little rolls of sausage and roasted potatoes and cannoli, which were very yummy for dessert. We were entertained by two musicians, one an accordionist and one a guitarist and they sang many native Sicilian songs which are usually about women and love. They were very good and we had a lot of fun.

On Friday we went to Agrigento which is in the southern part of Sicily and we saw the Valley of the Temples. These temples made us feel as if we were in Greece. They were beautiful and we had a very good guide from the area. After the tour of about 90 minutes it was time for lunch. You are probably thinking that all we did was eat. Well, you are right. There was a little bar and we only had about 1/2 hour before we went back to the hotel and there were some arancini again in the food case. Carlo said we should try again to see if these were better than the last ones. We did try them and they were delicious. They were filled as they should be and now I can tell our friend Barbara that there must be someone else with the right sized hand.

We left for Palermo from Agrigento. Palermo is on the north side of Sicily so we actually crossed the island of Sicily to get to Palermo. That evening we all went to a restaurant near the hotel but we went by bus. After dinner we had to wait for the driver to bring the bus around for us to be taken back to the hotel. As we were waiting, the owner of the restaurant came up to the group and was talking to the tour director and Carlo and I were nearby. Carlo and I were just about the only ones who were fluent in Italian so we complimented the restaurant owner on the delicious meal. He was so happy and then he asked where we were from. When we replied, "California," he asked more questions and when we said, "near San Francisco" he said he worked for a while in San Jose, on 2nd Street at Palermo"s. I came back with "Oh, we know that restaurant and the owner is Renato Cusimano." He jumped back in amazement and said "He is my friend, I can't believe it!" Here we were 5,000 miles away from San Jose and we met someone who worked there. I think we left him very happy to be able to talk about his time here in California. Since this restaurant was so close to the hotel some of the people, Carlo included, decided to walk as the weather was just right. On the way back they stopped at a gelateria for another dessert or coffee. The gelato in Italy is so good that one feels as if they can't get enough.

The next day, Saturday, we visited some cathedrals and we went up to Mt. Pellegrino and Santa Rosalia's Grotto. The bus could not go all the way up to the Grotto and church so he dropped us off in a piazza and then we would have to walk up. We were given a choice of walking or taking a taxi up the short distance to the top. The price would be one Euro per person and five people could get into a taxi and be taken up. One taxi left with 5 people and 3 more of us got into a taxi to go up. The taxi didn't move. There was no one else around in the piazza and I asked him why we weren't moving. he said it didn't pay for him to just go with three people. Gas was expensive and he needed at least five people to make it worthwhile. He was going to wait until two more showed up. I told the other two people if they were willing to pay one more Euro I would also so he could get going and away we went. The taxi driver spoke the Sicilian dialect, which was a bit difficult to understand, but I did all right. He gave me a compliment, however, after asking if I was born in Italy and I explained that no, I wasn't, but I learned Italian from my parents.

The cathedral at the top was so ornate with gold leaf and mosaic, but very beautiful. Since the cathedrals are crowded with people the tour director gave us all an ear piece with a small receiver to wear and she would speak into a tiny microphone so that her talking wouldn't bother other people in the church. We could hear her explain everything and she would also tell us if she was moving into another area. I thought this was a good way for us to hear everything and not have to try to be in a group close to her.

That evening we went to a small town near Cefalu called Sferracavallo and we ate an all fish dinner at a restaurant called "La

Barca" or The Boat. This was the second all fish dinner we had in Italy and everything was delicious.

The next day was Sunday and we visited two more cathedrals in Cefalu. We were going to have a late lunch as we would be getting on an all night ferry trip to Naples from Palermo. We went to a farm house and ate lunch around 2:00 which lasted until about 4:00. We went to a harbor to load onto the ferry and we pulled out at 8:00. As the crossing to Naples would take twelve hours and we would be sleeping on the ferry, we were a bit apprehensive as to what the accommodations would be like. We were a bit surprised to find a small but nice cabin with bunk beds, bathroom facilities and a shower.

We didn't have anything to eat since we had a late lunch but if one wanted, there was a smack bar and small area where one could get something. Also, some young people who didn't want to pay for a cabin rented bedding and a deck chair where they slept for the night. The deck chairs were inside, not out on the deck. We arrived in Naples at 7:00 a.m. to a gorgeous sunrise.

The bus took us to the Hotel Medusa in Naples which was beautiful. Then off to a tour of the City of Pompeii which was buried almost 2,000 years ago when Mt. Vesuvius erupted. I enjoyed this tour very much to see how much there is to Pompeii. I had no idea how advanced the civilization was at that time. Then it seemed to go backward.

Later that evening which was a Monday, we had dinner at the hotel on the back patio. There was a rather large wedding inside the hotel and we could get a glimpse of the doings through the windows near our table. The drapes were sheer and we were interested in what was going on. At the end of our dinner we heard explosions which at first we thought was thunder. When we asked our waiter, he said that the fireworks were being shot off because of the wedding. This is the custom for weddings, baptism, babies being born, etc. The next evening we again saw fireworks from our hotel window around 11:30 at night and they were about three blocks from the hotel. Something was being celebrated again.

The next morning we awoke to rain. We were to tour a factory that made furniture and gift items with inlaid wood or "intarsio" and then in the afternoon we were to go to the Island of Capri and see the Blue Grotto. We decided to go to the factory as we would be inside and we were given a short talk on how the inlaid furniture and items were made. All the pieces were beautiful and we ended up buying something, a set of three nesting tables which finally arrived two days before Christmas. We decided to cancel the tour to Capri as we didn't want to be walking around in the rain and we wouldn't be able to go into the Blue Grotto because of the rain. Some of the people opted to go so the bus driver took one group back to the hotel and the others continued on with the tour. Our group was then on our own at the hotel and we found a restaurant nearby called "La Brace" or The Embers so 14 or us descended on the restaurant. We were just about the only ones there but it was good. Carlo and I had ravioli filled with fish and a cream sauce. Some of the ravioli pasta was streaked with black which meant that it was made from squid ink and they were delicious.

I forgot to mention that the Hotel Medusa was a really beautiful hotel with palm trees all around the grounds and inside the floors were covered in large tiles. Each floor had a different design in the hallways and into the rooms.

That evening was a relaxing evening as we were going back to Rome the next morning and then home after the day in Rome.

We arrived in Rome on Wednesday and went to visit St. Peter's basilica. Again our tour director used the personal hearing aids and her small microphone which was really useful in the basilica. There was such a difference from when we visited St. Peter's in 1969 with the children. Then we were there in August and tourists were able to walk freely in the basilica and cars and buses were able to park in St. Peter's Square. Now cars and buses are not allowed in the square and the basilica is so crowded and this was the end of September. There are now chairs for seating in the square and a platform with a canopy over it for the Pope. After visiting St. Peter's, we went to the Coliseum. Everyone was again told to use the hearing aids. The bus had to park about 1 1/2 blocks away and we were given directions on where and when to meet after we toured. We were also left on our own for about 1/2 hour. At the end of the tour and free time we were called back by the tour director. One of our group didn't like wearing the ear piece so he removed it and couldn't hear the guide. When we gathered to go back to the bus, John was missing. It was no use calling him as he wasn't wearing the earpiece. Three people went in search of John as they knew what he looked like. They came back without him. So we had to go to the bus as it would be waiting and the driver couldn't park too long where we were to meet him. John's wife and the tour director stayed behind to search for him and told the bus driver to make a loop around the block and then perhaps they would be back, if not they would take a taxi back to the hotel. The bus driver made two loops around the block and during the second one, he got a call on his two way radio that they had found John and would be back at the pick up point. We were all worried that they wouldn't find him with all the tourists but he was just at the wrong meeting place. If you are ever in that situation, wear your hearing aids, they come in handy.

That evening we all went to a restaurant called Papa Rex. Across from the restaurant there are some rather wide steps and the group gathered there and a commercial photographer took a photo of the group and as most tourists do, we bought the photo. Also when we entered the restaurant, there was a young man dressed up in a gladiator outfit and another photo was shot of us with the young man. The meal was good and again there were singers singing during the meal. That evening we said goodbye to all of our tour friends as we were the only ones leaving the hotel at five in the morning. The others had a later flight or they were continuing with travels of a few days or more. We got up at 4:00 and our driver was right on time at 5:00 to drive us to the airport. We flew to London and had a three hour layover, then we flew to San Francisco arriving at 5:00 in the afternoon. After a month of being away, it was great being home with many happy memories of Italy, our relatives, and spending two weeks with new friends, seeing new things, and enjoying all of it.

In February of 2008 we received word that one of Carlo's young cousins was getting married in June. With all the cousins we both have in Italy, you would think at one time or another we would have attended one of their weddings. Well, we hadn't so now was to time to celebrate with them. We met Lorenzo and his sister Elisa in 1986 and they were such nice children, we immediately took a liking to them. Elisa now was already married and had two little girls, Alice and Serena. Lorenzo's family, the Verdis were living in Genova but Lorenzo had been working near the city of Piacenza which was about a two-hour drive north of Genova. He met his future wife while working there and both worked in the environmental field.

We departed on Tuesday, June 17, and landed in Milano the next evening around 6:00. Since we would have to go through customs, rent a car, and drive one and a half hours to reach Zia Pina's home in Quargnento and then talk endlessly to relatives, we decided to stay overnight in Milano. Our travel agent suggested the Villa Malpensa near the airport. She said it was only five minutes away. That settled it. We called for the shuttle which arrived in five minutes and drove us to a beautifully renovated villa. The villa was the summer home of the Caproni family who were rich industrialists from nearby Milano. The family money dried up after WWII as the Italian government seized businesses and properties of fleeing Fascists. The Malpensa airport now covers a major portion of the original Caproni farm lands. This information immediately brought to mind the fact that the customs building my mother and I went through in 1953 really was like a chicken shack because of the white-washed windows all along the side wall. The new customs building had not been built yet. The goat is the symbol of the Caproni family and appears in many places in and around the hotel.

The next morning Carlo went to the airport to rent the car and when he returned to the hotel we started off for Quargnento. We arrived before lunch to once again be greeting by Zia Pina who is getting shorter and shorter and her daughter Rosita. They are always so welcoming. During the winter, until the weather warms up, they live in town not at the cascina. In town, their apartment had only one bedroom so we rented a room at the hotel which is right next door to their apartment. The hotel is now called I Quattro Gatti", or The Four Cats. We slept there but ate at Zia's house. The owner said she would give us a rate of 60 Euros because we were unofficially citizens of Quargnento because of my aunt. This was a savings of 10 Euros.

During the afternoon, my cousins from Torino all came to visit us as they knew we would be leaving the next day for the wedding and wouldn't be back for about ten days. With an extra six people in my Zia's apartment it was a bit crowded but my Zia always enjoys company.

The next afternoon we left for the town of Agazzani which is near Piacenza. It is a two hour drive east of Quargnento. The hotel "Il Cervo" (The Deer) which was designated for attendees of the wedding was in the town of Agazzani. The church was in the tiny suburb of Tuna. I had to take a photo of the sign of Tuna as I believe Tuna is the tiniest town in Texas and we had seen a play called Red, White, and Blue Tuna in San Francisco.

The hotel is a family-owned operation, very nice and clean and their restaurant was very good. The ceremony was to take place at 4:30 the next day, so we decided to roam around a bit that morning. There are many castles in the area and some are open to the public. The desk clerk gave us a map and circled the ones he knew to be open so we went exploring one of the castles which was close by.

We found Castello di Rivalta which was interesting. Some of the family members still live on the grounds. There are also little shops and eating establishments such as a gelateria, a bar, a restaurant, etc. It was a very warm day so before heading back, we had an aperitif, a Crodino which is a bitter over ice. Whenever one orders a drink at a bar or outdoor café, they also bring little dishes of nuts, chips, pretzels, etc. So we were set before the wedding. We returned to the hotel, rested for a while and then got ready to attend the wedding.

We arrived at the church and I was expecting a small wedding. We were surprised to see about 200 people milling around, many of them Carlo's relatives and all looking for a bit of shade under the trees. Soon we heard a motorcycle coming down the road with the horn blasting all the way. Lorenzo was riding on the back of the motorcycle in his wedding suit behind his friend and big smiles on their faces.

The ceremony was not formal like many of our weddings. There were no bridesmaids, no ushers, no wedding march. The choir situated behind the alter sang as the bride walked in on her father's arm with two little nieces in long white dresses preceding them. The two male witnesses were on either side of the aisle near the alter. The groom's sister was next to one of the male witnesses. The ceremony was an hour long and it was a bit uncomfortable in the church which did not have air conditioning. After the ceremony, the wedding party and some of the relatives got on a small sleek rental bus which held about 20 or 30 people. We all followed the bus to the reception.

The bride's family owns a farm which is being converted into a bed and breakfast or agriturismo. Agriturismos are gaining popularity in Italy and this one is also on the internet. It advertises that they raise animals (veal) and different grains and during harvest time one can help to harvest asparagus. So, here we were at the farm, it was almost 6:30 and white linen tablecloths were on tables set on the grass in front of the beautiful farm house. There were bushes or trees ringing the grassy area along with light standards to light the area. The place settings were beige straw chargers under the plates and the centerpieces were glass bowls holding greens, flowers and fat candles inside them. There were appetizers set up in two or three places with chefs cooking some of them on the spot. Then we sat down to a multi-course feast. One of the courses was a scallop shell containing slices of tiny octopus legs or tentacles marinated in oil and vinegar. They were about four of five inches long and delicious. The pasta course was similar to raviolis but instead of being squares or rounds of filled pasta, these were caramelle - squares of filled pasta and then the ends were twisted to look like candies and the sauce was butter and sage. The wedding cake was not the traditional cake with all the white frosting. Instead there were several fruit and custard-filled tarts laid out to simulate a wreath or ring on a table and there was a white mosquito netting hanging over the table as was once used over baby cribs or bassinets so that the insects couldn't get to the desserts. There was also a help-yourself table of different gelatos and liquors.

It was almost midnight when things began winding down after an evening of eating, visiting and singing. Many of Lorenzo's friends who are still single made up songs with American tunes and Italian lyrics as to why he should not get married — all in good humor. They also went around with a microphone to interview people to get advice for the newlyweds. They were actually looking for negative comments and when they came to us and asked if we were married and how long, we told them it would be 50 years in March, they said "Forget about it."

Some of the young people came from many different places around the world. Lorenzo and Monica speak English and perhaps other languages. We heard a young Asian man speaking English and Carlo struck up a conversation with him. He found out that the young man met Monica in Denmark while on vacation once and he said he was from Indonesia. They also had guests from Washington state and Florida.

When our waiter was clearing off our table, he looked exhausted. I am sure that walking back and forth over uneven turf can be very tiring. I asked if they had to do all the dishes and he said that thankfully they just loaded everything up and brought them to a central warehouse where other people took over washing of the dishes. I figured with about six or seven pieces of china and three or four glasses for each guest they must have had at least 1,400 dishes and 800 glasses to wash. We left around 12:30 and later heard from Lorenzo's mother that some of the young people cele-brated until 5:00 a.m. and just camped out on the lawn. What a fun wedding!!

The morning after the wedding we met Carlo's cousin, Maria Teresa and her son Luca in the lobby of the hotel and had a quick breakfast together. They took off to return to Genova and we also left for Sassello which would be about two hours away. We took the autostrada until Fellizzano and then took the state highway to go directly to Sassello. Along the way, the weather was warm and we both wished we had a cool drink when we saw a sign for a bar/ trattoria. It was a small building out in the middle of nowhere and I told Carlo that a beer really sounded great and he agreed. We pulled up to the place, went inside and there were two very small and tall tables with two tall stools next to them. The bar was about six feet long. The proprietress came out and served us two beers and made a bit of small talk and of course immediately found out we were from California. When ever Italians found out we were from California they would start asking questions and would make comments on how beautiful California must be, etc., etc. A few steps up from the bar was the restaurant part of the building and there was a gathering of about 20 people all enjoying a Sunday banquet and we could smell some delicious aromas coming from the kitchen. The bar/trattoria was called Locanda del Mare which means Inn of the Sea, which was strange because it is located a bit far from the ocean. There is a river nearby but not very big. When she brought over two small dishes or cups of peanuts, party mix, etc. Carlo asked what the specialty of the house was and she replied that she cooked mostly seafood.

She returned to the kitchen and we sipped our beer. Ten or fifteen minutes later, she returned with two small oval dishes filled with fried seafood and marinated seafood and she insisted we try them. She wanted to see if we liked them. Did we ever — they were delicious and they were on the house. We said to ourselves that we would try to come back to this spot and eat dinner, but unfortunately we never got there Perhaps next time.

We arrived in Sassello around five o'clock at Carlo's cousin's home at the mill and store. Gianna and Rinaldo were waiting for us and said that Rinaldo's sister was treating us all to dinner as her birthday was two days prior but she waited for us so we could all go out to a restaurant in Savona. Anything for a celebration!

The next day, Carlo went with Rinaldo to get produce and other goods in the city of Cuno which is a two hour drive from Sassello. So with a four-hour round trip and at least a two hour shopping spree, they were gone most of the day. When they returned, all the goods had to be unloaded and stored into place. Gianna was by herself manning the store which is open from 8:00 to 12:00 and then closed until 3:00. Then they reopen from 3:00 until 7:00. They are constantly running. That week Rinaldo went to Cuneo twice but during the summer, he goes anywhere from three to four times a week.

Rinaldo also grinds the wheat and corn into flour and corn meal for polenta. His grist mill is 400 years old and he inherited it from his father. Rinaldo also has to cut the grooves into the stones which grind the wheat and corn when the grooves get worn. It is an art that was passed down from his father. Rinaldo's son Diego also learned the art but he had other ideas. He owns a business with a friend where they make cartons or boxes for anything such as candy, cookies and they are all designed and made by computers which are huge.

Diego also is the head of a fund to help children in the Congo in Africa. There is a school run by nuns from Savona, Italy and Diego gets donations from people and then delivers the money with his friend. The two men with their two Land Rovers ship the cars to Africa and meet the ships and then drive from Morocco down all of Africa until they reach the Congo. Then Diego's girlfriend Federica and another girl fly down to the Congo with the money to hand over to the nun. Then the four of them drive down to South Africa and fly back to Italy and the cars are shipped back. He has done this twice and is planning on another trip the day after Christmas. They are usually gone about two months.

After visiting all of Carlo's relatives in Liguria for about 10 days, we headed back to see my relatives before heading for home. We decided to stay again at the Villa Malpensa the night before catching our plane in Milano as we had an early flight and since we had to return the rental car and be there at least a few hours ahead of time, we thought this idea was best.

We said our goodbyes to all my relatives and got to the hotel around 6:00. We made reservations for dinner in the restaurant. The maitre'd said, "Oh, you are our clients." We replied that we did stay once three weeks prior. We had dinner wih a glass of wine each. Then we ordered dessert and then the waiter offered an after dinner liquor and poured ice cold limoncello. I drank mine rather quickly and he said teasing, "I see you did not like the drink" and he filled my glass again, even though I protested. Well, when he presented the bill, he had Carlo note that he did not charge us for the wine, the dessert, nor the limoncello. Wow! But, that is how many Italians in Italy are. Just as the owner of the small bar/trattoria, they want you to enjoy their hospitality and their food and drink. They are proud of their country and what they have to offer.

During this trip we had gone to a realtor in Sassello to list the house that Charlie and Lee built in Pontinvrea so that it could be sold. The following year she wrote to us saying that she had a problem with searching for the title and Carlo's name was not on title. We thought we had changed everything in 1986 when we were there with Lee but she said she couldn't find it. So in June of 2009 we made plans to make a quick trip since Carlo had to do this in person in Savona at the equivalent of the Hall of Records where deeds were recorded.

So, we left on June 19 we left San Francisco two hours late in leaving because of a problem with two of the bathrooms on the airplane. Consequently we missed our flight from Frankfurt to Milano and arrived in Milano at 10:30 in the evening. We had breakfast and left the next morning for the cascina. Checked in at the Hotel Quattro Gatti which is next to Zia Pina's apartment and went to lunch with her and Rosita. Later had a light dinner and then my cousins came to visit. Rosanna who was diagnosed with ovarian cancer last year looked terrific and her new short hair growth after the cancer treatments looked very stylish. Next day was Saturday and we ran some errands and then later in the afternoon other cousins from Torino came to visit. That evening we had lightning, thunder and then rain. The next day was Sunday and we went for lunch at Rosanna and Dalmo's summer home in Quargnento and it is called "Il Ronchetto".

The next day we checked out of the hotel and headed for Sassello. On the way we stopped in a town called Strevi. There is a winery called Marenco Winery and we had stopped years before to ask if we were related. No, we aren't but there wine is good and we again bought some Marenco wines. Then we stopped again at the Locanda al Mare where we had stopped the year before and had the wonderful seafood. Then we continued on to Sassello.

Instead of staying at Gianna and Rinaldo's home we decided to stay at the Hotel Ligure because Diego and Federica now had a baby and Gianna and Rinaldo would be busy. The Hotel Ligure is between Pontinvrea and Sassello and the new owners are someone we have known for years. The rate for the rooms include breakfast and either lunch or dinner. We stopped at Gianna's before we went to the hotel and met the new baby whose name is Giorgio. He is a beautiful baby.

The next morning we went to Savona to the Office of Territorio and two ladies there were very helpful. We were expecting to spend the whole day trying to get something resolved but were very surprised when it took only about an hour. Papers were found regarding the property being passed on to Carlo's mother and since she gave up her right to the property, it was passed on to Carlo.

So naturally with the free time we went to the shopping mall in Savona which is called Il Gabbiano which means "The Seagull". The super market in the shopping mall is called Ipercoop and you can find everything and much more. We ate at a fast food place called "Flunch".

The next day we went to Genova to see more relatives and it was not a very nice day. We met for our usual get together at the Arvigo Restaurant on the hill and this time there were only ten of us. We also made plans with Marta, the nineteen year old daughter of Maria Enrica and Bruno, as she would be coming to California two days after we left Italy.

Sunday was Rinaldo's birthday and we said we would treat him and his family to a dinner at the Hotel Ligure. Carlo's cousin Marino and Mariu called us and said they wanted to get together with us so we asked them to join us during the birthday celebration of Rinaldo. The owner, Antonella fixed a beautiful dinner and we had a beautiful fruit tart instead of a birthday cake.

The next day was another big dinner or I should say lunch as Italians always make the main meal at lunch time the biggest meal of the day. We had asked my relatives from Sangano near Torino to join us at the Hotel Ligure. Marisa and her husband Beppe, her brother Mario and his wife Fulvia all came for lunch. We had a great lunch and then just sat around and talked. Then we brought them to Sassello to meet Gianna and Rinaldo and see their store and mill.

The next evening we went to Varazze at the beach to meet up with Rosanna, Franco and Marco Zunino and had dinner at one of the restaurants. Rosanna and Franco have a condominium in Varrazze as Franco still works although he is retired. He works during the summer on the beach renting and putting up beach chairs, umbrellas and working the small bar and snack shop on the beach.

The next day was July 3 and we packed our bags, said our good-byes and headed for the cascina. Stayed two nights in Quargnento, had one last dinner with Rosanna and family at their place at Ronchetto. We left during the afternoon to go to the Villa Malpensa as our flight was for the early morning and we would have to return the car before that. So we checked our car in and then went to dinner at the Villa. The waiter was the same one who was so nice to us the last time we were there. When Carlo told him we were back again, he hesitated as if he didn't remember us but then he looked at me and said "Oh, yes, I remember the senora." Yes, I guess he remembered me gulping down my limoncello, but he didn't elaborate. We had a nice dinner and at the end of the meal without saying anything, the waiter came over with two limoncellos and he had a knowing smile on his face and again the drinks were on the house. I thought to myself— "That is one very cool waiter."

31

TRADITIONS

Whenever I hear people talk about traditions, I think of years and years of something being done or carried out. In our family we never really had many traditions but when I think about it, we did some things over and over again for a few years but then we switched and started something else.

When I was a young girl in McCloud, we didn't have Christmas dinners at our house with a lot of relatives because we just had our family of four. I only remember one Christmas when we went to someone else's house for dinner. I asked my mother a few years ago if we ever celebrated Christmas dinner with others and she said we went to some other people's homes a few times but I don't really remember them. I guess the events didn't make an impression on me. My mother said she would usually roast a capon because a turkey was too large for us.

Also, on Christmas Eve, my father sang in the adult choir of the Catholic church so we would go to midnight mass. My brother and I would have to go to bed for a couple of hours and then we were awakened to get ready for mass at midnight. We would get our present early from Santa because my father would go and take a bath and my mother would sit with Lou and me in the kitchen around the stove and shut the doors which led into the living room or bedrooms. Then we would hear the front door shut and we would say "Santa came!" We would run into the living room, peek out the window to see if we could still see him and there would be the gifts under the tree. I finally got wise to the fact that my gift was not from Santa but from my parents when I read the tag on the box of the beautiful doll I received. My mother had a very distinct handwriting of a European person with all the curly-cues and I said to myself "Ah-ha! This looks like mom's handwriting." We would go to church after this and then the next morning we would open the three or four gifts we received from other prople.

When we moved to San Jose, we lived a few doors down from a Sicilian family who invited us over for Christmas Eve open house in the evening. There were many people as it was a large extended family and there was food everywhere. Catholics were supposed to be fasting on Christmas Eve and the food was mostly made up of fish. Sicilians are noted for their fish dishes and I never ate so many types of fish dishes.

After Carlo and I married, we would go out to the Sunnyview Family Club for New Year's Eve. One year my brother Louis said we should have something for the employees in my dad's store for New Year's Eve such as a bagna cauda. I have written about this dish previously and it consists of a hot dip made of oil, lots of garlic and lots of anchovies into which raw vegetables are dipped like a fondue. Well, you can say that this started a tradition which grew from a beginning of about 15 people to a high of 54 people and lasted about 25 or 30 years. Lou had to stop because his wife Betty had a heart attack and it was just too much to do.

We have tried to revive the tradition somewhat in memory of my nephew by different people having this dinner at their houses because David was always the last person at the table because he loved this dish, but it just isn't the same.

Where we would have the holidays also started with my Zia Adriana and Zio Angelo of San Martin having Thanksgiving at their home, my brother Louis or myself or my mom and dad would have Christmas dinner and Carlo's parents would have Easter. Fall was always beautiful being at Zia and Zio's house with all the trees sporting their fall colors. Easter was always great at my in-law's place because they had a lot of land where the children could look for Easter eggs. We always painted a plastic egg gold and hid a two dollar bill in it. This changed also because Zia Adriana and Zio Angelo changed from having a prune orchard to growing row crops such as all types of squash, butternut, acorn, spaghetti squash, kabocha, sweet dumpling, etc. She grew them for the wholesale market in Los Angeles. Big semi trucks came to pick up her harvest and the late fall was when they were extremely busy so the dinners were switched around to my in-laws having Thanksgiving and Adriana having Easter.

We alternated Christmas and Christmas Eve, for instance, if I had Christmas dinner, Christmas Eve was at Lou's house and vice versa the next year. Then when Lou's children married and had children and sometimes he had Betty's brother's family over, the count got to be too much so we each had just our families over. The most we ever had at our house was 28 and now it is down to about 13 or 14. Also, we never know where we will be as our daughter lives in the Lake Tahoe area, our son and his family often go to Sonora to his in-laws where we have also been invited, or we go up to Lake Tahoe, so everything is changed.

Some of the traditions we still keep are what we will eat for the holidays. We almost always have raviolis besides the meat and side dishes. One dish Carlo's mother always made as an antipasto was beef tongue with a tuna sauce spread on it. We didn't think the younger people would like it, but every year when we had dinner, some of the young ones would ask, "Did Lee make tongue?" They would always love this. Another dish is called "antipasto" and my mother would make it with different vegetables cooked in vinegar and water and other ingredients which consisted of different olives, pickles, and then boiled in tomato juice or sauce and tuna was added to this. This was a side dish during the antipasto course.

A dessert that was always a tradition was a type of flan or custard but it also contained chocolate and brandy.

Easter was always barbecued lamb and after the first Easter we had at Carlo's parent's home, my nephew asked if Charlie was going to barbecue lamb when the second year rolled around for Easter. When we answered "yes" he licked his lips and said "Yummy." We ate outside at a long table with benches under a huge tree and you could say it was very Italian.

At Christmas, the traditional meal would be turkey but sometimes we change and have prime rib roast. One year I thought I would be traditional with a Christmas goose. Never again! There was so much fat and it spattered all over the oven. I think it was an inch deep at the bottom of the oven. I have cooked a wild goose which Marco shot and it was not fat and it was very good but a domestic goose has been fattened and makes a mess in the oven. Perhaps I have to take some cooking lessons.

32

THE BO AND STANCHI FAMILIES

My father's father was born in Franchini, Italy. He was one of five children. The oldest of the five as far as I know was Carlo Bo born in 1875. He was a small man with curly black hair and a curly handlebar mustache. He was married to Lina Scarsoglio and they had four children. The next child was my grandfather, Luigi Bo, born in 1876 and married to Maddalena Baralis. My nonnis had two children, my father Stefano and my aunt Maria Bo who married Giuseppe Mordiglia. My nonno Luigi and his brother Carlo didn't look alike at all. Where Carlo was small, my nonno was a husky man and later, almost balding. There were three other children in the family, Rosetta, Matilde, and Albino. I know nothing about these other children except that Albino died very young. I did meet Carlo's widow and one of her children.

My grandmother, Maddalena was born in Acceglio in 1876. There were six children in the family. There was a nun, three other females and two males. One of the males, Stefano, came to America in 1906 after having been called for by his wife's three nephews. His wife was Anna Donadei. Stefano and Anna had three girls, Maddalena (Lena), Angela, and Maria. Stefano is the one who called for my grandfather, Luigi Bo. I don't know when Stefano brought his family over but we have a photo of Stefano and his family plus my grandparents and all their family. My father was about 14 and Steve Memeo, son of Lena Baralis Memeo is in the photo and he is about 18 months old. I think it was taken right after my father came to America in 1920.

Angela Baralis is the cousin married to Antonio Galletti whose family we stayed with in Klamath Falls during a visit. Angela and Tony had two children, Gaetano (Guy) and Eleanor. Guy never married and Eleanor and Ralph Suckraw had two children, Lee and Louise.

My aunt Maria married Giuseppe Mordiglia and had three children.

Zia Maria Bo Mordiglia & Zio Giuseppe Mordiglia 1967

The first is a daughter Marisa born in 1938, and married to Giuseppe Cane. They have two children, Luca born in 1973 and Elisabetta born in 1977. Elisabetta's husband is Marco and they have a daughter named Camilla born in 2009. Pietro is the next child born in 1942 and married to Vittorina Busso. They have two sons, Riccardo born in 1968 and Silvano born in 1972. Riccardo is not married and Silvano is married to Gianna and they have a little girl, Elena born in 2008 and a little boy, Matteo born in 2010. The third child is Mario Mordiglia born in 1944 who was married to Chiara Deambrogio and from that marriage two sons were born. That marriage ended in divorce and Mario is now married to Fulvia Bella. Mario's sons are Marco, born in 1969 and Enrico born in 1972. Marco is not married and Enrico is married and has twin boys, Luca and Riccardo born in 2008.

My mother's families are the Zeppa and Stanchi families. My maternal great-grandparents were Evasio Zeppa and Giovanna Longo.

Maternal great-grandfather Evasio Zeppa

THE BO AND STANCHI FAMILIES

Maternal great-grandmother Giovanna Longo Zeppa

Giovanna Longo had nine siblings and they lived in Fubine. I was fortunate to meet my great-grandmother when I went in 1953 as she would spend the summers at the cascina and then move into Fubine for the winter. She was a very sweet lady with apple red cheeks and would sit outside against the wall of the cascina so the sun could warm her.

My grandfather's father was Giuseppe Stanchi born in 1841 and came from Valenza, Italy and settled in Quargnento, Province of Alessandria, Italy. My great-grandfather built a large farm house or cascina on a slight hill and it had quite a bit of land around it for growing hay, corn, wheat, etc. He married Maria Mairo and they had two sons, my grandfather Domenico, and Francesco, and a daughter who became a nun. My grandfather had four children, Giuseppe or Pino born in 1910 and died in 2006, my mother Maria, born in 1912 and died in 2007. My mother was baptized

Maria but from the day she was born she was called Marina. The
story is that when my grandfather brought his sister to enter a con-
vent the Mother Superior was such a sweet person and her name
was Marina. My grandfather vowed that if he ever had a daughter
he would call her Marina. The third child Evasio was born in 1917
and died in 1996 and the fourth child Adriana was born in 1925
and lives in San Martin, California.

Zia Giuseppina Mantelli Stanchi & Zio Evasio Stanchi

Zio Pino married Francesca Bisoglio and they had one daughter,
Rosanna born in 1942. I first met Rosanna in 1953 and she is one
of the kindest and sweetest cousins I have. I always enjoy talking to
her. She married Dalmo Picchio and they have two children, Paolo
and Laura. Laura is now married to Marco Iannarelli. Rosanna
and Dalmo live in Torino and have a second home near the cascina
in Quargnento so they usually go there on weekends during the
summer so they can harvest the vegetables from the garden or fruit

from the trees as it is impossible for them to have a garden in the city of Torino. The home was Rosanna's parents' home and Dalmo's parents had a cascina right next to this home.

Dalmo and the family skis and they have a condominium up in the Valle de Susa area. A few years ago Dalmo retired from his job at Pininfarina on a Friday. He and his son went skiing near the Dolomites on Saturday. He fell and hit his head on a rock and was in a coma for 30 days. Rosanna went to be by his bedside and he finally came out of the coma. After a lot of therapy and nursing, one cannot tell that he suffered a head injury. Dalmo skis again but now it is with a helmet.

Zio Evasio married Giuseppina (Pina) Mantelli and had one daughter Rosita, born in 1947, who lives with her mother in the town of Quargnento during the winter and at the cascina in the summer. During the summer the daughter-in-law of my grandfather's brother who owns half of the cascina, spends the summer there also. This is company for Zia Pina and Rosita. Francesco had three children, Aurora, Giuseppe and Ausilia. Giuseppe was married to Carla Prigione and she is good company for Zia plus she still drives. The cascina is a bit out in the middle of farm land and Carla usually has one of her two daughters with her.

My grandfather's children whom I already mentioned were Pino and Evasio and then my aunt Adriana, born in 1925 who came from Italy in 1950 and stayed here after marrying Angelo Robba. They have two children, Rosemary born in 1953 and Henry born in 1956. Henry is not married and Rosemary has two children from her marriage to Greg Bridwell which ended in divorce. David was born in 1982 and is now married to Laura and Michael who was born in 1984 and is not married and now working in Colorado. My mother married Stefano (Steve) Bo and had my brother, Louis and myself. My brother had three children, Steven Bo born in 1952 and is a dentist in Sunnyvale, David Bo born in 1955 and was a Sunnyvale Public Safety Officer until his death in 2004, and Elizabeth Bo born in 1957 who married David Smith who also died in 2004. Steven married Patti Quinlan and had two children, David born in 1980 and Stephanie born in 1985. Steven and Patti are now divorced. David married Michele Joesten and had four children, twin girls, Alysha and Andrea born in 1990, Marina born in 1992, and Stephen born in 1994. Elizabeth or Betty Lou as she is called has one son, Daniel born in 1991.

I think I have mentioned our children before, Marina born in 1960 and Marco born in 1963. Marina has a long time companion Bill Smallfield whom we think of as a son and they live in Truckee, California. Marco married Kristen Popovich and they have a son James David Marenco whom we think is the greatest thing to happen to our family. Marco and Kristen are now divorced but it is an amicable divorce.

As you might notice, the same names are repeated many times as children are often named after grandparents or aunts or uncles. Also there are many ladies named Maria and many men named Giuseppe which means Joseph. In such a Catholic country as Italy, there are many Josephs and Marys.

33

WRAPPING THINGS UP

Now as I near the completion of my memoirs I can reflect back on my life with a satisfaction of what I have done so far and what a beautiful and full journey. Of course there are still things I would like to do and places I would like to visit, but I if I don't fulfill these dreams, I am still content with all I have done.

We are extremely proud of our two children, Marina and Marco. Marina moved to the Lake Tahoe area in 1984 after graduating from Chico State with a BS in business finance and began working by doing accounting for small businesses. She also married Dale Roberts in 1984 but this marriage lasted only four years and there were no children as a result of this marriage. She had a computer which she would take with her from place to place. During the winter when she couldn't take her car because of snow, she would put her computer in a padded case, strap it onto a sled and away she would go to her accounts. Then she settled at one business, Dave's Sports. Dave's Sports grew into five outlets, Truckee, Kings Beach, one at the entrance of Squaw Valley and two places in

Tahoe City. Her office is in Tahoe City and she is the chief finan-
cial officer, also known as "The Shark." She got that knickname
because at the beginning of her life in that area she worked for a
mortgage company, hence being a "loan shark". Dave Wilderotter
owns Dave's Sports but he was quoted as saying that Marina just
about runs the business. In fact when he wants to do something
and he presents the idea to the managers of the outlets, they say
immediately, "Well, what will Marina think?' Dave answers, "Wait
a minute — that's my name on the store."

Marina and her partner Bill Smallfield love the Tahoe area and
are always skiing, either downhill or cross country. They also
bicycle, camp, fish, backpack, hike and they love to just be around
nature. They are both good cooks and they work so well in the
kitchen. It always seems to be a well orchestrated production when
they cook a meal together.

Bill was born in the province of Ontario, Canada and moved to
St. Croix in the Virgin Islands when he was about eighteen or nineteen years old. He lived there for about seventeen years and
worked at a restaurant or café when the owner offered him a job as
a cook in a small coffee shop he was going to open in Tahoe City.
Imagine his shock after coming from a warm, mild climate in the
islands to the snowy and sometimes sub-zero weather of the Lake
Tahoe region. He had to learn to adjust and buy different clothes
in a hurry. The coffee shop had to close after a few years because
the building had to be closed due to non-compliance to building
codes. Bill has worked as a bartender at Squaw Valley during the
winter and during the summer he works in construction.

Our son Marco went to DeAnza College in the automotive
department and then attended College of San Mateo to get his Air-
frame and Power Plant certificate and when he finished he got a job
with United Airlines at the maintenance base in San Francisco. He
worked on the jet engines for 18 years. The last few years had been
bad ones for United and he was dissatisfied with the way things

looked for him and his future so in 2007 he applied and got a job with Hewlett-Packard at their jet aviation center in San Jose. He worked there for almost a year and a half. He was very happy there working on the beautiful Gulfstream jet airplanes but then the department had to downsize so he was laid off along with some pilots, flight attendants and other mechanics.

Now Marco is looking into buying his own business and it has to do with airplanes of course but I will not elaborate further as it is still in the works.

Marco and Kristen's son Jimmy is like a dream come true for us as we think he is the smartest little boy around, but then isn't that what all grandparents think of their grandchildren? Carlo's mom didn't think she would live to see the day that she would have a great-grandchild. When Jimmy was born she said that she could now die happy.

I am still amazed with all that my parents and Carlo's parents did after coming from Italy with just a few years of formal education. It just proves that if one is willing to work hard and does his best, good things will happen and they will be satisfied beyond belief.

34

FAMILY TREES

THE MARENCO FAMILY TREE

> **GRANDPARENTS ANTONIO MARENCO AND MARIA GAMBETTA**

I. Angelina Marenco + Unknown
    A. Maria Luisa
    B. Ivana
    C. Valentina
    D. Piero
II. Maddalena Marenco + Carlo Lepra
    A. Emma Lepra + Charlie Leiduano
        a. Aida Leiduano + 1. John Fiscus
                           2. Matthew Bullock
        1. Vanessa Fiscus
        2. Renard Fiscus
    B. Inez Lepra
III. Giovanni Marenco + Unknown
    A. Maria Marenco
    B. Aurelio Marenco
        a. Gianni Marenco

    b. Roberto Marenco

    c. Federico Marenco

  C. Pierina Marenco + Unknown Bruzzone

    a. Claudio Bruzzone

    b. Simone Bruzzone

  D. Gino Marenco + Teresa Boretti

    a. Marica Marenco + Unknown Delepiane

      1. Emilio Delepiane

      2. Elisa Delepiane

IV. Pietro Marenco + Rosa Rivera

  A. Josephine Marenco + Everett Dahlin

    a. Jacqueline Dahlin + Frank Bertoni

      1. Mark Bertoni

        * Vito Bertoni

        * Vanessa Bertoni

      2. Ken Bertoni

        * Anthony Bertoni

      3. Theresa Bertoni

  B. Pierina Marenco + Otto Gaschk

    a. Robert Gaschk

    b. Lori Gaschk + Christopher Mack

      1. Chris Mack

      2. Andrea Mack

  C. Roy Marenco + Virginia Janowicz

    a. Paula Marenco + Jeffrey Lindeman

      1. Jeffrey Lindeman + Stephanie Fridley

        * Alexis

        * Curtis

        * Norine

      2. Andrew Lindeman + Mahsa Adami

      3. Heather Lindeman + Brian Anderson

    b. Linda Marenco + Henry Castillo

      1. Henry Castillo + Stacy Samaniego

        * Josie
        * Lola
  c. Virginia Marenco + 1. Brook McMahon
                    2. Richard Towner
      1. Cotie McMahon + Courtney Daleg
          * Mason
          * Ashton
      2. Jason McMahon + Dave Shirley
          * Isabelle
  d. Steven Marenco + Valerie Whipple
      1. Shannon Marenco
          * Zoe
          * Ethan
  e. Gregory Marenco + Maureen Foley
      1. Brett Marenco
      2. Rory Marenco
  f. Andrew Marenco + Cherie
      1. Brandy
      2. Josie
      3. Samantha
      4. Jayd
      5. Anglei
      6. Lucinda
  g. James Marenco + Elaine Kitchens
      1. Lauren Marenco
      2. Melissa Marenco
  h. Jeanne Marenco
  i. Victoria Marenco + Manuel Favela
      1. Jesse Favela + Autumn Plount
      2. Robin Favela
      3. Veronica Favela
  j. Marian Marenco + Dennis Salazar
      1. Natalie

2. Nina

3. Gregory

V. Teresa Marenco + Ignacio Biale

A. Maria Biale + Henri Mitteau

  a. Danielle Mitteau + Jacques Nugues

    1. Jean Nugues

      * Alexis

      * Thibault

      * Matthieu

    2. Didier Nugues

      * Jeremie

      * Ophelie

    3. Michel Nugues

B. Giovanni Biale + Rina Olcese

  a. Franco Biale + Laura Barozzi

    1. Paola Biale + Massimo

      * Camilla

      * Carlotta

C. Luigi Biale + Lina Marini

  a. Maria Enrica Biale + Bruno Lantero

    1. Marta Lantero

D. Emma Biale + Paolo Lagana

  a. Ivana Lagana + Luigi Verdi

    1. Elisa Verdi + Christian Trana

      * Alice

      * Serena

    2. Lorenzo + Monica

E. Pierina Biale + 1. Unknown Morando

             2. Franco Ferighetti

  a. Maria Teresa Morando + Pietro Timossi

    1. Luca Timossi

    2. Gian Pietro Timossi

VI. Giuseppe Marenco + Maria Drocco

A. Charlie Drocco
B. Eddie Drocco
C. John Drocco
VII. Edoardo Marenco + Aurelia Risso
  A. Bruno Marenco + Adelia Mochafige
    a. Maura Marenco + Fulvio Molfino
      1. Michele Molfino
  B. Aldo Marenco + Anna Pozzolo
    a. Rosanna Marenco + Franco Zunino
      1. Marco Zunino
VIII. Luigi Marenco + Caterina Castagna
  A. Roberto Marenco + Yolanda Romero
  B. Walter Marenco
IX. Caterina Marenco + Francois Quillerou
X. Marco Marenco + Lucresia Gillio
  A. Carlo Marenco + Rose Bo
    a. Marina Marenco + William Smallfield
    b. Marco Marenco + Kristen Popovich
      1. James David Marenco
XI. Adolfo Marenco + Santina
  A. Maria Rosa Marenco + Francesco Margiocco
    a. Mario Margiocco + Mariu
      1. Francesco + Laura Cartaneto
        * Giovanni
      2. Silvia Margiocco
      3. Marta Margiocco
  B. Antonio Marenco + Giovanna Badano
    a. Maria Rosa Marenco + Raffaelle Guarino
      1. Valentina Guarino
      2. Michela Guarino
  C. Tullio Marenco + Letizia
    a. Loredano Marenco + Alessandro Campo
XII. Ignacio Marenco

XIII. Marinin Marenco

THE ALLERA FAMILY
GREAT GRANDPARENTS DOMENIC ALLERA & LUCREZIA ENRICO

I. Rosa Allera + Ralph Vacco
  A. Fred Vacco + Ruth
  B. Teresa Vacco + Sylvester Santoro
  C. Norine Vacco
  D. Lynette Vacco
  E. Robert Vacco
II. Caterina Allera + Ferdinando Bartodatto
  A. George Bartodatto
III. Maria Allera + 1. Giacomo Gillio (Carlo's maternal grand-parents)
                          2. Bartolomeo Rosetto (second husband)
        A. Teresa Gillio + Joseph Massara
  B. Lucresia Gillio + Marco Marenco
    a. Carlo Marenco + Rose Bo
      1. Marina Marenco + William Smallfield
      2. Marco Marenco + Kristen Popovich
        * James David Marenco
  C. Joseph Gillio + Cesira (Jessie) Venturi
  a. Sandra Gillio
IV. Luigi Allera + Rosina Quillico
  A. Katie Allera + John Bonessa
    a. Frank Bonessa + Rose Mary Quartuccio
      1. Frank Bonessa
      2. John Bonessa
    b. Rosemary Bonessa + William Crawford
      1. Kenneth Crawford + Shannon
        * Colin Crawford
        * Cody Crawford

    2. Nancy Crawford + James Drazenovich

  c. Louis Bonessa + Sandra Allred

    1. Susan Bonessa + Matthew Henry

      * Lauren Henry

      * Jacob Henry

    2. Louis Bonessa + Timmy Thompson

      * Jack Bonessa

      * Cooper Bonessa

B. Nora Allera + 1. _____ Durandetto

             2. John Lyons

  a. Leroy Durandetto

C. Domenic Allera + Mary

  a. Gary Allera

  b. Denny Allera

  c. Mary Jean (Mimi)

D. Mabel Allera + 1.

         2.

         3.

E. Jack (Giovocino) Allera + Thelma Shaffer

  a. Randy Allera + Chris Filo

    1. Kimbery Allera

    2. Ryan Allera

  b. Jackie Allera

F. Jim Allera + Loree Held

  a. Jim Allera + Jean

    1. Jess Allera

  b. Tina + Tom Turnbaugh

V. Gaspare Allera + Mary

  A. Olga Allera + Pete Ravicchio

    a. Donald Ravicchio

  B. Elda Allera + Pete Arduino

VI. Vittorina Allera + 1. Pasquale Bella

           2. Giuseppe Rudari

A. Adolf Bella + Louise
   a. Norma Bella
   b. Lynette Bella
B. Domenic Bella
   a. Kathleen Bella
VII. Marco Allera + Eve

THE BO FAMILY
PATERNAL GRANDPARENTS LUIGI BO AND MADDA-LENA BARALIS

I. Stefano Bo + Maria (Marina) Stanchi
   A. Louis Bo + Elizabeth Rakowski
      a. Steven Bo + Patti Quinlan
         1. David Bo
         2. Stephanie
      b. David Bo + Michele Joesten
         1. Andrea Bo
         2. Alysha Bo
         3. Marina (Mimi) Bo
         4. Stephan Bo
      c. Elizabeth Bo + David Smith
         1. Daniel Smith
   B. Rose Bo + Carlo Marenco
      a. Marina Marenco + William Smallfield
      b. Marco Marenco + Kristen Popovich
         1. James (Jimmy) Marenco
II. Maria Bo + Giuseppe Mordiglia
   A. Marisa Mordiglia + Giuseppe Cane
      a. Luca Mordiglia
      b. Elisabetta Cane + Marco Lonegro
         1. Camilla Lonegro
   B. Piero Mordiglia + Vittorina Busso
      a. Riccardo Mordiglia

b. Silvano Mordiglia + Gianna Aimone-Bonanima
1. Elena Mordiglia
2. Matteo Mordiglia
C. Mario Mordiglia + 1. Chiara Deambrogio
2. Fulvia Bella
a. Marco Mordiglia
b. Enrico Mordiglia + Giuseppina (Giusy) Nardi
1. Luca Mordiglia
2. Riccardo Mordiglia

THE STANCHI FAMILY
MATERNAL GRANDPARENTS DOMENICO STANCHI & ROSA ZEPPA

I. Giuseppe Stanchi + Francesca Bisolio
A. Rosanna Stanchi + Dalmo Picchio
a. Paolo Picchio
b. Laura Picchio + Marco Iannarelli
II. Maria (Marina) Stanchi + Stefano (Steve) Bo
A. Louis Bo + Elizabeth Rakowski
a. Steve Bo + Patti Quinlan
1. David Bo
2. Stephanie Bo
b. David Bo + Michele Joesten
1. Andrea Bo
2. Alysha Bo
3. Marina Bo
4. Stephen Bo
c. Elizabeth Bo + David Smith
1. Daniel Smith
B. Rose Bo + Carlo Marenco
a. Marina Marenco + William Smallfield
b. Marco Marenco + Kristen Popovich
1. James (Jimmy) Marenco

III. Evasio Stanchi + Giuseppe Mantelli
    A. Rosita Stanchi
IV Adriana Stanchi + Angelo Robba
    A. Rosemary Robba + Greg Bridwell
        a. David Bridwell + Laura Boardman
        b. Michael Bridwell